Risk Issues and Crisis Management in **Public Relations**

1

Praise for *Risk Issues and Crisis Management in Public Relations*

"It used to be said that 'reward is commensurate with risk'; now I fear more apt is 'risk is likely to end in crisis'. Who better to guide us through the risk/crisis minefield than Mike Regester and Judy Larkin, who have guided so many so well for so many years. Read it before you need to would be my advice."

Sir Robert Worcester, Chairman, MORI

"Reputation is about what you do, what you say and what others may say about you. But in complex organizations reputation can be a tricky thing to manage. This book, full of examples both good and bad, shows how reputation should be managed in corporate life."

Lord Tim Bell, Chairman, Chime Communications plc

"As one involved in MBA teaching and executive development, I find this book invaluable – not only for students, but also for managers seeking insights into these crucial areas of modern management. It's a clear and highly readable overview of the requirements of risk, issues and crisis management, informed by the expertise and experience of two leading practitioners and consultants, as well as by skillfully chosen and 'classic' case studies. The book is recommended early reading for any manager involved in risk assessment, in trying to understand and manage issues, and concerned to prepare him or herself for the demands of crisis management."

Dr Jon White, Associate, The John Madejski Centre for Reputation,
Henley Management College

"In a world where the hardest won corporate reputation can disappear overnight, this is required reading. Industry has learned little from the mistakes of the past, say the authors, who go on to give a compelling account of just how much there is to learn. Their first-hand experience in dealing with reputational issues and managing crisis shines through."

Robert Phillips, CEO, Edelman Public Relations

"An issue ignored for too long. Dusty emergency plans nobody ever tested. An injudicious aside on air. Reputation destruction comes in many forms. Fortunately, so do the lessons learned, assembled here in this essential handbook of avoidable corporate catastrophes. A compelling and lucid analysis by leading practitioners with many years of first-hand experience in the field."

Matt Peacock, Group Director of Communications, BG Group plc

"Regester Larkin is a key business partner helping us to shape our thinking on proactively managing our reputation. This book is a leading work on reputation management."

Isobel Hoseason, Director of Communications, National Grid Transco

Risk Issues and Crisis Management in Public Relations

A Casebook of Best Practice

Fourth Edition

Michael Regester
& Judy Larkin

KOGAN
PAGE

London and Philadelphia

for

Paul
Lucinda, Alice, Kimberley and Daniel

Publisher's note

Every possible effort has been made to ensure that the information contained in this book is accurate at the time of going to press, and the publisher and authors cannot accept responsibility for any errors or omissions, however caused. No responsibility for loss or damage occasioned to any person acting, or refraining from action, as a result of the material in this publication can be accepted by the editor, the publisher or any of the authors.

First published in 1997 as *Risk Issues and Crisis Management*
Second edition published 2002
Third edition published 2005
Reprinted 2005, 2006
This edition published in 2008 as *Risk Issues and Crisis Management in Public Relations*
Reprinted 2008, 2010

120 Pentonville Road
London N1 9JN
United Kingdom
www.koganpage.com

525 South 4th Street, #241
Philadelphia PA 19147
USA

© Michael Regester and Judy Larkin, 1997, 2002, 2005, 2008

ISBN   978 0 7494 5107 3

British Library Cataloguing in Publication Data

A CIP record for this book is available from the British Library.

Library of Congress Cataloging-in-Publication Data

Regester, Michael.
    Risk issues and crisis management in public relations: a casebook of best practice / Michael Regester and Judy Larkin. -- 4th ed.
        p. cm.
    Rev. ed. of: Risk issues and crisis management, 2005.
    Includes bibliographical references and index.
    ISBN 978-0-7494-5107-3
    1. Issues management. 2. Social responsibility of business. 3. Crisis management. 4. Public relations. I. Larkin, Judy. II. Regester, Michael. Risk issues and crisis management. III. Title.
    HD59.5.R44 2008
    658.4'056--dc22

                                                                    2008006549

Typeset by Jean Cussons Typesetting, Diss, Norfolk
Printed and bound in Great Britain by MPG Books Ltd, Bodmin, Cornwall

Contents

PR in Practice Series

Published in association with the Chartered Institute of Public Relations
Series Editor: Anne Gregory

Kogan Page has joined forces with the Chartered Institute of Public Relations to publish this unique series, which is designed specifically to meet the needs of the increasing numbers of people seeking to enter the public relations profession and the large band of existing PR professionals. Taking a practical, action-oriented approach, the books in the series concentrate on the day-to-day issues of public relations practice and management rather than academic history. They provide ideal primers for all those on CIPR, CAM and CIM courses or those taking NVQs in PR. For PR practitioners, they provide useful refreshers and ensure that their knowledge and skills are kept up to date.

Professor Anne Gregory is one of the UK's leading public relations academics. She is Pro Vice Chancellor of Leeds Metropolitan University and Director of the Centre for Public Relations Studies in the Business School. She is the UK's only full time professor of public relations. Before becoming an academic, Anne spent 12 years in public relations practice and has experience at a senior level both in-house and in consultancy. She remains involved in consultancy work, having clients in both the public and private sectors, and is a non-executive director of South West Yorkshire Mental Health NHS Trust with special responsibility for financial and communication issues. Anne is Consultant Editor of the PR in Practice series and edited the book of the same name and wrote *Planning and Managing Public Relations Campaigns*, also in this series. She was President of the CIPR in 2004.

Other titles in the series:

Creativity in Public Relations by Andy Green
Effective Internal Communication by Lyn Smith and Pamela Mounter
Effective Media Relations by Michael Bland, Alison Theaker and David Wragg
Effective Writing Skills for Public Relations by John Foster
Managing Activism by Denise Deegan
Online Public Relations by David Phillips
Planning and Managing Public Relations Campaigns by Anne Gregory
Public Affairs in Practice by Stuart Thompson and Steve John
Public Relations: A practical guide to the basics by Philip Henslowe
Public Relations in Practice edited by Anne Gregory
Public Relations Strategy by Sandra Oliver
Running a Public Relations Department by Mike Beard

The above titles are available from all good bookshops. To obtain further information, please go to the CIPR website (www.cipr.co.uk/books) or contact the publishers at the address below:

Kogan Page Ltd
120 Pentonville Road
London N1 9JN
Tel: 020 7278 0433   Fax: 020 7837 6348
www.koganpage.com

About the authors

Michael Regester is an international authority, author and lecturer on crisis management and is regarded as having pioneered many of the systems, procedures and training programmes which companies can put into place to handle the communication aspects of crisis situations.

His involvement in crisis management started in 1979 when, as public affairs manager for Gulf Oil Corporation, Europe, West Africa and the Middle East, he had to handle the communication aspects of one of the oil industry's worst disasters – at Bantry Bay in Ireland.

In addition to many papers on public relations and crisis communications, he is author of *Crisis Management*, published by Century Hutchinson in 1987. His second book, *Investor Relations*, co-authored with Neil Ryder, was published by Century Hutchinson in 1990. Both are the first books on their respective subjects to be published outside the USA and have sold internationally.

He is a former board member of the International Public Relations Association, a Fellow of the UK Chartered Institute of Public Relations, and a regular visiting lecturer on crisis management at British universities.

He is a founding partner of crisis and issues management consultancy, Regester Larkin.

Judy Larkin is a founding partner of Regester Larkin and has 30 years' experience in international reputation management and risk communication. She advises organizations on how to anticipate and assess threats and opportunities from emerging issues and to develop response strategies designed to align operational and reputational objectives with stakeholder expectations.

Judy's experience includes working for research and development-based corporations, both as an in-house senior executive and as a consultant running reputation management practices for leading US and UK firms. She is a senior research fellow, advisory board member and lecturer at the Risk Management Centre of King's College London and also lectures at a number of universities and business schools, including the Centre for Risk Analysis at Harvard University's School of Public Health. She is a Fellow of the Institute of Public Relations, the Royal Society of Arts and the Royal Institution. Judy has written numerous articles and has had two books published on best practice approaches to reputation management and risk communication.

Foreword

We live in a world where corporate reputations are fragile and where crises seem to be occurring more and more. The role of the communicator in this environment is critical. Furthermore, the communication planner who might foresee and prepare for such eventualities is a significant player in our interconnected and changing world.

In this book, Michael Regester and Judy Larkin outline a comprehensive approach to managing situations that may turn into crises and handling crises once they occur. Their proposition is that it is impossible to live without risk and, therefore, it is important that organizations are in constant dialogue with all the stakeholders with whom they operate. This means that lines of communication must be open, regularly evaluated and that a basis for understanding needs to be established.

The authors go on to define issues and how they can be managed and, critically, who should be responsible for issues management. They discuss in detail the issues lifecycle, from the point at which an issue is just a potential, right through to its development into a crisis, when it is either resolved or left to lie dormant and pop up at some later stage.

Despite the best endeavours of the most insightful and professional managers and communicators, crises do happen. So what happens then? Well, it depends on the type of crisis! Regester and Larkin carefully outline a number of scenarios illustrating different crises and take the reader through the practicalities of the legal issues involved, the crisis-management planning process and the nitty-gritty of handling crises as they unfold. This includes setting up a press centre, managing the media, handling relatives, keeping employees informed and dealing with the emergency services.

Of course, it doesn't end there. Work is still to be done after the immediate crisis is over. Again, the authors suggest the necessary steps that have to be taken to manage the aftermath of a crisis and to learn from it.

Sprinkled with detailed and informative examples and case studies, *Risk Issues and Crisis Management in Public Relations* is a must for the modern-day public relations practitioner. The authors have gained a great deal of knowledge and experience of issues and crises management over many years, having been involved in developing issues and crises management practices and handling a number of large-scale crises. The public relations practitioner who is able to manage risk issues and crises for his or her organization is an invaluable asset, so a good knowledge and understanding of the issues covered in this book is a must for anyone involved in public relations today.

Professor Anne Gregory
Series Editor

Preface

If your responsibility involves managing or advising on any facet of communication which has a bearing on corporate reputation or operational performance, this book is intended for you.

No matter how well organized and in control you may feel about your day-to-day tasks, extraneous events may suddenly place you and your colleagues in a vulnerable position.

Something as seemingly trivial as an opinion advocated in a trade publication, a minor but continuing increase in product complaints, an unsubstantiated claim about your company's performance or an apparently unconnected trend in social behaviour could have the potential to emerge as an issue, the maturing and long-term consequences of which could be devastating for your business.

Equally, the totally unexpected could happen – in the next hour or week – in an alarmingly fast and dramatic way, creating a true crisis situation. In either case, if you are unsure of your organization's ability to anticipate the probability of such a risk actually happening, let alone have the expertise, resources and infrastructure to cope, these 12 chapters are designed to provide a practical operational framework for pre-emptive action planning.

Risk Issues and Crisis Management in Public Relations is a best practice casebook, completely updated in 2008, drawing on the authors' considerable experience in working alongside senior management teams from many different industry sectors and on a cross-border basis. In addition, they refer to many well-documented case study examples and assess the lessons – both positive and negative – to be learnt from each.

This book attempts to define and apply the emerging discipline of issues management with particular reference to assessing and dealing with risk in a communication context. A principal focus is on techniques for anticipating, planning and proactively managing issues to minimize negative commercial impact and create competitive opportunities.

Furthermore, while there is a greater acceptance on the part of business of the need to plan and organize for potential crisis situations, the continuing failure of senior executives to seize the initiative in explaining what has happened, what is being done to sort out the mess and, crucially, how the organization feels about what has happened, is amply demonstrated in the continuing succession of damning cases that fuel the appetite of a global media and sophisticated advocacy industry.

Guidelines for anticipating, planning, preparing and training are provided together with suggestions on how they can be applied inside your organization. These are summarized from the personal advice and experience of the authors who have made a detailed study of, and been directly involved in, handling major risk issues and corporate crises.

Acknowledgements

We would like to thank Regester Larkin colleague Jonathan Howie for research for this book and Regester Larkin global affiliate companies for case study contributions.

Introduction

WHAT PRICE REPUTATION?

There is no doubt in our minds that business is a formidably positive force in society today. Good business – performing and behaving with a sense of responsibility – underpins successful communities. It influences who we buy from, work for, supply to and invest in, and plays to both the rational and emotional attachments that we have with an organization. Strategic business development and revenue growth are reflections of a company's performance, but so is perceived leadership through greater visibility. Reputation is, therefore, a vital commercial asset and one which companies squander at their peril.

The influence and resources of big business today are huge, and that is not necessarily a bad thing. At the turn of the millennium 51 out of the world's top 100 economies were corporations, representing annual revenues of US$4 trillion (Anderson and Cavanagh, 2000). The annual revenues of Royal Dutch/Shell are greater than the GDP of Morocco; those of Wal-Mart greater than the GDP of Poland, and those of General Motors greater than the GDP of Denmark. Against a backdrop of economic globalization, political transition and technological transformation, business has emerged as the principal engine of growth and development in the new world order, and so it has everything to play for.

Companies can, on occasion, lose sight of the right course to navigate by focusing on short-term requirements at the expense of longer-term impacts – no surprise when share-price is king and the average life expectancy of a CEO is three years. Ignoring the wider consequences of what companies are doing can, however, create unwanted market volatility, negative scrutiny and opportunities for the growing influence of anti-business activism. Companies travelling along this route are charting a course towards a field of operational and reputational icebergs that can quickly sink the most water-tight business strategies.

Threats to reputation – whether real or perceived – can destroy, literally in hours or days, an image or brand developed and invested in over decades. These threats need to be anticipated, understood and planned for. Public perception of risk has become a constant and recurring threat to reputation. Understanding and communicating effectively around risk perception can help to reduce conflict and gain support and trust – critical attributes in securing and maintaining customer, investor and employee loyalty. This is even more important at a time when the forces of globalization and the internet are pushing us from a so-called 'old world' or 'industrial' economy, dependent on the value of physical assets such as property and equipment, to a 'new world' or 'knowledge' economy characterized by the intangible assets of reputation, knowledge, competencies, innovation, leadership, culture and loyalty.

Why is it then that corporations are still surprised when they are faced with controversy? Exxon, Shell, British Airways, BP, Coca-Cola, McDonald's, British Nuclear Fuels, Nike, Marks & Spencer, Singapore Airlines, Renault – some of these companies are potent symbols of globalization, others are or were powerful local or regional brands, some successfully reinvented themselves from nationalized backgrounds – most have spent fortunes developing or redesigning and promoting their corporate or brand image. And yet all have failed at some point to acknowledge the commercial impact of adverse public perception on reputation in a risk setting, with chilling results.

In many Western societies today, we are living in an environment of unprecedented risk aversion and perceived lack of trust. This is strange, because for much of human history we have relied on gut instinct in the face of uncertainty and fared pretty well.

Reputation is built on trust and belief. Our own reputations matter to us a great deal – whether we are good at what we do or fun to be around. But in the commercial world reputation appears to have become a Cinderella asset – easily overlooked but with terrific potential. After all, it should be the biggest asset in most corporations and a high priority in the boardroom. Yet reputation isn't properly valued, is rarely fully understood and is seldom managed in a cohesive way by the people at the top.

As the examples cited above demonstrate, traditional models simply don't work any more because they ignore the essential building blocks of trust and belief. Senior managers need to think and behave differently: first, by demonstrating a clear acknowledgement of the importance of reputation in the boardroom, and second, by adopting an integrated approach to reputation management across the organization in exactly the same way that conventional operational risks are assessed, audited and managed. The maxims explored in this book for avoiding the pitfalls and delivering successful reputation risk management are as follows:

- Acknowledge that reputation is a valuable asset and needs to be actively managed at board level.
- Develop a finely tuned radar and become a listening company.
- Design clear and robust management systems that integrate with routine risk management processes.
- Create your own code of good behaviour and assure your licence to operate.
- Treat your stakeholders intelligently.
- Work as if everything you say and do is public.

While companies must listen to stakeholders, build bridges where necessary and seek solutions wherever possible, they also need to take a stand where necessary.

Research quoted in Chapter 1 indicates that business is regaining trust among opinion formers. Business, nonetheless, needs to be more assertive about setting, rather than following, the terms of debate on key issues. And it should do this with the confidence and assertiveness that comes with millions of 'votes' a day from those who buy its products and services.

Part 1

Risk Issues Management

1

Outside-in thinking

WHO CAN WE TRUST?

Minds are like parachutes; they work best when open.

Lord Thomas Dewer

When we last updated this book, in 2005, we wrote:

Business today suffers from the perception that its leaders are complacent, greedy and unconcerned about the long-term welfare of their companies and the employees that have not been shown the door through downsizing. Government regulators are considered to be in the pockets of industry, examples of bureaucratic sloth. The media is widely believed to sensationalize the news as a means to establish its own agenda. Consumer activists, often considered to be agents for constructive change, are being criticized for exaggerating the dangers facing society.

Well, the good news is that some perceptions of business, at least, have changed for the better since then. In its eighth annual trust and credibility survey, the 2007 Edelman Trust Barometer, which surveys 3,100 opinion leaders in every region of the globe, found business to be more trusted than either government or media in the 18 countries surveyed.

Business is more credible than government or the media in 13 of the 18 countries surveyed in 2007. The survey also found that more respondents in 16 of the 18 countries felt that companies have more of a positive impact on society than a negative impact.

In the United States, 53 per cent of respondents reported trusting business, which marked an all-time high for the survey. This is a recovery from a low of 44 per cent in 2002, which came in the wake of the Enron and WorldCom debacles. In the three largest economies of Western Europe, France, Germany and the United Kingdom, trust in business stands at 34 per cent, which is higher than trust in media and government at 25 per cent and 22 per cent respectively. The 2007 survey marks the lowest levels ever of trust in government across these three European countries.

In Latin America, represented in the survey by Brazil and Mexico, trust in business is at 68 per cent while trust in media stands at 62 per cent and trust in government at 37 per cent. Asian trust in business is 60 per cent while trust in media and trust in government are both at 55 per cent. China, Japan, India and South Korea represented the Asian nations in that year's survey.

In three of the four fast-growing developing nations known as the BRIC countries (Brazil, Russia, India and China), business is more trusted than government, media or non-governmental organizations (NGOs). In China, business is trusted by 67 per cent of respondents but trails government, which is trusted by 78 per cent. Russia, where the survey finds respondents much less trusting of institutions generally, is the only BRIC country where a minority of respondents, 39 per cent, trusts business, but they trust it more than government (32 per cent) or media (35 per cent).

In the 2007 survey, NGOs are either the most credible institution or were level as the most credible institution in 10 out of 18 countries. This puts NGOs even with business, which also leads or ties for most trusted in 7 out of 18 countries. In the 2006 survey, NGOs were the most trusted in 7 of 11 nations surveyed.

The reason for increased trust in business is put down to strong economic growth, visible consequences for executive malpractice and some success in solving problems facing society. Commenting on the survey, Richard Edelman, president and CEO of Edelman, said: 'Business has a clear opportunity to assume a leadership role on major issues, from climate change to privacy.'

'A person like me' is the most trusted spokesperson across the European Union, North America and Latin America. In Asia, it is second to physicians. For the second consecutive year, a 'person like me' or a peer is the most trusted spokesperson in the United States at 51 per cent. A peer is tied with doctors as the most trusted messenger across the big three economies of Europe, at 45 per cent.

CEOs are trusted by only 18 per cent of opinion leaders in Europe's three largest economies (the UK, France and Germany), the lowest rating ever recorded in the survey within this group of nations. In the United States, 22 per cent of respondents trust CEOs and 36 per cent trust an average employee, while in the three largest economies of Europe 28 per cent trust these employees, making rank-and-file employees more trusted than CEOs in both the United States and Europe.

This would suggest that companies need to design their communications as much on the horizontal or the peer-to-peer axis as on the vertical or top-down axis. However, there is certainly no room for complacency.

There are many dynamic forces – political and regulatory, economic, social and technological – that are shaping the way organizations work, perform and behave. They are expanding:

- the quantity, quality and speed of information globally;
- the impact of new broadcast and multimedia technologies on public opinion;
- the competition for reaching and influencing consumers;
- the knowledge, values and behaviour of constituents;
- the association between product and corporate brand reputation.

Second, the role of government and corporations in society is being challenged to a much greater degree than before. Here are some examples.

Public policy formulation is still an evolutionary process. We are quite naturally confused over government roles at local, regional, national and federal levels. This is characterized by uncertainties at a national level of the benefits of a unified Europe and the perceived responsibilities of newly democratized systems of government in central Europe.

Corporate and institutional behaviour is under much greater scrutiny. Critical media reports highlight concerns over excessive profits and senior executive pay, a lack of adequate corporate governance and corruption scandals in the financial and public services sectors. Monopolistic practices are questioned as industries consolidate and integrate for global competitiveness. 'Dirty tricks' campaigning, aggressive lobbying tactics that compromise the credibility of executives and public officials, and too much interference by business in government typify the populist braying of newspaper and broadcast editors alike.

We are less trusting of those in authority. In most developed countries, government promises on taxation and healthcare reform continue to be broken, and we are challenging industrial performance, for example, over the environmental reputation of oil and chemical companies. Even the ethical stance of companies focusing on socially responsible business practices, such as Body Shop, Ben & Jerry's and Levi Strauss, is being called to account.

Corporate loyalty is no longer a given. Redundancies, relocations, the erosion of workers' rights and job security have taken their toll. Demographic changes mean fewer young people are entering the market, the demand for skilled workers is gradually increasing while unskilled jobs are in decline. Employment is likely to become a sellers' market.

The social landscape is changing. Populations are getting older, resulting in several European countries raising the retirement age at a time when people generally want to stop work earlier. Our traditional family structures are under intense pressure. Nearly one in two marriages are ending in divorce in the UK. Coupled with declining job security, domestic property prices, pension and elderly welfare provision, a staggering change in family cash flow through an average lifecycle is illustrated in Figure 1.1.

Opinion polling in the United States and Europe indicates that some of the principal shifts occurring in society that give rise to concern relate to:

- safety and security, including both social and economic security;
- environment, including workplace;
- gender/equality;
- service quality/value for money;
- institutional accountability;
- empowerment.

Changes in these and other areas are bringing about a big increase in activism. We are now much more likely to vote with our feet on issues of major concern, by picketing, boycotting and litigating. In the past 10 years, the proliferation of single-issue groups has outstripped anything in the past. Powerful and well organized, there is rarely a sandal-wearing extremist in sight. They have money and are well connected, often with sophisticated cross-border links.

CONSUMER POWER AND THE RISE OF A NON-GOVERNMENTAL ORDER

More often than not we now trust ourselves. We have much greater access to information through the internet, greater confidence in the validity of our own opinions and our 'consumer rights', and we increasingly back our ability to make a difference.

As business is becoming the main target for evidence of 'responsible behaviour', consumers are becoming the most vocal task-masters. Now, the active consumer:

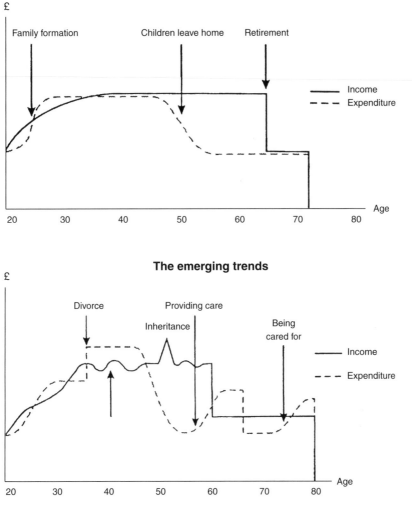

The traditional model

The emerging trends

Source: Henley Centre Future of Work Forum, 1996, London

Figure 1.1 *Family lifecycle cash flows changing*

- demands and exercises personal choice;
- responds to single-issue politics;
- is more likely to question the value of new developments;
- regards environmental issues as fundamental.

Research organization Populus, in association with Good Business and *The Times*, launched in 2007 the Concerned Consumer Index – a monthly measurement of attitude among the increasing number of consumers who take social, environmental and ethical issues into account when making purchasing decisions.

Results of the first survey showed that 9 out of 10 people feel companies have a wider responsibility than just delivering goods at the lowest possible price. Three-quarters of the population claim to weigh up a company's reputation before buying its products or services, and nearly three in five say they actively avoid purchasing from certain companies because of questions they have about their social, environmental and ethical track record.

What marks out 'concerned consumers' is that they do all these things. They belong to that half of the adult population who not only care about social, environmental and ethical issues but actually do so enough to change their purchasing behaviour. They make decisions based on values as well as value. They are prepared to reward companies that they feel care about more than just selling to them as cheaply as possible.

According to the research, 50 per cent of concerned consumers seek out information about companies before buying from them on a regular basis. They are also ready to urge others to follow their lead. Two in five of them say they recommend goods and services to others on a frequent basis, nearly half as many again as the rest of the population. They are also more likely to pick up on stories both good and bad about the way businesses conduct themselves, to register these and to translate them into future buying decisions.

NGOs in Europe are masterminding increasingly sophisticated campaigns. Their own research reinforces the view that social as well as environmental responsibility is a key issue for the public. According to Peter Melchett, former Executive Director of Greenpeace UK, 'The vast majority of people are not anti-science, nor are they Luddite. But people are increasingly aware, and mistrustful, of the combination of big science and big business.' He continued, 'people scorn patronizing assumptions based on the premise that they don't know what is good for them. On the contrary, people insist that it is their society and their world, and they will decide what is acceptable, and what is not.'

This vocal and energetic movement is growing in line with corporate unpopularity, tackling issues as diverse as food and health safety, pollution and climate change, animal welfare, trading standards, ageism, racism, nuclear disarmament, sexism in the workplace, litter, noise, pornography, pesticides and disclosure of information. There are now more than 2,000 single-issue campaign groups in the UK, ranging from big organizations like the multinational Greenpeace with 4 million members to specialist outfits such as Surfers Against Sewage. One way or another, they have the power to inflict long-term damage on companies, and like shareholders and politicians, they need to be factored into corporate planning and decision making.

Effective consumer campaigns have contributed to a rise in popular sensitivity to a range of environmental and social issues and a plea for restraint in corporate activities. Global companies are the main targets of these demands because of their visibility and their perceived ability to shape economies and politics for their own ends. In our newly transparent, internet-driven world, businesses have no place to hide, no time to think and no second chances.

Charities, consumer groups and other NGOs are building enormous influence. Direct action campaigns clearly pose threats to reputation risk. Protestors at the World Trade Organization (WTO) meetings in the United States, Europe and China over the last eight years expressed concern about growth of big corporations, environmental degradation and the widening global gap between the 'haves' and 'have-nots'. They also criticized the IMF, the World Bank and WTO as three undemocratic institutions whose policies deprive people of food and water, and thus start wars.

NGOs have become increasingly sophisticated and powerful in targeting government and business at local, national and international levels. Under greater scrutiny and with expectations of more open governance and accountability, businesses are being pressured from many different quarters to respond to a culture of growing individuality and assertiveness, where every opinion is perceived to matter.

Campaign tactics are varied, often well managed and increasingly coordinated through internet and mobile communication technologies. The emergence of internet-based social networking sites and phenomena such as Wikipedia is having a profound effect on defining present-day and emerging issues. The boycott is one of the oldest and most effective – a threat that can haunt any company today that fails to consider the ethical as well as environmental consequences of its commercial activities. This has ranged from student boycotts of Barclays Bank in the apartheid South Africa of the 1980s, through boycotting Exxon products over the Valdez spill in Alaska in 1989 and Shell gas stations over Brent Spar and its interests in Ogoniland in 1995, to PepsiCo in Myanmar through the mid-1990s, and clothing manufacturers such as Levi Strauss, Nike, Gap and Marks & Spencer over employment practices in developing countries.

One of the longest running boycotts has been against Nestlé. Baby Milk Action has been waging a record 25-year-long war against the company over the way it has marketed infant formula products, which it claims contravene the World Health Organization (WHO) code. In the 1970s, when the company was accused of selling infant formula in developing countries at prices that could not be afforded and where clean water was virtually non-existent, the company decided to ignore allegations of irresponsible behaviour and greed. Baby Milk Action became a powerful, critical force against Nestlé, generating negative media coverage and succeeding in targeting the company where it hurt – for example, through campaigning for boycotts of its market-leading Nescafé coffee brand. Nestlé suffered significant reputational and commercial damage by refusing to debate the issues in public. By the time the company woke up to the need to build bridges with campaigners and other stakeholders, the iceberg had well and truly struck. No amount of resource or attempts to align with the WHO through the development of a health code for infant feeding and nutrition made a difference. Furthermore, the student leaders and activists of the 1970s have become the media and social commentators and business people of today, consolidating the polarization of opinion.

Source: Regester Larkin

Figure 1.2 *NGO tactics*

The effect of these developments has been to shift the power of 'voice' in the formation of corporate reputations away from companies themselves and towards their stakeholders. Regester Larkin's Managing Director Andrew Griffin argues in his book *New Strategies for Reputation Management* that this balance of power has shifted too far and that companies need to wrest back control of their reputations. As new opinion leaders emerge via the internet, reducing the share of voice of corporations, reputation risk management is becoming defined increasingly by external stakeholder perceptions of what they believe corporations should say and do rather than by what a company says and does.

Activists have traditionally focused on problems; companies have tended to deal with issues, and there is a difference. A problem has a wide context: pollution; bad employment practices; poverty; human rights abuse; hunger; racial discrimination. An issue tends to be more specific, and involves considering potential solutions – regulation to curb emissions; codes of practice to improve workers' rights or reduce bad behaviour; financial or regulatory penalties for failing to meet required standards. Activist groups today are focusing more on winning issues and seeking solutions, rather than merely creating awareness of problems. A key maxim for avoiding a collision course with activists is for companies to switch on and monitor the radar. The objective is to scan stakeholder attitudes in relation to emerging, current or linkage issues that may have the potential to impact on commercial or reputational objectives, and become familiar with the profile, personalities and working practices of activist groups.

The activist's checklist for developing a campaign strategy around an issue is likely to consider whether it will:

- result in a real improvement for people;
- give people a sense of their own power;
- be worthwhile and winnable;
- be felt in an emotional way;
- be easy to understand;
- have a clear target and timeframe;
- build leadership;
- have a financially beneficial angle;
- enhance profile to support subsequent campaigns;
- raise money and membership;
- fit with objectives and values.

(Source: Adapted from *Organizing for Social Change*, Midwest Academy, 2000)

In the same way that an NGO will develop its campaign agenda, a company facing potential direct action from an NGO must *analyse the problem and decide what kind of solution to work towards*. It requires answers to these questions:

- Can a credible argument be made against the company's position on the issue?
- Does the issue evoke emotion?
- Is the issue media and internet-friendly?

- Are there linkages to other issues, and are there legacy problems?
- How strong are the key activists?
- How far have the dynamics of the issue lifecycle developed?
- What impact will dealing with this issue have on the organization?
- What are the risks (and opportunities) if we ignore the issue?
- How are the company's key stakeholders likely to react, and how strong is our support base on the issue?
- How confident are we that we can influence the issue in the way we want?
- What potential resources will be required?
- What is the simplest solution and what is the most far-reaching?
- What are the potential benefits from actively seeking a solution?

(Source: Adapted from Winter and Steger, 1998)

Once again, accountability and transparency are the watchwords for corporate response to NGO attack. The view of one senior reputation risk practitioner is that 'public opinion demands accountability and transparency from business today and it will expect performance delivery on social and environmental issues pretty soon after'.

Post September 11, the global economic justice agenda championed by these groups is once again gaining momentum. However, the vast majority of NGOs are seeking solutions and change, not all-out war. Activists are far more willing to enter into partnerships with business to achieve their objectives. A greater self-confidence has emerged from the more militant tendencies of the 1970s and 1980s – a shift in mindset from 'anti-business' towards a more goal-oriented approach that accepts that partnerships that deliver results is not a compromise of principles.

Companies are seeking NGO advice on strategies for environmental, social and supply chain management. The WWF (formerly the World Wide Fund for Nature), for example, has worked extensively with industry to establish the Forest Stewardship Council and Marine Stewardship Council.

Even Greenpeace, among the most aggressive of campaigners, is collaborating more with business. It cultivates industry outsiders that could be potential allies, encourages them to adopt environmentally friendly technology, and then targets its members to place orders. This approach led to the launch of chlorine-free paper and Greenfreeze, a CFC-free refrigerant. The group also developed smILE, a fuel-efficient prototype car based on a Renault Twingo and designed to demonstrate that a 50 per cent reduction in carbon dioxide emissions from cars is feasible. Greenpeace has established a unit to find technical solutions to environmental problems, and believes that it can bring technology to the market which would not otherwise happen. Marketing pressure is a key driver for the organization's campaigns, together with a streamlining of tactics based on research, the use of the media and the law, and targeted lobbying.

However, the strength of NGOs should not be misinterpreted as an issue fait accompli. No company should feel bullied into automatic capitulation over NGO demands if the tactics employed involve unfounded allegations or misinformation. These should be rebutted in a clear, credible and consistent manner. Many companies by their nature are involved in complex manufacturing and supply chain issues where accidents can happen or trade-offs need to be made. And many NGOs get their facts wrong or don't consider secondary issues or consequences of their demands. There is no doubting, however, that NGOs are among the most sophisticated and effective communicators, backed up by greater latent trust from the public. Business needs to be attuned to the issues communications 'playing field' defined by NGOs, and to be well equipped to succeed on those terms.

CASE STUDY: OXFAM ATTACKS STARBUCKS

US coffee chain Starbucks has built a reputation for being a socially responsible company that pays higher prices for its coffee to ensure fair trade with 'third world' producers. It is also widely acknowledged that the company has created trickle-down benefits for other businesses.

In October 2006, Oxfam UK accused Starbucks of attempting to block a move by the Ethiopian government to trademark the names of three of its most famous coffee beans in the United States. The charity said that Starbucks asked the National Coffee Association (NCA), the trade association of US coffee companies, to block the country's bid. Oxfam claimed that, by blocking the trademarks, Starbucks was denying Ethiopia earnings of £47 million per year. Should Ethiopia gain the trademarks, it would allow the country to negotiate purchasing conditions with roasters or retailers that want to use the names. The Ethiopian government filed its applications to trademark the three bean names – Sidamo, Harar and Yirgacheffe – in the European Union, Canada, Japan and the United States in 2005. Coffee is Ethiopia's largest export.

Dub Hay, Starbucks senior vice-president, denied that Starbucks approached the NCA and claimed that the trade body actually contacted Starbucks over the issue. Robert Nelson, head of the NCA, confirmed this, saying that the trade association was against the move because it would damage Ethiopian farmers economically. He said that the Ethiopian government had been badly advised and the move could result in the government setting coffee bean prices unreasonably high, resulting in fewer exports. In a press release, the NCA said that trademarking a geographical area was not consistent with US law. It added that, even if other intellectual property methods were used to trademark the coffee beans, no value would be added to Ethiopian coffees.

The Ethiopian government offered Starbucks a loyalty-free licensing agreement, which the company refused to sign, but which was signed by its rival

Green Mountain. Oxfam maintained that coffee bean pricing should be left to the Ethiopian government to decide for itself. The charity seemed to turn the problem into an industry-wide issue by saying that it was an opportunity for Starbucks to 'show leadership'.

In December 2006, Oxfam posted a clip on video-sharing website YouTube that criticized the company's policies in Ethiopia. The video has received almost 50,000 hits. Starbucks also released a short clip on the site of Dub Hay saying that trademarking a geographical area was 'against the law'. This received more than 30,000 hits, but caused anger from various quarters, resulting in Dub Hay apologizing for accusing the Ethiopian government of doing something illegal. Starbucks said: 'Since this video was posted, a lot has happened. When we posted this video, we felt the information was correct and since we've learnt a lot and realized the information about the legality of the trademark was not accurate.'

On 16 December 2006, Oxfam organized the 'Starbucks Day of Action', which encouraged people to protest at branches of Starbucks around the world. And in January a representative of an Ethiopian cooperative coffee union met with Tony Blair to kick-start a fair-price campaign that included a film called *Black Gold* that sought to 'expose' the global coffee industry.

In November 2006, Starbucks CEO Jim Donald visited Ethiopia to talk to prime minister Meles Zenawi in order to resolve the trademark issue. However, Ethiopian officials said that the meeting had failed to end the tensions. Jim Donald said of the meeting: 'We believe the meeting was very cooperative and productive and we are committed to working with the Ethiopian government to find a solution that supports the Ethiopian coffee farmer.'

At the time of writing, Starbucks and the Ethiopian government are still in discussions, having had two meetings described as 'fruitful' by Jim Donald. In February 2007, the company softened its position, promising to drop its objections to Ethiopia's desire for intellectual property rights. But critics say that the NCA will simply lobby on the company's behalf. And, crucially, Starbucks has not said that it will sign a licensing agreement with Ethiopia if the country successfully registers its brands. The company also announced plans to double purchases of East African coffee within two years and increase credit to farmers in the region to improve bean quality.

This slight change of policy was coupled with a public admission of misjudgement from Alain Poncelet, vice-president of coffee and managing director of Starbucks Coffee Trading Company. He said it was:

> very clear to us that we have not engaged as much as we should have in East Africa. We all agree that we are looking for the same results and that the farmer should be the one benefiting. We are not in a position to tell the Ethiopian government what to do. We are a coffee company; we do not set the rules… We have got so many letters from Central American farmers saying that this is not the Starbucks they know.

Press comment on this issue was perhaps less voluminous than one might expect for a case involving a large multinational. This was perhaps due to the complexity of trademarking, which contributed to making the situation unclear.

And so it was not easy to frame the debate as 'corporate greed vs innocent victim' and it was therefore more difficult for the press to condemn the company.

As the issue emerged, one of Seattle's local newspapers, the *Seattle Post-Intelligencer*, said that Starbucks' CEO was playing 'Russian roulette' with the brand: 'It's ironic that Starbucks' anti-development stance likely will lead to a greater impact on profits than any increase in commodity prices the company might encounter was it to support Ethiopia. Ethiopians cannot dig themselves out of poverty unless they are allowed to participate meaningfully in the value chain. Let's hope Starbucks allows them to do so.' Seattle's other daily newspaper, the *Seattle Times*, said the dispute had 'rattled' Starbucks image. The *Houston Chronicle* condemned the company: 'Shame on Starbucks, whose revenues in 2005 were US$6.4 billion, for trying to strong-arm a country whose entire gross domestic product is US$6 billion.'

In a business analysis article, the *Sunday Times* said that Starbucks' image has suffered: 'The spat has landed Starbucks in a public-relations nightmare, with the ethically minded company accused of acting tough with one of the world's poorest countries.' In a news report, the *Independent* described the incident as a 'public relations disaster'.

Result

The issue of whether Starbucks actively attempted to veto Ethiopia's trademark via the NCA is now looking irrelevant. From an Oxfam/Ethiopia perspective the result so far has been favourable. Oxfam has successfully forced the issue into the public domain and has forced Starbucks into admitting and explaining to the public why it opposes the trademark initiative.

Oxfam also hinted that the problem was an industry-wide issue and appeared to offer Starbucks the opportunity to take the lead in tackling the problem.

Perhaps Starbucks could have coordinated an industry-wide response, because there seem to have been subsequent accusations against the industry. And this issue will almost certainly spread to other coffee companies because, if the ethical Starbucks cannot be trusted to give third-world farmers a fair deal, who can?

However, the company had built up considerable reputation capital, which perhaps led its stakeholders to believe that it would not behave in such a way towards one of the poorest nations in the world. Importantly, the company realized it wasn't going to win the perception battle by sticking to its argument of Ethiopian farmers being wealthier without the intellectual property rights. And so it conceded that it shouldn't have been seen to take on a foreign government, thereby halting further reputation damage.

In today's complex environment, organizations have to understand and respond to our rapidly shifting values, rising expectations, demands for public consultation and an increasingly intrusive news media. It is no longer enough to focus on internal objectives alone: *outside-in thinking*, illustrated in Figure 1.3, is an essential prerequisite for achieving the tacit acceptance of society to continue to operate.

There is a growing expectation, on the part of a broad range of stake-holder groups, that organizations should perform and behave in a more open, socially caring and responsible way. These principles are even more important in times of intense pressure, for example where there is a *real* or *perceived* risk to public health, safety or the environment.

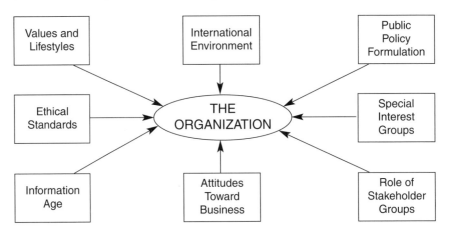

Source: Ashley and Morrison, 1995

Figure 1.3 *Outside-in thinking*

DEALING WITH RISK

The so-called 'risk society thesis' identifies new patterns of political and public anxiety. This conflict is being brought about by a combination of:

- continuous societal change and uncertainty;
- the remorseless pace of industrial and technological innovation;
- time and cost pressures that do not allow for adequate scientific evaluation of the risks versus the benefits of innovation;
- a trend towards greater individuality and assertive public opinion.

In combination, these factors are intensifying a host of risk issues.

Traditional reliance on the judgement of experts to interpret levels of risk in using new products and processes is now paralleled by a growing ability on our part – reinforced by a modern media – to challenge political and corporate reassurance couched as scientific or technical fact. The perceived risk of contracting CJD through BSE-infected cattle is an example of the potential and real business impact of exaggerated public fear.

Risk is a measure of the adverse effect of an issue. It is about assessing and communicating the possible *hazards* associated with a particular process relative to the *safeguards* and *benefits* which it offers. This helps us, as consumers, to make choices about our health and safety, and the protection of the environment in which we live.

Risk assessment is essential when:

- a *new risk emerges* – such as the threat of avian flu or concerns relating to genetic manipulation;;
- the *degree of existing risk changes* – such as the safety of train travel in the UK following a series of fatal train crashes over the last several years or the perceived risk of thrombosis from sitting still during long-haul flights; or
- a *new perception of risk occurs* as in the potential impact of so-called gender-bending chemicals (phthalates) on animal and human health, and the environment.

All too often during public health and safety scares, the basis for sensible decision making has remained buried beneath an avalanche of scientific or technical data. According to US crisis management specialist Peter McCue, each crisis follows a similar pattern:

1. a special interest group sounds the alarm;
2. the media creates widespread awareness of the claim;
3. industry responds with reams of data and proclaims its products safe;
4. in the face of increasing shrillness, the public becomes anxious and avoids the products in question until more reliable information is available;
5. sales decline as regulators equivocate and issue confusing guide-lines;
6. relying on exaggerated public fear, the activists step up the campaign;
7. the media faithfully covers everything they do and say;
8. industry reacts strenuously, occasionally resorting to exaggerations of its own in an attempt to restore calm and boost sales;
9. for a period of time everyone loses perspective on the issue;
10. eventually, a more accurate and balanced assessment emerges;
11. industry braces itself for another day;
12. those who make their living from consumerism find somewhere else to spread doom and gloom;

13. the media moves on to the next crisis, giving little attention to clarifications of the original inflated charge;
14. government returns to studying the issue so that it can write new and confusing legislation.

So, there are a number of dilemmas facing organizations endeavouring to understand and manage the dynamics of a risk issue:

- *Risk means different things to different people* – we overestimate sensational risks, like flying or contracting CJD, while we underestimate common risks such as driving a car or taking a short cut through an alley at night.
- *Basic attitudes are hard to change* – they are forged by a range of social and cultural factors and reinforced by our own contact with and opinions advocated by friends, colleagues, family members and others. These attitudes shape the way we interpret, understand and act upon new risks.
- *The public is not looking for zero risk* – we each constantly make risk/benefit choices, consciously or unconsciously, but there is a basic unease about two things: where is the benefit and can the people responsible for managing the risk be trusted? This is particularly true in areas of food and health safety, for example in food processing, biotechnology and synthetic chemical usage.
- *The source of information about risk is critical* – research in the UK indicates that consumers are totally confused about whom to trust on food safety.
- *Emotion* is the most powerful influencer of all. Emotional symbols – water cannon jets aimed at Greenpeace activists attempting to occupy the Brent Spar, aerial shots of the oil spill in Alaska, the cloud hanging over Chernobyl, debris floating in the water off Long Island following the crash of TWA flight 800 and the Snowdrop campaigners at Parliament – can overwhelm and *totally negate scientific fact*.

CASE STUDY: MMR

The government's failure to listen to people's worries and answer their fears led to a reduction in the uptake of the measles, mumps and rubella (MMR) vaccine and confusion about whom to trust on the issue. Although the MMR vaccine has been given to children in the UK since 1988, in 1998 research led by Dr Andrew Wakefield of the Royal Free Hospital appeared in *The Lancet*, claiming a possible link between the vaccine and bowel disorders and autism in children. Organizations such as the Medical Research Council (MRC) reacted by dismissing these claims. The government set out to persuade parents that giving the MMR vaccine to their children would be the most sensible option, considering that the alternative would be to deal with a measles epidemic.

Dr Simon Murch, one of the doctors involved in the original research, changed his opinion and announced that he did not believe a connection exists between MMR and autism. Tony Blair would not comment on whether his son Leo had received the MMR vaccine or not. Parents very quickly became deeply confused. The then Prime Minister's silence led to understandable assumptions that Leo had not received the MMR jab, and this contrived to create a feeling of deep mistrust in the government's advice. This, combined with conflicting medical opinion and a clear lack of authoritative scientific facts to alleviate the perceived risk, caused parents to refuse the combined jab.

Although many reports were published rebuking Dr Wakefield's original claim, this did little to ease parents' minds. The number of parents willing to allow their children to receive the jab fell significantly from 92 per cent in 1996 to 82 per cent in 2003 and even 60 per cent in some areas. Public calls for the introduction of single vaccinations grew louder. The government responded by claiming that the rejection of the combined jab in favour of single vaccinations could potentially lead to a measles epidemic. The number of laboratory-confirmed cases of measles rose from 112 in 1996 to 736 in 2006; and cases of mumps rose from 94 to 4,408 over the same period.

It is important in emotive cases to understand and be sensitive to the emotional triggers of those affected. Not many things are as emotive as the health and welfare of children. The government failed to do this, and instead of listening to and answering health concerns in the call for single vaccines, it concentrated on pushing the MMR jab. Added to this was its attempt to fight fear with fear, telling parents that if their children weren't given the vaccine they could die from a measles outbreak. This was a clear case of pouring oil on the fire. Rather than seeking to address the emotional concerns, sensitively and dispassionately presenting the risks and benefits and taking the emotion out of the debate, it heightened the scare factor.

The government's immediate reaction to the original 1998 research was handled through a rapid and effective report from the MRC. Unfortunately, over the next five years there was no commitment to monitoring the issues and maintaining an open flow of information. Public mistrust evolved rapidly on the back of dismissive behaviour and a lack of openness, capped by doubts surrounding Leo Blair's inoculation.

As Liam Donaldson, Chief Medical Officer for the Department of Health, said, 'People are entitled to make claims, and when those claims cause anxiety to parents then we have a responsibility to respond to parents' concerns and look at the evidence again and continue looking at it every time that a claim is made.'

The safety debate continued apace and, in February 2004, the UK's General Medical Council – the medical profession's supervisory body – announced it would investigate the allegations surrounding Dr Wakefield's research work. Dr Wakefield welcomed the decision as an opportunity to defend his reputation.

At the same time, *The Lancet* revealed that Dr Wakefield had also been working on a study investigating possible links between the MMR jab and autism to see if legal action would be justified. Dr Richard Horton, editor of *The Lancet*, said that at the time the original research was published this second study had not been disclosed to them. 'If we knew then what we know now, we certainly would not have published the part of the paper that related to MMR', he told BBC News.

As the controversy continued, and prompted by media reports reigniting concerns about the safety of MMR, 30 paediatricians and vaccination experts published, in June 2006, an open letter calling on journalists, politicians and health professionals to 'draw a line under the question of any association between MMR and autism' in the light of evidence that shows the vaccine is safe.

In October the final nail in the coffin of the belief that the MMR vaccine is associated with autism in children seemed to have been hammered home by a new Canadian study carried out by researchers at McGill University Health Centre. This argued that earlier studies suggesting that vaccination with MMR could lead to autism were fundamentally flawed and that the techniques used in the original molecular study revealed errors that led to false identification of the measles virus.

Through 2007 public health officials urged parents to vaccinate as new figures showed a sharp jump over the summer in confirmed cases of the potentially life-threatening infection and only a 74 per cent take-up for the recommended two-dose vaccination. At the time of writing the GMC disciplinary hearings were due to finish in October 2007 but will remain subject to legal appeal.

HANDLING THE ORGANIZATIONAL RESPONSE

For organizations facing emerging risk issues, some of the principal guideposts for effective risk communication are:

- To understand the dynamics of public emotion and the working practices of special interest groups and the media who may strive to raise and legitimize a stance on an issue for public debate and, ultimately, public policy formulation.
- To familiarize the organization with the cyclical development of an issue; to focus appropriate resource on early identification and monitoring of information relevant to the emerging issue and organized activity for response. This should include a clearly defined policy and associated communication strategy.
- To appreciate that it is not realistic to change public opinion about the *size* of the risk (even if the true risk of an unfamiliar hazard is small), and so for the organization or industry:
  - to communicate in language that relates to and alleviates public anxiety;
  - to establish and build *trust* about the commitment to *control, reduce and contain it.*

THE ADVOCACY APPROACH

According to Howard Chase (1984), more often than not activist groups are setting the public policy agenda by combining propaganda techniques with computer-age technology.

First, they create a perceived need for their reform idea (eg, that phthalate levels in synthetic chemical manufacture are destroying our reproductive systems and the environment) in both special interest and establishment press and before groups of opinion leaders.

Second, they create the appearance of legitimacy for the idea through studies, third-party validation and, ultimately, through public opinion polling and public policy lobbying.

Finally, they use other information dissemination techniques such as widespread editorial, direct mail and grass roots mobilization to extend their viewpoint on a cross-border basis.

At its simplest, a campaign may consist of gathering information and passing it on to the media and government. Often, by using research, a pressure group can win public support for its cause and the courts can be brought into the equation to challenge corporate performance. Members and supporters can be mobilized to write to companies complaining about actions and policies. More pressure can be exerted by a boycott. Lufthansa agreed to stop transporting animals for laboratory testing 10 days after European anti-vivisection groups launched a campaign urging travellers to use another airline, and pressure is currently mounting at an EU level for more precautionary policies relating to the use of animals in medical research. The student boycott of Barclays Bank due to their operating in South Africa lasted 15 years, and was one factor that contributed to its eventual withdrawal in 1986.

Shareholders can also be tapped for support. Pensions and Investment Research Consultants claim there has been a rapid rise in ethical unit trusts over the last five years. Demonstrations at company annual meetings are now regular events. Furthermore, financial institutions have experienced the damage inflicted by legal claims resulting from environmental pollution. Claims relating to toxic waste, asbestos and radioactive waste contributed about 20 per cent of the recent serious losses at the Lloyd's of London insurance market.

The new litigious culture of the late 20th century is costing corporate America $43 billion a year in product liability insurance. Even a small high street solicitor in the UK who paid an annual premium of £1,000 for professional indemnity 20 years ago is faced with a bill of £60,000 today. The burgeoning lottery of compensation claims for personal injury – physical and emotional – is achieving Alice in Wonderland status. UK health authorities are among many public bodies in the firing line, anticipating an annual increase of between 15 per cent and 20 per cent in compensation claims. Recent landmark judgments have centred on significant awards to young adults over claims of bullying at school.

In the United States, the top 12 environmental pressure groups have operating budgets totalling around $400,000,000 a year, from a donor base of around 13,000,000 contributors. That works out at over 10,000,000 more people and an extra $250,000,000 than the entire combined Democratic and Republican parties have available to them.

The volume of work created by these advocacy groups, particularly in the area of environmental protection, is forcing organizations to focus on the introduction of issues management systems and new functions to manage them. In recent years, big businesses have shifted their thinking, believing there are commercial as well as social advantages to communicating about the steps they are taking to reduce their impact on precious resources without redressing the imbalance in some way. Many companies now publish environmental policy statements and employ specialists to devise strategies for cleaning up manufacturing processes and developing environmental initiatives in the community. Similarly, some organizations are implementing marketing and sponsorship programmes designed to promote brand awareness but in an ethically sustainable manner. 'Advocacy advertising' and 'cause-related marketing' campaigns are run by companies such as Levi Strauss, Benetton, J&B, Body Shop and many retail banks.

In his book, *The Critical Issues Audit* (1994), Eli Sopow refers to news content analysis research which shows a consistent pattern by advocacy groups or individuals who are attempting to gain public support for their action. The steps are listed below and shown in Figure 1.4:

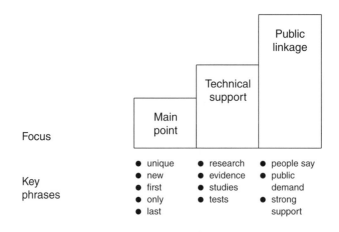

Source: Sopow, E, 1994

Figure 1.4 *Advocacy approach*

Step 1: A key point of conflict is established, generally presented in simple terms. Action words are used by advocates to create a sense of urgency. Those words include *unique, new, first, only, last.*

Step 2: Once the issue has been identified as important/urgent it requires legitimacy. This is provided through apparent scientific and technical confirmation, with action words like *research, evidence, studies, tests.*

Step 3: The issue now has a sharp focus, and is backed up with scientific research. This step incorporates the necessary ingredient of broad-based public support. Action words are *people say, public demand, strong support.*

In formulating a potential strategy relating to an emerging issue, it is possible to anticipate some of the types of tactics that advocacy groups are likely to adopt. These tactics help to mobilize public opinion in such a way that pressure for public policy change – ie greater industry regulation – can be brought to bear.

Using our phthalates example, these tactics will include:

- Advocating, through the media and independent scientific experts, the need for a (long-term) comprehensive and independently commissioned research programme (to be funded by government and industry) to established 'benchmark criteria'; the aim is to pressurize government to take action to eliminate synthetic chemicals that disrupt hormones and a key objective here is to shift the burden of proof to chemical manufacturers.
- Proposing the development of a model similar to the 1987 Montreal Protocol, an international treaty that mandates the phase-out of CFCs and other ozone-depleting chemicals on an international basis.

In addition, advocacy groups could encourage activists at grass roots level via calls to:

- prevent exposure to hormone-disrupting chemicals through their total elimination;
- regulate every new compound so that before it is allowed to enter commercialization it is subjected to tests by manufacturers to ascertain what risks the chemicals pose;
- protect against the vulnerability of children and the unborn, taking into account that the effects of exposure on developmental processes are usually irreversible;
- change specific regulations and laws to take into account the additive and interactive effects of chemicals, not simply the effects of each individual chemical;

- assess contaminant levels from any single source within the context of total cumulative exposure rather than on an individual basis;
- manufacturers to provide comprehensive labels for their products so consumers have the information they need to protect themselves and their families from hormonally active compounds;
- force manufacturers/distributors to accept responsibility for monitoring their products for contamination;
- companies to detail the quantity of hormone-disrupting compounds incorporated into their products;
- collate comprehensive records of birth defects and symptoms of impaired function to determine whether significant changes are occurring;
- force governments to collaborate cross-border to act in the face of a genuine threat to human welfare.

So, the industry or organizational 'issue action plan' needs to factor in the methods of working and approaches of special interest groups in order to effectively respond to this type of agenda setting. In addition, companies now need to be taking steps to actively consult with the communities of which they are a part.

PUBLIC CONSULTATION – BUILDING DIALOGUE INTO THE COMMUNICATIONS PROCESS

In today's disaffected political environment in many Western countries, leaders in government and business are being called upon to embrace genuine public input. Public consultation is an increasingly important facet of *outside-in thinking*. It is about building dialogue into the communications process to minimize conflict and to achieve as much consensus as possible in balancing the scales of protectionism and developmentalism.

Simply assuming that being aware of upcoming issues, distributing some literature, placing some ads and holding a few 'town hall' meetings would create the result the company wanted in the first place is completely outdated. Public concern over what constitutes 'sustainable development' will continue to increase. As we learn more about the real pressures on the environment, it is argued that many of us will feel a desire to push for a slow-down in the remorseless progress of industrialization. The result is that a company's well-researched and very reasonable proposal relating to seeking planning permission for a new development on the edge of a green belt area may not seem so reasonable to people who already feel threatened by environmental degradation.

We were involved in such a case some years ago, when a company waiting for confirmation of planning permission to operate a low-level radioactive waste facility was confronted – much to its surprise – by a well-organized, articulate and highly vocal local community campaign. In spite of stressing that the type of waste that would be stored at the facility posed virtually no risk to human health, local teachers, parents, children and government officials, already living in a catchment area of research establishments working with nuclear materials, felt that enough was enough. One more facility, however safe it might be, was one too many in the risk/benefit equation. Anxiety over the perceived additional risk to their health and that of the environment, and a failure on the part of the organization involved to develop a more proactive public consultation process during the application for planning permission, created mistrust and a militant response. Parents and children marched on the premises of the company, under the watchful eye of local television, radio and newspaper reporters. Although we don't expect zero risk, we do want to get as close to it as possible.

THE RISE OF THE PRECAUTIONARY PRINCIPLE

A lack of *outside-in thinking* by organizations is giving rise to the 'precautionary principle', with potentially disastrous consequences for both business and society.

In this era of the triple bottom line – the achievement of a balance between commercial success, environmental responsibility and social justice – the stakes are becoming much higher for companies in their dealings with the outside world.

The cumulative effect of a succession of highly publicized health and food safety issues in recent years has contributed to a culture of blame and uncertainty. While consumers have become better informed and sophisticated – with rapidly rising expectations in relation to product and service choice, quality, value and access – they have also become more anxious about the complexity and pace of change that both drives and serves these demands.

Businesses should by now understand that successful companies are those which are outward-facing and which understand not only who their audiences are, but also what they think and what they want. So why are companies so often surprised by controversy? Probably because they are used to rational decision making based on technical and scientific data. They fail to understand that an issue can be viewed in many different ways and that emotion is a powerful changemaker.

There are many examples over the last 10 years of companies that have failed to put this into practice: Monsanto, Merck, Cadbury, Nike, McDonald's and Coca-Cola are just a few.

Added to which, some parts of the media have been directly responsible for manipulating sensible and justified calls for greater accountability to create a situation in which the public has become totally risk-averse. The genetically modified food furore during 2000 was punctuated by media coverage that *campaigned* rather than *reported* – to the extent that the media was driving the issue to fit its own agenda. Sensational head-lines of the 'Frankenstein Food' variety quickly influenced a British public which has, for the most part, only a basic scientific education.

This, in turn, has been amplified by the workings of sophisticated pressure groups. Such situations can all too readily be channelled through pressure on government agencies to introduce tougher and costlier legislation and, ultimately, litigation.

In the wider context of corporate responsibility, the precautionary principle is a gift to those campaigning for greater restraints on business. It was first mooted in 2000 as justification for the delay in approving GM crops across Europe and there are now demands for a no-testing policy.

More recently, a government-sponsored report on mobile phones advocated a precautionary stance, while acknowledging the absence of evidence that mobile phones are damaging to health. The result has been a very confused British public.

If this trend continues, there is likely to be a stalemate with all new technologies. The discovery of the genetic blueprint for life was triumphantly welcomed in headlines around the world – but in today's climate of hostility to change, the ability to apply this new knowledge for the benefit of mankind may well be hampered.

It is clearly time for the balance to be redressed. This can only be done through early and open communication. Policy-makers need to work alongside industry to communicate in ways to which the public can relate; they need to reclaim the 'middle ground' and demonstrate both competence and honesty. Unless they do, the gap between their own efforts and the machinations of the media and other self-interested groups will grow ever larger, and 'caution' will undermine progress.

CASE STUDY: PHTHALATES IN TOYS

Phthalates have been used in a wide range of products for almost 50 years, because of their ability to turn rigid polyvinyl chloride (PVC) into a flexible product. In the mid-1990s the safety of phthalates, particularly in children's toys, was called into question amid claims that they could cause cancers, liver damage and hormonal disruption. Environmental NGOs in Europe and the United States launched a concerted campaign to ban phthalates in children's toys, and despite a lack of clear scientific evidence that phthalates could pose a health risk, the EU eventually banned phthalates at the end of 1999 in teething rings and toys that could be sucked by children under the age of three. Similar measures were subsequently introduced in the United States.

Greenpeace was the most influential campaigner against phthalates in toys, and for many years had highlighted environmental health risks from chlorine and associated plastics manufacture. In 1996 it began contacting leading toy manufacturers requesting meetings to discuss concerns about PVC toys, and began targeting the European Commission.

By April 1997, the Danish Environmental Protection Agency (EPA) stated that the level of phthalates in teething rings was 'unacceptable', and Danish importers voluntarily withdrew teethers from the market pending further research. The European Commission referred the concerns regarding phthalates to the newly appointed Scientific Committee on Toxicity, Ecotoxicity and Environment (CSTEE) for investigation.

In September 1997 Greenpeace launched its 'Play Safe' campaign in New York and London, 100 days before Christmas. The campaign increased direct action against manufacturers and retailers – a list of PVC and non-PVC infant toys was made available to parents in an attempt to target manufacturers such as Mattel and retailers such as Toys'R'Us. Greenpeace's claims continued to be widely and sensationally reported by the media. The following month saw requests from the Austrian consumer affairs minister and Belgium's public health minister for the voluntary withdrawal of PVC toys on the basis of precautionary consumer protection. A domino effect followed across Europe, with similar restrictions being introduced in Italy, Germany and Spain. Retailers in these countries began to withdraw branded PVC products from sale. In December 1997, a German toy retailer association responded by calling for a total withdrawal of PVC toys.

Although scientific evidence indicated no adverse human health effects, under growing media and NGO pressure, the European Commission requested that the CSTEE set up a working group to investigate the impact of phthalates on children's health, and to suggest appropriate limits and test methods. The Commission removed all PVC toys from its childcare facilities as 'a precautionary measure' in February 1998.

Throughout 1998 there was considerable scientific debate on phthalates, but not much in the way of a concerted response from industry. The World Health Organization (WHO) denied phthalates had carcinogenic properties, but under concerted NGO and media pressure the European Commission still agreed a non-binding recommendation to withdraw teething rings from use. Member states were invited to adopt appropriate safety measures while Community legislation for permanent protection was prepared. Between 1998 and 1999, eight EU countries introduced their own restrictions on the production and sale of phthalates. The government bans gave Greenpeace considerable ammunition to advance its crusade against the plastics industry.

In July 1999 the European CSTEE reported that scientific research showed there was no immediate health risk. However, in December 1999 the EC went ahead with a three-month renewable ban on PVC toys and teething products intended to be put in the mouths of children under three, pending future legislation. The ban has been continuously renewed since then. On 6 July 2000 the European Parliament voted on a draft Council Directive on phthalates in toys, requiring the banning of all phthalates in plastic toys for children under three years of age. This was followed by a demand by the European Parliament for a policy to replace soft PVC.

In the United States, industry capitulation was also swift. Government agencies, toy manufacturers and toy retailers came under pressure to remove phthalates from their products following the regulatory action in EU countries. Greenpeace accelerated its campaign in the United States during this period; at the opening of the International Toy Fair in New York in autumn 1998, activists abseiled down the side of a building to unfurl a banner that said 'Play Safe, Buy PVC Free'. Relentless pressure from Greenpeace and the US environmental NGO Environmental Defense (ED) led some larger US manufacturers to remove phthalates from their products, and Mattel announced voluntary action to remove phthalates from soft toys in 1998.

In December 1998 the US Consumer Product Safety Commission (CPSC) asked industry, as a precautionary measure, to remove one particular phthalate (DINP) from soft rattles and teethers in spite of a CPSC study demonstrating that 'the amount ingested does not even come close to a harmful level'. The plastics industry was requested to remove phthalates from soft toys and teethers to 'alleviate the mood of fear and as a precaution while more scientific work is being done'.

Environmental Defense maintained the pressure. In October 2000, it wrote to 100 US toy manufacturers requesting voluntarily disclosure of the chemical constituents of their products 'either targeted for young children or that in

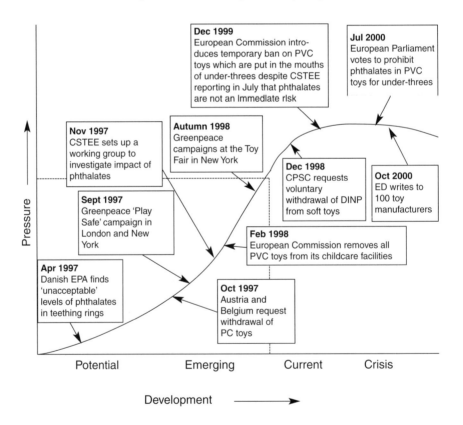

Figure 1.5 *Phthalates in toys issue lifecycle*

use involves mouthing or extensive skin contact by children including older children'. Unwisely, the Juvenile Product Manufacturers Association (JPMA) and the Toy Manufacturers Association (TMA) responded by saying that they did not think this was necessary, enabling Environmental Defense to claim that 'they would say that, wouldn't they?' through ongoing media articles and advertising campaigns.

European and American regulatory reaction towards the phthalates campaign ultimately forced the plastics industry to withdraw its products. Companies producing, selling and using phthalates took a wholly unnecessary hit to their reputation and to their financial performance. Why? Because of a total failure to understand the dynamics of the issue lifecycle curve, the triggers that can escalate a risk issue out of control, and a complete inability to communicate early on and in any concerted way to offset public perception of a wildly exaggerated health risk. If you see national regulatory agencies calling for voluntary restrictions on products, recognize that you are already forfeiting any chance of navigating your way round the risk perception icebergs! (Source: Larkin, 2003.)

CASE STUDY: CHINESE TAKEAWAYS HIT NORTH AMERICAN AND UK BUSINESS

There was a steep rise in concern over products imported from China in 2007. Many companies were affected by tainted products from the Far East, ranging from pet foods and proteins to toothpaste and tyres, fish and Fisher-Price. Two companies, in particular, were affected – Canada's Menu Foods Income Fund and America's Mattel.

The saga kicked off in March 2007 after three weeks of complaints from consumers that certain brands of pet food were leading to ill health and death among animals. Menu Foods, the largest maker of wet cat and dog food in North America, responded with a voluntary recall on 16 March after company tests confirmed kidney failure in test animals. Several other companies followed suit, and the source was discovered to be contaminated wheat gluten and contaminated rice product from China. Overall, several major companies recalled more than 5,300 pet food products, most from Menu Foods. The company said that it would compensate pet owners who could trace their pets' illnesses to the company's products. Menu Foods said that a 'clerical error' had resulted in a recall delay in Canada. A spokesman told the *USA Today*: 'Humans are not perfect. Someone made a mistake.' The company later estimated the recall had cost it at least US$42 million (without taking into account reduced sales).

The widespread reports of possible melamine contamination (a chemical used to give the impression of increased protein content) in pet food led to fears that food supply for humans from China could be affected too. Subsequently, the US Food and Drug Administration (FDA) subjected all vegetable proteins imported from China, intended for human or animal consumption, to detention without physical examination. The US Department of Agriculture said that between 2.5 and 3 million people in the United States had eaten chickens that had been given feed containing contaminated vegetable protein from China, but that the threat to human health was minimal. The whole event prompted an increase in sales of natural pet food in the United States. One report said that Menu Foods faces 90 class-action lawsuits as a result of the contamination.

In May 2007, China announced that two company managers had been detained, accused of adding melamine to food additives. It also sentenced to death its former head of the State Food and Drug Administration for corruption and dereliction of duty. Dozens of people in China have died in recent years because of poor-quality drugs.

China's State Cabinet also announced a crackdown on corruption in the food industry, as well as plans for a new product recall process for 'potentially dangerous and unapproved food products'. Subsequently, China's former head of the State Food and Drug Administration was executed for corruption.

Then, in June, Colgate-labelled toothpaste sold in discount shops in the United States was found to contain a toxic chemical used in anti-freeze. The same chemical had been found in toothpaste sold in Nicaragua a few weeks earlier, which had prompted the US FDA to warn US consumers against buying toothpaste exported from China. The US FDA said the toothpaste was a low health risk to humans. Colgate said the products were counterfeit and it would never use such a chemical in its toothpaste. However, it did recall the 100-millil-itre tubes (the size of the fake tubes) from retail stores in several parts of the United States. It also said it would work with the American Dental Association and the American Dental Hygienists to help answer queries. Colgate-Palmolive's chief executive and chairman, Reuben Mark, said: 'We will spare no effort to help consumers avoid counterfeits and support regulators in their efforts to remove these products from the marketplace.'

Next, US regulators ordered a major recall of tyres made in China. A New Jersey firm (Foreign Tire Sales) was ordered to recall 450,000 truck tyres and was in the process of suing the Chinese manufacturers over safety fears. The company said a full product recall would result in bankruptcy and said that six other US firms had also imported the defective tyres. It is understood that Foreign Tire Sales is being sued by relatives of two men killed in 2006 in a crash involving a vehicle that apparently used the faulty tyres. The Chinese manufac-turer, Zongce, denied these safety claims and said it had received no complaints from its other US customers. The Chinese government later defended the company, saying the tyres were 'qualified to be sold in the US'.

Also during June, the US FDA announced that it had halted the import of five types of farmed Chinese seafood, which contained antibiotics not permitted in North America.

The Chinese government later admitted that nearly a fifth of goods made and sold in the country were 'sub-standard'. China's General Administration of Quality, Supervision, Inspection and Quarantine tested a variety of products, but did not include exported products. The government later admitted the country had failed to fully protect the public over the food and drug safety issues.

However, China then suspended imports from several US meat suppliers, saying that officials had found salmonella and growth enhancers in chicken products. Beijing named Tyson Foods as the company whose products contained salmonella. Other companies indicted by China were Sanderson Farms, Cargill Meat Solutions, AJC International and Triumph Foods.

In response to the spate of product safety breaches, President Bush set up the Import Safety Working Group to look at the safety of food and other products imported into the country. The US FDA faced criticism for not adequately monitoring the safety of goods consumed in the United States.

In August 2007, Mattel recalled nearly 1.5 million Chinese-made Fisher-Price toys in the United States and the UK over fears that their paint contained too much lead. Fisher-Price's general manager said there would be a 'dramatic investigation'. Days later, the boss of the Mattel Chinese contract manufacturer committed suicide. Mattel chief executive Robert Eckert said: 'In the long term I think we won't be judged by the fact that a mistake was made in a vendor's plant, but instead we'll be judged on how we respond.'

The following days saw the number of recalls from Mattel reach 18 million from around the world. The company is believed to source its products from about 3,000 factories across China. There are over 10,000 toy factories in China (mostly working for export), producing around 80 per cent of the world's toys. The company said on 20 August 2007 that it had recovered only 8,000 of the 2 million items it had recalled in the UK. Mattel set up an arm of its website with the slogan 'Your children are our children too'. It contained detailed information and a personal video message from CEO Bob Eckert addressing 'fellow parents'. On 16 August, the hotline dealing with the Mattel recall in Britain and Ireland crashed owing to 'sheer volume of calls'. At the time of writing, the recall is still in full flow.

Soon after the recall announcement, China banned pork imports from several US suppliers, saying they contained a banned growth hormone, ractopamine. It has also sent back shipments of soya beans and pacemakers. On 24 August, the Chinese government then blamed changes in international safety standards for the recalls, saying that some foreign media reports were 'hyped' and 'untruthful' and had hurt China's image.

August also saw other companies in the United States, the UK, New Zealand and Saudi Arabia pulling Chinese products off their shelves.

China announced that it would spend US$1.1 billion to improve food and drug safety by 2010. This plan had begun two years previously, but was only announced in August 2007.

Most press reaction focused on the spate of recalls in relation to the damage to the 'Made in China' brand. US press reaction was largely focused on the dangers to the US consumer. It was unsympathetic toward Menu Foods. The *Seattle Post-Intelligencer* said: 'Pet owners deserve their day in court over the massive tainting of cat and dog food... The suits could be one way for people who lost pets to encourage companies to prevent repeats.' The *Pittsburgh Post-Gazette* said: 'Not only will the class-action suits seek justice for pet lovers, but they will also put manufacturers on notice that they are producing food for valued members of the family. In other words, handle with extreme care.'

However, Mattel garnered favourable press in the United States, with some commentators saying their handling was 'textbook' crisis management. *The Financial Times* said the Mattel Fisher-Price recall came as a surprise because 'Mattel is considered to have some of the best practices for monitoring overseas manufacturing, including owning many of the factories it uses in China.' The Lex column in the *FT* said that the Chinese economy would not be affected at any significant level by the recalls. It said that toys account for 1–2 per cent of Chinese exports, which total at US$1,200 billion. At the time of writing, the amount of items affected by recalls is US$700 million.

After the announcement of the Fisher-Price recall, the *Wall Street Journal* said: 'Most notably, Mattel has taken the lead in identifying and recalling the toys... Some American companies doing business in China have been slow to wake up to the challenge and responsibility of managing quality control there. They're waking up now, as they realize their brand reputations depend on it.'

However, after the announcement of the major recall, the *Wall Street Journal* said:

Mattel's second major toy recall in as many weeks is giving executives a public-relations migraine and investors the jitters... The key point is that companies like Mattel and its suppliers have every incentive to do something about faulty products, not merely to appear to be doing so... Mattel knows all too well that the cost of salvaging its brand would far exceed any marginal profit gain from winking at quality in the name of squeezing its suppliers on price... For toy makers – and their suppliers – getting a reputation for unsafe toys could be fatal... Parents will decide in coming months how much they trust products made for Mattel in China... Most investors know that consumers will punish companies for safety problems, but that politicians pose an even greater threat if they use the product recalls as an excuse for protectionism.

The *Guardian* said the toy recall was 'the latest trade tiff between the US and China... So far, there is no record of harm done – unless you count manufac-turers' reputations, the orthodoxy of outsourcing and free trade... This toy scare will only add to the misgivings over freer markets.'

Outcome

It is still unknown how much each recall will cost the numerous companies involved. However, Mattel estimated the Fisher-Price recall to cost US$30 million, but the company's share price has not been significantly hit.

It appears that one or two companies have been caught up in a so-called trade war between the United States and China. The move by China to ban US pork imports after the Mattel recall was seen by many as retaliation for the toy recall and raised the spectre of trade wars. Indeed, the *Financial Times* said that non-tariff barriers, including product standards, are being used and will be used frequently to regulate global trade.

Supply chain issues have been on the radar of businesses for a while, but rarely have the issues exploded into life as they did in 2007. This may herald a raft of regulatory measures imposed on manufacturers at home and abroad. On 23 August 2007, US lawmakers said that they were requesting information from 19 US companies affected by the tainted Chinese imports. In the UK, Gary Grant, chairman of the Toy Retailers Association, said: 'As a retailer and as a parent, I would be happy to give my children products that are sourced from China. But to quantify that, it would need to be known brands, such as Mattel and Hasbro, which have stringent testing in place.'

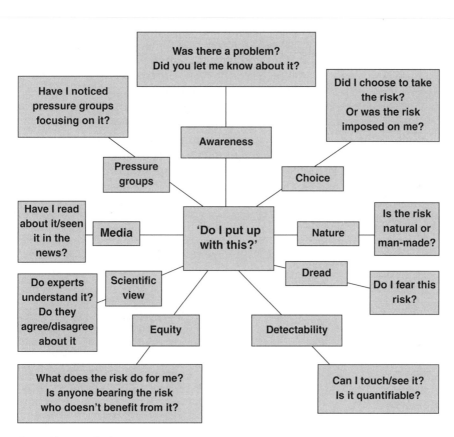

Source: Regester Larkin

Figure 1.10 *Risk perception wheel*

SUMMARY

The difficulty for companies setting off down a more assertive public consultation route is that they should be prepared not to get their own way on every occasion. Unsuccessful consultation can actually polarize or further divide public opinion. Nevertheless, taking an active role in communicating about issues through adopting a more 'inclusive' approach in the influencing and consultation process will, we believe, prove to be an essential requirement if the current fault-line between financial and sustainable success is to be removed.

Outside-in thinking depends on an organization's ability to move away from one-way information flow towards active *dialogue* with a wide range of stakeholder groups. Institutions and companies, upon which we depend to provide and protect, must run much faster both to resolve potential conflict *and* achieve consensus about their role and relationship in society. Those who fail to address the need for this type of change, as we shall illustrate in the following chapters, may simply forfeit their licence to operate.

2

Issues management defined

One moment of patience may ward off disaster; one moment of impatience may ruin a whole life.

Anon

As we described in the previous chapter, organizations are running just to stay in place in their chosen markets as rapidly shifting public values, rising expectations, demands for public consultation and an increasingly intrusive news media present greater challenges.

A recent US public opinion survey of 1,000 consumers showed that half had actively boycotted a company at some time, with a further 26 per cent saying they had joined a boycott within the past year. Their outrage was caused by bad customer service, poor quality products and environmentally unsound actions. They objected to corporations whose values were out of sync with their own. The mismatch between political and public priorities, as we shall see in the following chapters, is even more pronounced. The actions of politicians and political institutions today are inconsistent with changing public attitudes leading to greater frustration, anxiety and lack of trust in the integrity and effectiveness of elected officials (Sopow, 1994).

How issues are handled can mean the difference between a crisis out of control and a proactive solution – between profit and loss. From our own experience, many issues can be anticipated and successfully managed. On the negative side, however, many organizations still fail to see there is a problem.

WHAT IS ISSUES MANAGEMENT?

Issues management has been around for almost 30 years, but while it has been adopted by some major corporations as a powerful strategic planning tool, it has not attracted the widespread attention we believe it deserves.

In the mid-1970s, an atmosphere of increased hostility towards corporations led business communicators to rethink the role of corporate communication. The groundswell of public suspicion about private sector management was reflected through two trends. While some 40 years ago public opinion surveys reflected a clear majority in favour of the practices of business management (an 85 per cent score was typical), 35 years on that figure had slumped to around 10–15 per cent. During the same period companies, increasingly subject to criticism, hired public relations firms in droves to defend them in the face of growing public opposition. Budgets grew tenfold, running into billions of dollars annually, but this did nothing to stop the decline of public support for corporate enterprise.

Issues management was an attempt to define the strategies that companies needed to use to counter the efforts of activist groups which were putting pressure on legislators for stricter controls of business activity. 'Despite the billions of dollars companies and their associations have spent on *external relations* business in general has been ineffective in defining and then validating its position on public policy issues' (Jones and Chase, 1979). So, a new area of corporate communication emerged – issues management was first implemented as a way in which companies could deal with their critics.

In 1978, the US Public Affairs Council defined it as 'a program which a company uses to increase its knowledge of the public policy process and enhance the sophistication and effectiveness of its involvement in that process'. Heath and Cousino offer their own explanation of issues management as 'a product of activism and the increasing inter- and intra-industry pressures by corporations to define and implement corporate social responsibility (CSR) – as well as the debate in public about what the standard of CSR should be' (1990).

Many saw the early role of issues management in the United States as an effective means to avoid large sums of clean-up money and a way to forestall incoming government legislation on employment and other social issues.

Tradition has it that in 1977 W Howard Chase coined the term 'issue management'. Chase drew upon his experience at American Can Company and the lead of another specialist who introduced the term 'advocacy advertising' to recommend a new kind of corporate communication response to the critics of business activities. Companies were advised to move from an information base to an advocacy position because 'companies should not be the silent children of society' (Chase, 1984). Since then, the relationship between business and society has become an important strategic factor in reputational and financial performance terms.

Chase and his colleague Barry Jones defined issues management as a tool which companies could use to identify, analyse and manage emerging issues (in a populist society experiencing discontinuous change) and respond to them *before* they became public knowledge. They felt that most companies reacted after the fact and were forced to accept what new regulations and guidelines were given to them.

> When challenged by today's activism, business tends to react to overt symptoms, rather than by identifying and analyzing fundamental causes of the trend which has led to a critical issue. It is not surprising, then, that when a critical issue reaches the public policy decision-making point, business finds itself the defendant in the court of public opinion.
>
> (Jones and Chase, 1979)

Public policy also needs defining and one expert says:

> Public policy is a specific course of action taken collectively by society or by a legitimate representative of society, addressing a specific problem of public concern, that reflects the interests of society or particular segments of society.
>
> (Buchholz, 1988)

Some experts describe the formation of public policy in terms of the interplay of government, the media and the public. As an issue gains momentum, a climate of opinion is created that puts pressure on government to do something about it. If, however, interest flags in any one of the three components then the issue will lose momentum (Ito, 1993).

Any section of society can and will exert some sort of pressure on government and its influence over corporations. Jones and Chase describe the formation of public policy as the result of interaction between public and private points of view. They state that a corporation has every moral and legal right to help formulate public policy instead of waiting for governments to pass legislation. As a result, more organizations, particularly in the United States, see issues management as an integral part of strategic planning and a basic ingredient for corporate survival.

Hainsworth, in a 1990 article, describes the importance of issues management:

41

Where legislation and regulation are concerned, issues are always resolved to someone's advantage and to someone's disadvantage. If it is the object of corporate management to maximize the organization's profits and minimize its losses in a socially responsible manner, then issues management should be seen as a critical element in overall corporate planning and management.

WHAT ABOUT THE SCEPTICS?

Critics of the term 'issues management' feel that it implies manipulation – 'of conditions or events which are the natural and freely occurring output of a pluralistic society' (Brown, 1979). Others argue that no organizational management can allow its environment to stand still, nor can it decide the direction in which the environment will change.

Scepticism about adopting issues management as a clearly defined function exists in the following areas according to Tucker and Broom:

Financial risk – the link between issues management and the bottom line is a tenuous one, normally only realizing benefit over the long term, if at all. *Boundaries* – issues-based communication is just one tool used in conjunction with, for example, research, corporate planning, change management and other media and communication activities. It is both difficult to define and evaluate in isolation. *Diversity* – the people actively conducting and taking part in the issues management function are not only from public relations backgrounds; they may include lawyers, corporate planners and analysts, researchers, etc. It may be inappropriate to assume that the public relations practitioner is the single driving force behind issues management.

Furthermore, some specialists question the degree to which a disciplined acceptance of and approach to issues management is actually applied inside the organization.

Research conducted in 2006 across a sample of 22 major public corporations in the UK on behalf of Regester Larkin indicated that:

- Recent world events, particularly 9/11, have resulted in companies developing a more robust approach to preparing for bad times, with serious interest at board level. The companies interviewed had clear structures and procedures.
- Issue management is usually driven by communications, public affairs – or a designated team.
- Issues are prioritized using a matrix, and a team is allocated to each priority issue. Issues reports go to the board of directors.
- Crisis or incident management is usually driven by a designated senior team with cross-functional support.

- There is a tendency to devolve issue and crisis management to the businesses, with guidelines and oversight from the centre.
- The barrier between operational crisis management and communications no longer exists, and communications people are an integral part of the team.
- External public affairs and investor relations support plays an important role, but generalist PR company support is rarely employed.
- Industry associations are seen to play an important role in educating members about the need to prepare for the bad times and in sharing best practice.
- The term 'issue management' was generally used, well understood and interpreted as follows:
  - 'Slow burn, with a potential for crisis.'
  - 'Things to watch that can affect the industry.'
  - 'There is still an opportunity to influence and manage it.'
- The few companies that did not use the term 'issue management' thought in terms of potential crises: 'We don't talk about issues, just degrees of crisis.'

Academic research and practical case study examples demonstrate that effective use of issues management techniques can:

- increase market share;
- enhance corporate reputation;
- save money;
- build important relationships;
- protect business continuity; and
- mitigate risk and associated regulatory impacts.

Failure to do so can lead to market share erosion, impact reputation, incur significant expense, put management in a negative spotlight and reduce corporate independence through increased regulation.

Having worked across both areas for many years, our experience tells us that issues management is not crisis management and the two terms should not be used interchangeably. Part of the difficulty in defining and understanding the principles of issues management is that it is less action-oriented and more anticipatory in nature than crisis management. Issues management is proactive in that it tries to identify the potential for change and influence decisions relating to that change before it has a negative effect on a corporation. Crisis management tends to be a more reactive discipline dealing with a situation *after* it becomes public knowledge and affects the company. It is needed after there is public outrage.

Dealing with crisis situations is much more immediate and we have learnt to have an overnight bag at the ready wherever we are. There is normally a clear focus, and a finite set of actions and audiences and information that needs to be communicated within a short timescale. With issues management, organizations should be aiming to eliminate any possibility of outrage, often by trying to anticipate trends, changes and events that may have a bearing on the ability of the corporation to continue to operate or, indeed, achieve competitive benefit.

Issues management involves looking into the future to identify potential trends and events that *may* influence the way an organization is able to operate but which currently *may* have little real focus, probably no sense of urgency and an unclear reference in time.

According to US issues management specialists, Tucker and Broom (1993):

> Issues management is the management process whose goal is to help preserve markets, reduce risk, create opportunities and manage image (corporate reputation) as an organisational asset for the benefit of both an organisation and its primary shareholders.

WHAT IS AN ISSUE?

It will come as no surprise to discover that there are many definitions of an issue offered by business communicators and academics on both sides of the Atlantic.

An issue arises, according to US specialists Hainsworth and Meng (1988):

> as a consequence of some action taken, or proposed to be taken, by one or more parties which may result in private negotiation and adjustment, civil or criminal litigation, or it can become a matter of public policy through legislative or regulatory action.

Chase and Jones describe an issue as 'an unsettled matter which is ready for decision'. Others suggest that, in its basic form, an issue can be defined as a point of conflict between an organization and one or more of its audiences. A simple definition that we like to use is that an issue represents 'a gap between corporate practice and stakeholder expectations'. In other words, an emerging issue is a condition or event, either internal or external to the organization, that if it continues will have a significant effect on the functioning or performance of the organization or on its future interests.

Example triggers for issues management include the potential for new legislation, an opinion or claim advocated through the media or other channels, a competitive development, published research, a change in the performance or behaviour of the organization itself or individuals or groups to whom it is linked.

Managing issues frequently involves dealing with change. An overall aim is to bring some control to the impact caused by discontinuity in the environment (Heath and Nelson, 1986). The ultimate goal, according to Hainsworth and Meng, is to shape public policy to the benefit of the organization through:

- early identification of the potential impact of the change; and
- organized activity, based on sound management principles and techniques, and allowing time for analysis and creative thinking to influence the evolution and, ultimately, the outcome of that change.

It is important to remember, however, that managing issues should not be considered a defensive activity. Although most of the time we are asked to advise companies on how to minimize the commercial risks associated with change, positive opportunities for repositioning a product or process, or communicating new benefits do exist *if they are looked for.* The creation of new issues or the gathering and management of information and opinion relating to an issue can be harnessed by an organization for significant competitive or social advantage.

WHO SHOULD PRACTISE ISSUES MANAGEMENT?

A major question relating to issues management is who is best placed to practise it? Chase feels that issues management derives strength from public relations, and from its various disciplines – public affairs, communications and government relations. He goes on to say that issues management is the highway along which public relations practitioners can move into full participation in management decision making (Chase, 1984).

> Public relations practitioners understand that they are expected to play increasingly complex and involved roles in promoting the bottom line, building harmonious relations with stockholders, and protecting corporate interests in ways that must be sensitive to the needs of a variety of external interests.
>
> (Heath and Cousino, 1990)

We believe public relations practitioners are well placed to help manage issues effectively but often lack the necessary access to strategic planning functions or an appropriate networking environment which encourages informal as well as formal contact and reporting.

WHAT ARE THE FUNCTIONS OF ISSUES MANAGEMENT?

The US Public Affairs Council (1978) states that the functions required of issues management are identifying issues and trends, evaluating their impact and setting priorities, establishing a company position, designing company action and response to help achieve the position and implementing the plans.

These functions must occur constantly and be integrated and focused on the central task of helping the organization – through its management. The key tasks of this activity are *planning, monitoring, analysing* and *communicating.*

Heath and Cousino (1990) identify four broad functional requirements for a company to maximize its position and positively sustain its public policy environment, with a principal focus on nurturing relationships with stakeholders.

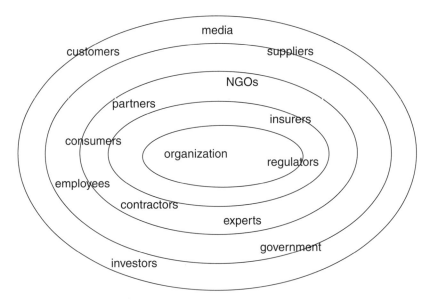

Figure 2.1 *Stakeholder risk radar screen – charting the importance to organization and influence on issue*

Smart planning and operations

If issues managers are doing a good job of capturing the critical changes in the public policy environment then that information should be integrated into the strategic business plan and corporate management strategies. The rationale is that this kind of information can offer business opportunities, justify the curtailment or change of business activities, and guide the standards by which the company operates. 'Issues management can positively affect corporate performance by enhancing the firm's responsiveness to environmental change' (Wartick and Rude, 1986).

Tough defence and smart offence

Issues management offers the rationale, tools and incentives for becoming involved in the discussion of public policy issues as early as possible. If companies get involved before issues have solidified, they can increase the likelihood of their communication campaigns succeeding. In other words, what needs to be said to whom and with what intended effect to exert influence in the public policy arena?

Getting the house in order

According to the authors this is about examining requirements to achieve appropriate commitments to matters of corporate social responsibility. Research in the United States found that market forces alone do not shape the fate of corporations – public policy change plays its role. In addition, public affairs must be sensitive to public policy forces and assist in corporate planning and in the formation of business ethics. The essence of being a responsive organization in the modern world is to move from coping with external demands to anticipating how demands can best be met within the technical and economic context of the organization (Post and Kelley, 1988).

Scouting the terrain

What companies believe to be the nature of the marketplace is likely to influence their strategic business plans. The same can be said of businesses that use issues monitoring to assess the public policy environment. Greater sophistication has been used in an effort to refine strategic management information systems. In addition to straightforward polls and surveys, futurists, for example, have used social scientific techniques to offer valuable insights into the ways issues can be identified, monitored and analysed. The key to making this activity effective is understanding a corporation's culture, its organizational and political structures and the nature of public policy issues analysis. Companies can then determine what issues to monitor and analyse as they refine their public policy and strategic plans. This process requires more than periodic public opinion surveys.

SUMMARY

The importance of anticipation – forward-thinking skills inside the organization – and *outside-in thinking* skills in relation to the role of new and diverse stakeholders, should not be underestimated. The push towards globalization and the requirement for organizations and institutions to understand and respond to the sophisticated demands of consumers and constituents emphasize the critical connection between business and society in the decades ahead.

While practical experience demonstrates that barriers exist to understanding, resourcing and managing the impact of change in the future, we are convinced that the implications of failing to examine the farthest reaches of the lighthouse loom – how issues emerge, mature and are resolved at a political, regulatory, economic, social or technological level – can deprive an organization or an industry of its ability to continue to sustain a viable existence. Equally, evidence exists to suggest that organizations can gain influence and commercial advantage through positively shaping the progress of trends, conditions and events which spawn issues. The rationale for anticipation, planning and progression to minimize risk and capitalize on opportunities in the issues arena are explored in the next chapters.

3

Planning an issues management programme – an issues management model

You can't build a reputation on what you are *going* to do.

Henry Ford

Issues generally evolve in a predictable manner, originating from trends or events and developing through a sequence of identifiable stages that are not dissimilar to the cyclical development of a product. Because the evolution of an issue often results in changes in public policy, the earlier a relevant issue can be identified and managed in terms of a systematic organisational response, the more likely it is that the organisation can resolve conflict and minimise cost implications to its advantage. For this reason, understanding the cyclical development of an issue is critical to effective issues management.

Hainsworth, 1990

Meng (1987) identifies six possible groups or publics that make issues:

associates, employee associations, the general public, government, media and special or general interest groups. Their influence on organizations may vary from controlling the operations of a company to forming internal and external coalitions to increase the potential influence of an issue. So, when issues are ready for decision, organizational response can be critical. Meng characterizes issues into several types: demographic, economic, environmental, governmental, international, public attitudes, resources, technological, and values and lifestyles.

An issue originates as an idea that has potential impact on some organization or public and may result in action that brings about increased awareness and/or reaction on the part of other organizations or publics (Hainsworth, 1990). In a model developed by Hainsworth (1990) and Meng (1992), this process can be described as a cycle made up of four stages: origin, mediation and amplification, organization, and resolution. In Figure 3.1, the vertical axis of the diagram represents the level of pressure exerted on an organization by a developing issue; the horizontal axis represents the various stages of development. At each stage of evolution

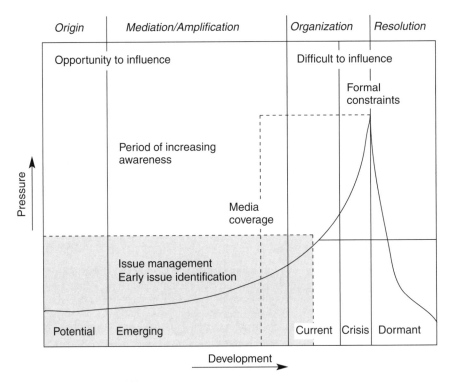

Source: Hainsworth and Meng

Figure 3.1 *Issue lifecycle*

pressure mounts on the organization to respond because of the increasing importance of the issue. An issue can fail at any point in the process for any number of reasons, but issues that continue to mature appear to consistently evolve from one stage to the next.

ISSUE LIFECYCLE

Stage 1 – origin: potential issue

An issue arises when an organization or group attaches significance to a perceived problem (or opportunity) that is a consequence of a developing political/regulatory, economic or social trend (Crable and Vibbert, 1985). From a management perspective, trends must be identified from which issues at some points may emerge. Trends probably first become identified and articulated by academics or specialists participating in working groups, policy and planning units, who may become concerned with some problem, situation or event that has potential impact and demands response from an institution, organization, industry or other group. If a response is forthcoming, it frequently results in counter-responses from those benefiting from the status quo and those desiring change.

An issue begins to gain definition when an organization or group plans to do something that has a consequence for another organization or group (Grunig and Hunt, 1984). Awareness and concern on the part of a group brings about a resolve to 'do something'. Lines become drawn and conflict emerges (Crable and Vibbert, 1985).

So, what we see in the early *potential* stage is a defined condition or event which has the potential to develop into something of importance. The types of issues which exist in this phase, however, have not yet captured significant expert or public attention, although some specialists will begin to be aware of them.

From our own experience in the healthcare sector, an example could be a trend in the increased incidence of a disease or knowledge of forthcoming research that highlights adverse side effects of a drug. At this stage, however, the issue often lacks sufficient form or substance to justify deliberate external intervention, for example by competitors who seek to shape or redirect it. Issues that make it past Stage 1 are alive, have a momentum of their own, and are capable of being modified as they move towards resolution.

In Stage 1, groups or individuals generally begin to establish a certain level of credibility in areas of concern and seek out support from other influencers and opinion leaders who are involved to some degree in that particular area of interest. At this point it is common for those involved to feel a bit uneasy as they begin to recognize that, in some situations, a point of conflict could exist.

The constant scanning of this process and early identification of potential issues is important and should be an integral part of the corporate planning process itself.

(Nagy Hanna, 1985)

Stage 2 – mediation and amplification: emerging issue

As groups emerge and lines become drawn, a process of mediation and amplification occurs among other individuals and groups who may have a similar viewpoint and may be expected to react in a similar way. Initially, this takes place within the relevant specialist media of interest groups, industries, professions and others with comparable opinions, values or concerns. As momentum builds within the mass media, the issue becomes amplified into a public issue that may become part of the public policy process.

The *emerging* issue stage indicates a gradual increase in the level of pressure on the organization to accept the issue. In most cases, this increase is the result of activities by one or more groups as they try to push or legitimize the issue (Meng, 1987). Using our healthcare example, this may involve competitors of a pharmaceutical company using published data to gather support from opinion leaders and influencers such as the media to gain medical community and, ultimately, public/patient acceptance of *their* interpretation of the issue.

At this stage in the issue's development it is still relatively easy for the organization to intervene and play a proactive role in preventing or exploiting the evolution of the issue. However, it is often difficult to determine the urgency of the issue, and we have often found the issue slipping away at this point as management attention evaporates in favour of more immediate and pressing matters. Although it is hard to know whether the issue will remain moderate or increase in intensity, stay confined to a particular area or become pervasive, it can be folly simply to pursue the status quo. We have seen this in recent public health scares and in increasingly persistent and professionally organized grass roots campaigning on animal welfare and environmental issues.

A dominant factor in the development of the issue in this phase is media coverage. Frequent editorial, initially specialist/trade and then broader general/business, begins before the issue reaches the shaded area in Figure 3.1. Before the issue reaches the next stage, those involved usually try to attract media attention as a means of progressing the issue. Sporadic in the beginning, this coverage will eventually become regular and is a critical factor to be considered in the advancement of the issue (Meng, 1987). Time and time again we have been involved in situations where regular competitor assessment, early media scanning and the decision to communicate with the media have happened too late.

According to Hainsworth the process of mediation is critical and has the effect of accelerating the full development of the issue. It is therefore essential that companies which are targeted conduct regular and effective monitoring of the commercial, regulatory and social environment in order to identify Stage 2 issues and begin to formulate action plans to deal with them.

Stage 3 – organization: current and crisis issue

Mediation brings varying degrees of organization. Positions solidify. Groups begin to seek a resolution to the conflict that is either acceptable to their best interests or at least minimizes potential damage.

In the context of the public policy process, publics or groups should be viewed as dynamic. They are often groups of individuals with varying degrees of commitment who face a similar problem, recognize that the problem exists and unite in some way to do something about the problem (Hainsworth, 1990). These groups are not static and their level of organization, funding and media literacy can vary enormously. At one end of the spectrum, they may be informal networks of people sharing only one passing interest in the resolution of the conflict, or they may be highly organized, well connected and funded with an intense and focused commitment.

As these groups work out their viewpoints and objectives and seek to communicate their respective positions, conflict achieves a level of public visibility that is likely to push the issue into the public policy process (Hainsworth, 1990). In turn, increased public attention motivates influential leaders to become a part of the emerging conflict and pressure mounts on institutional bodies to seek a resolution to the conflict.

An example of this process was the establishment of the Snowdrop Campaign in the UK in 1996 which called for a ban on hand guns in the aftermath of the Dunblane massacre. The impact of an individual can be equally effective. In early 1997, a village resident campaigned successfully against his local parish council in Yorkshire, England, to protect 56 yards of hawthorn hedge from being removed to develop a bowling green, with knock-on implications for the protection of 40,000 miles of hedgerow in the UK.

In the *current* phase, the issue has matured and is displaying its full potential upon those involved. It becomes very difficult to affect the issue as it has now become enduring, pervasive and increasing in its intensity. The different parties involved recognize its full importance and, in response, place pressure on regulatory institutions to become involved.

As the issue lifecycle diagram illustrates, in no time at all the issue ramps up from *current* to *crisis* status to reach a formal institution such as a regulatory authority which has the power to intervene and impose constraints on the organization or industry as a way to resolve the situation. This was clearly demonstrated by Exxon Corporation's perceived failure to move swiftly enough to clean up the *Exxon Valdez* oil spill in Alaska in 1989, which led to stiff public policy requirements for ocean-going oil tankers to be built with two hulls.

Similarly, looking at our pharmaceutical industry example, there could be demands for additional safety data through costly new patient trials, blacklisting of specific drugs restricting patient indications, major changes in prescribing information, company-funded patient education programmes and, ultimately, product withdrawal. Options available to the organization to affect or influence the issue are now limited – it is in crisis response mode.

In 1982, Eli Lilly was the target of international media attention and protracted, costly litigation associated with the withdrawal of the anti-arthritic drug, Opren. With claims that the drug caused unpleasant side effects, including persistent photosensitivity, the company was forced into significant out-of-court settlements valued at millions of pounds.

Hundreds more alleged victims of the banned drug sought compensation some 10 years later, but the courts ruled that the majority of claimants had initiated their actions too late. The issue continued to be the focus of adverse media commentary, citing elderly arthritic sufferers attempting to seek compensation from an unsympathetic pharmaceutical giant.

Arguably, if Eli Lilly had moved more quickly to present an efficacy and safety database that could refute the severity of the claims being made against Opren and mobilized supportive opinion leaders to present a balanced case via the media, the company could have avoided such long-term negative consequences.

And, as we shall demonstrate more than once over the following pages, industry quickly forgets the lessons it could have learnt from previously mismanaged situations.

Since the Opren case, there have been many examples of similarly mismanaged situations. Vioxx is another.

CASE STUDY: VIOXX – NEVER IGNORE THE WARNING SIGNS

In 1999, the US Food and Drug Administration (FDA) approved Vioxx, a new Cox-2 selective inhibitor drug that treats acute pain in osteoarthritis. Vioxx was considered to be more effective and better tolerated by patients than other arthritis drugs. It was hailed by the media as a wonder drug for broad pain relief and had achieved record worldwide sales of US$3.5 billion by 2001.

In 2003, the European Committee for Proprietary Medicinal Products said that the benefits of Vioxx outweighed the side-effect risks. However, it recommended stronger warnings of cardiovascular risks associated with the drug.

The Vioxx saga began when Merck voluntarily withdrew the drug after a study linked the drug with an increased prevalence of heart attacks and strokes. At the time, around 2 million people worldwide used the drug. Merck's share price fell to an eight-year low, and Merck said it took the action 'because it best serves the interests of the patients'. The European Medicines Evaluation Agency decided to carry out a safety review of five other arthritis drugs suspected of increasing the risk of heart attacks and strokes. Merck's shares then fell by 10 per cent in November when the *Wall Street Journal* published evidence suggesting the firm had ignored problems with one of its drugs. The newspaper quoted internal company e-mails with a senior official apparently writing that cardiovascular problems 'are clearly there'.

In November 2004, a study in *The Lancet* said that Vioxx should have been withdrawn from the market years before it was. Richard Horton, the *Lancet's* editor, said that the FDA and Merck had acted with 'ruthless, short-sighted and irresponsible self-interest... the licensing of Vioxx and its continued use in the face of unambiguous evidence of harm have been public health catastrophes.' In the same month a US Senate inquiry was told that the FDA was guilty of 'profound regulatory failure' over Vioxx. Raymond Gilmartin, Merck's chief executive, told the inquiry that he believed in Vioxx and had followed correct procedures. The inquiry did not affect Merck's share price.

In December, the US National Cancer Institute (NCI) conducted a study for Pfizer, manufacturer of another Cox-2 drug, Celebrex, which concluded that patients on Celebrex had more than three times the risk of cardiovascular disease than those taking a placebo. The NCI suspended the use of Celebrex after the study, which hit the Pfizer share price. Pfizer said it had no plans to withdraw the drug. The study prompted the UK Medicines and Healthcare Products Regulatory Agency to advise patients taking Cox-2 inhibitors to contact their GPs.

In January 2005, the US FDA released a study in *The Lancet* that suggested Vioxx could have caused up to 140,000 cases of coronary heart disease in the United States. Merck responded by saying there were many risk factors and the report did not show that the drug was to blame. The Arthritis Research Campaign called the study 'shocking'.

In February 2005, a study by Australian scientists in the *Archives of Internal Medicine* said Cox-2 inhibitors caused higher blood pressure than other painkillers. The same day, the US FDA said it would create an independent drug safety oversight board to bolster its procedures. Mike Leavitt, the US House and Human Services Secretary, promised a 'new culture of openness'. Days later, the European Medicines Agency said people who had suffered heart disease or a stroke should not take Cox-2 inhibitors and that doctors should be 'cautious' about prescribing them. The Stroke Association said: 'Last year Vioxx was withdrawn because of this risk. It is now time that the whole class of these drugs be withdrawn too.' Soon after, the US FDA ruled that Vioxx should be allowed to be sold again in the United States, as well as Pfizer's Celebrex. Merck's share price rose 13 per cent after the ruling and, in an attempt to draw a line under the crisis, Richard Clark was named as the company's new CEO, replacing the embattled Raymond Gilmartin.

However, the story did not end there. In June 2005, the *British Medical Journal* carried a study suggesting that all NSAIDs (non-selective non-steroidal anti-inflammatory drugs – a class of painkiller of which Vioxx was one) could be linked with an increased rate of heart attack. The following year, the World Health Organization (WHO) called for stricter registration of clinical drug trials so that negative findings could not be kept secret, and in September 2006 the European Medicines Agency said it would investigate the cardiovascular safety of NSAIDs.

Meanwhile, litigation in the United States developed apace. In April 2005 a Texas jury found Merck guilty of negligence and ordered it to pay the widow of a heart attack victim US$253.4 million. This was the first lawsuit to be filed against Merck over Vioxx, and at this point analysts predicted Merck might end up paying out US$18 billion.

Outcome

The fallout over Merck's perceived poor handling of such a highly visible and damaging issue was significant, not only in terms of potential litigation impacts on the company's financial performance:

- Merck was censured for poor governance, secrecy and 'blindly aggressive marketing'.
- The FDA was accused of 'incompetence and complacency'.
- The company incurred considerable share price and reputational damage, leading to a major restructuring and knock-on consequences for the global pharmaceutical industry.
- The 'scandal' has impacted on trust levels in drug safety and in public health institutions.
- The potential for escalation in drug safety litigation is growing.
- There have been widespread calls for tougher drug safety regulation, greater transparency around clinical trials data management and more public participation as a means to regain trust. (Regulators have been responding via major internal reviews and public commitment to establishing more effective independent drug safety oversight mechanisms.)

Stage 4 – resolution: dormant issue

Once issues receive the attention of public officials and enter the policy process, either through changes to legislation or regulation, efforts to resolve the conflict become protracted and costly, as illustrated by the tobacco industry. The object of the public policy process is the imposition of unconditional constraints on all parties to the conflict – either to their advantage or to their disadvantage (Hainsworth, 1990).

So, once an issue has run the full course of its lifecycle, it will reach a height of pressure that forces an organization to accept it unconditionally. The pervasiveness of anti-smoking legislation in the United States can be viewed as an example of this stage.

The following case studies demonstrate this cyclical development of an issue and the implications of a slow organizational response.

CASE STUDY: MONSANTO WRECKED BRAND AND LOST OPPORTUNITY

Monsanto's plans for the introduction of genetically modified (GM) crops in the UK and more widely in Europe in the mid-1990s met a strong backlash from consumers, environmentalists, regulators and retailers.

Concerns about insufficient testing of GM organisms rapidly became a subject of national media debate. Despite refutations by senior scientists of health risk claims, the issue made front-page news in most national papers. The issue was picked up by the European media – particularly in France, Germany and Italy.

Monsanto continued to roll out its promotional plan, including a $1.5 million advertising campaign, and did not acknowledge stakeholders' concerns about GM products. It left the UK government, European Commission and retailers to respond to rising pressure, intensifying protests, boycotts and regulatory demands.

This resulted in a plummeting share price, and led to its merger with Pharmacia & Upjohn. Hostility to GM foods and Monsanto's attitude also led to the ruination of the UK and wider European markets for other GM producers: 24 of the top 30 European food manufacturers are now 'GM free'.

The story of Frankenstein food

Monsanto's biotechnology division had been very successful in the United States. The company had met little resistance from farmers or food producers to the concept of genetically modified food and its stock was high on Wall Street.

However, throughout the early 1990s, international environmental campaign groups Greenpeace and Friends of the Earth had been campaigning against the introduction of GM crops. In the United States, these campaigns remained marginal and were not viewed by Monsanto as a material threat. The dominant news story was Monsanto's commercial success and imminent expansion into Europe. In 1996, the European Commission approved imports of GM foods and the development of research and supply sites for GM foods.

In spite of growing concern among environmentalists and consumer groups following the EU's approval, it was not until early 1998 that Monsanto's strategy received sustained, hostile media and public attention.

Growing pressure on supermarket chains from environmental groups and consumer associations to label GM products were dismissed by Monsanto. Of key importance was the fact that the company did not acknowledge the different concerns held by European consumers and proceeded with the same strategy it had used in the United States.

Monsanto's attitude contributed to the decision by the frozen-food chain Iceland to announce the removal of GM products from its own-brand goods.

Iceland's decision immediately raised questions about the policy of other retailers and increased political pressure in Europe to regulate the sale of GM products and give consumers choice.

Monsanto responded to concerns in the European media with a misguided $1.5 million advertising campaign, including television advertising in the UK. It failed to address growing concerns about the long-term implications of GM and was seen by campaigners and consumers to be aggressive and dismissive.

The growing public and media perception of Monsanto as a company unwilling to address important questions about GM was compounded by its announcement at the beginning of 1998 that it planned to introduce a genetically modified potato. The announcement triggered a wave of critical media coverage.

In a *World in Action* programme screened in April 1998, one of the scientific researchers, Dr Arpad Pusztai, gave an unauthorized comment on the preliminary, unpublished results of tests in which modified potato had been fed to rats. He suggested that immune system damage was possible. Despite refutations of Dr Pusztai's claims by senior scientists at the Rowett Institute Laboratory where he worked, fears about the health effects of genetically modified organisms became the front-page story in many national newspapers.

In October of that year, a summit of international consumer groups accused Monsanto of 'bio-colonialism' and dismissed its claims that biotechnology could help the developing world. By now, the growing concern had reached investors and led to a fall in its share price of 11 per cent. This, allied to the mounting criticism of GM products in Europe, led to the collapse of Monsanto's planned merger with American Home Products. As a result, Monsanto came under increasing pressure from Wall Street to separate off its biotechnology function as the scale of opposition caused panic among shareholders. A report from financial specialists J P Morgan advised Monsanto to restructure.

Early in 1999, Monsanto's chairman, Bob Shapiro, confidently predicted that Europe was ready for the introduction of biotechnology and would provide a gateway for the company to markets in the developing world and the British Commonwealth.

This statement appeared to be at odds with the increasing resistance from European consumers and regulators. In February 1999, the UK's Health and Safety Executive successfully prosecuted Monsanto for its release of GM oilseed rape into the British countryside and the company was fined £17,000.

Oblivious to all, the company continued to roll out its plan and take an aggressive and uncompromising line with any opposition. In April, it failed to win its High Court action against the direct action group Genetix Snowball for destroying the company's crops.

Monsanto left the British government and European ministers to respond to public concerns, despite the fact that pro-GM politicians, including the British Prime Minister Tony Blair, were blatantly failing to stem the tide of negative perceptions towards GM food.

Throughout the summer of 1999, environmental activists kept the issue of GM fears in the news with high-profile direct action tactics. The head of Greenpeace, Lord Melchett, was arrested for uprooting GM crops and the subsequent court hearing was widely covered by the media. In other European countries, particularly Italy, protest centred on retailers that stocked GM products. The media debate intensified when Prince Charles aired his highly critical views on genetically modified organisms in an exclusive interview with the *Daily Mail* newspaper.

The situation in Europe resulted in further falls in Monsanto's share price, and increasing pressure from investors contributed to its merger in July 1999 with Pharmacia & Upjohn. Hostility towards GM foods and Monsanto's attitude also led to the ruination of the UK and wider European markets for other GM producers: 24 of 30 top European food manufacturers pledged that their own products would become 'GM free' over the course of the year.

The battle in Europe was undeniably lost for Monsanto. At Greenpeace's 1999 annual conference, Monsanto's US chairman Bob Shapiro encapsulated the realization of the mistakes made, 'because we thought it was our job to persuade, too often we have forgotten to listen'.

The impact of negative sentiment about GM products was captured by a Deutsche Bank report in August 1999 advising institutional investors to sell their shares in companies involved in the development of GM organisms. It drew attention to Monsanto spending $1.5 million on a wasted advertising campaign and the 11 per cent fall in the value of its stock over the previous six months. The Deutsche Bank report to investors also noted that European consumers had been through a number of food scares and 'hearing from unsophisticated Americans that their fears are unfounded may not be the best way of proceeding'.

It has proved impossible for the Monsanto brand to shake off its pariah status in Europe. In the summer of 2000, the Pharmacia Corporation announced proposals to sell off Monsanto's biotechnology subsidiary.

The outcome

Monsanto's strategy was for Europe to become a major supply and research base for GM products. The company intended simply to replicate its success in the United States. But in the United States, limited protest against GM had not impeded the company's continued expansion. Monsanto had dismissed its opponents as insignificant because they had inadequate scientific knowledge. It therefore rolled out its expansion strategy in Europe in the face of growing negative sentiment, confident that resistance would subside.

The UK government, European Commission, farmers and retailers were left to handle the public reaction. As a result, the company was seen to ignore the concerns of European consumers and opposition became entrenched. Commentators, politicians and even environmentalists who had been willing to support aspects of the GM programme were isolated and retracted their support. Anti-GM sentiment came to dominate Monsanto's attempted expansion into Europe.

CASE STUDY: ARLA PRODUCT BOYCOTT IN THE MIDDLE EAST – ISSUES MANAGEMENT PLANNING NEEDS TO BE GLOBAL

Arla Foods is a cooperative based in Århus, Denmark, and the largest producer of dairy products in Scandinavia. It is owned by 11,000 Danish and Swedish farmers. The company has a large presence in the Middle East, with annual sales there of US$480 million.

On 30 September 2005, Danish newspaper *Jyllands-Posten* published 12 editorial cartoons that depicted the prophet Muhammad. Besides depicting the prophet – which is blasphemy to Muslims – the cartoons were considered by many to be Islamophobic and racist. The newspaper said the cartoons were an attempt to contribute to the debate regarding criticism of Islam and self-censorship. Between October 2005 and February 2006, the cartoons were reprinted in several major European newspapers in Norway, the Netherlands, Germany, Belgium and France. This led to protests from Muslims across the world. Protest action included: setting fire to the Norwegian and Danish embassies in Damascus and Beirut; attacks on the Danish embassy in Tehran; and gunmen storming an EU building in Gaza City demanding an apology from Denmark and Norway.

Soon after the widespread publication of the cartoons, ambassadors from Muslim-majority countries requested a meeting with the Danish prime minister, Anders Fogh Rasmussen, to discuss the publications and perceived wider mistreatment of Muslims in Denmark. The Danish government declined the meeting, saying it could not influence the press. In his New Year speech, the prime minister chose not to apologize, but instead spoke of sensitivities when exercising free speech.

On 20 January 2006, Saudi Arabian political and religious figures called for a boycott of Danish products. Arla responded by placing advertisements in Saudi newspapers distancing itself from the cartoons. Arla told the offending newspaper, *Jyllands-Posten*: 'We fear that we will be hit by a wave of consumer anger.' The company also decided to put full-page advertisements in Saudi newspapers showing the official Danish stance on Islam. But Arla later admitted this action had not helped. On 27 January, the Confederation of Danish Industries appealed to *Jyllands-Posten* to print an apology for having commissioned the drawings, which they did on 31 January. The newspaper published two open letters on its website: one from the newspaper itself apologizing for the offence caused to Muslims; and the other from the artist who had depicted Muhammad with a bomb in his turban, justifying his cartoon. The prime minister welcomed the apology, but said: 'The Danish government cannot apologize on behalf of a Danish newspaper... independent media are not edited by the government.'

Meanwhile, Swiss giant Nestlé admitted to advertising in a Saudi paper telling consumers that two of the products it sold in the region were not of Danish origin. The company denied it was an 'anti-Danish' measure and justified the advert by saying it had achieved its purpose, with Nestlé sales normalizing.

At the end of January, Arla said the boycott of Danish products in the Middle East was almost total and that all its customers in the region had cancelled their orders. This resulted in 100 lay-offs. Arla said: 'We have found ourselves in the middle of a game we have no part in.' It added that it was very difficult to get this particular message across to its Muslim customers. 'We have taken 40 years to build up a very big business in the Middle East, and we've seen it come to a complete stop in five days.' January also saw an attack on two Arla employees, and in February Arla said the boycott was costing the company £1 million per day.

Outcome

On 1 March, Arla estimated the cost of the boycott would amount to US$64 million. But it reaffirmed its commitment to the Middle East: 'Even if the situation looks very difficult, we believe that Arla has a future in the Middle East.' Later that month, Arla began remarketing in the Middle East with full-page advertisements in 25 Arab newspapers. At the beginning of April, Arla products were beginning to be put back on the shelves of stores in the Middle East. It also said it would be sponsoring humanitarian causes in the region. However, it said: 'While we may be seeing a slow lifting of the boycott by retailers, it remains to be seen whether customers will in fact buy our products.'

By August, sales had returned to pre-boycott levels in most Gulf states with the exception of Saudi Arabia (Arla's largest market in the region). Arla's chairman, Knud Erik Jensen, said: 'With regard to the Middle East, the outcome has been slightly worse than expected last spring'.

Key lessons

This boycott was very unusual because such targeted campaigns are usually carried out against a company that has perceived to have transgressed in some way. This crisis did not evolve as an issue, but exploded into life almost totally unexpectedly. In the same way that Arla did not have control over the publication of the cartoons and subsequent outrage, it could not control the actions of the Danish prime minister or the reconciliatory actions of the newspaper. However, this type of crisis is not without precedent. In 1995, countries around the world boycotted French goods (especially wine) in protest over the French government's decision to resume nuclear weapons testing in the Pacific Ocean.

And so, although this particular crisis was unavoidable, it was not unmanageable. Arla's actions and communications were good, but it took too long to make itself heard. The company reacted only after Saudi calls for a boycott, by which time perceptions had been formed. It was not essential for the company to condemn the cartoons, but it should have been quicker to distance itself from them. It might also have been advisable for the company to adopt more robust messages. The company placed adverts in Middle Eastern newspapers that clarified the Danish government's position on Islam, which would not have helped the perception that Arla might have been in league with its national government. Perhaps Arla should have had a key message that severed any perceived

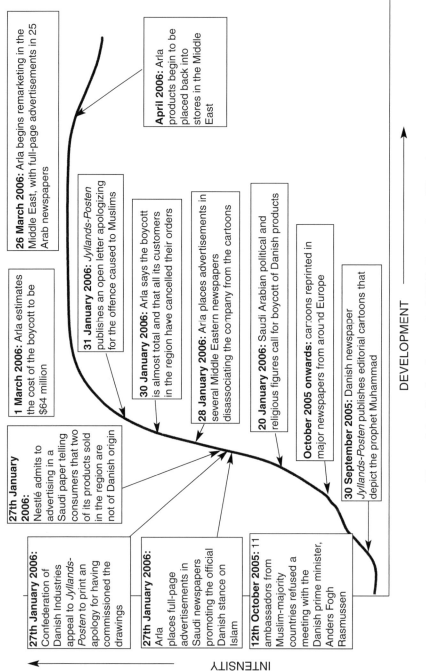

Figure 3.2 *Product boycott in Middle East – issue lifecycle*

INTENSITY

DEVELOPMENT

27th January 2006: Confederation of Danish Industries appeal to *Jyllands-Posten* to print an apology for having commissioned the drawings

27th January 2006: Arla places full-page advertisements in Saudi newspapers promoting the official Danish stance on Islam

12th October 2005: 11 ambassadors from Muslim-majority countries refused a meeting with the Danish prime minister, Anders Fogh Rasmussen

27th January 2006: Nestlé admits to advertising in a Saudi paper telling consumers that two of its products sold in the region are not of Danish origin

1 March 2006: Arla estimates the cost of the boycott to be $64 million

26 March 2006: Arla begins remarketing in the Middle East, with full-page advertisements in 25 Arab newspapers

31 January 2006: *Jyllands-Posten* publishes an open letter apologizing for the offence caused to Muslims

30 January 2006: Arla says the boycott is almost total and that all its customers in the region have cancelled their orders

28 January 2006: Arla places advertisements in several Middle Eastern newspapers disassociating the company from the cartoons

20 January 2006: Saudi Arabian political and religious figures call for boycott of Danish products

October 2005 onwards: cartoons reprinted in major newspapers from around Europe

30 September 2005: Danish newspaper *Jyllands-Posten* publishes editorial cartoons that depict the prophet Muhammad

April 2006: Arla products begin to be placed back into stores in the Middle East

links between it and the Danish government and should have positioned itself as a multinational business with equal interests in every country in which it operated. It could also have been more robust and confident in times of difficulty. The complaint from a company spokesman who said it was 'very difficult to get our message across' would not have given Arla's 11,000 owners much confidence.

A wider lesson from this crisis relates to the major political, cultural and social differences between the Middle East and Western Europe. There is a marked difference between media freedom and business protectionism between the two regions. The plethora of campaign groups in Western Europe is not mirrored in the Middle East, and consumer protection is less of an issue. With such marked differences, it is important for any company to understand fully the expectations and sensitivities of the culture in which it operates.

Businesses in the Middle East have experienced few reputational issues and crises to date, but this situation is likely to change in light of the international focus on the region. The 'war on terror', extensive natural resources and burgeoning commercial centres have been the main factors in drawing attention to the area. Growing numbers of international media outlets and increasing NGO interest suggest that reputational matters will become more significant for companies operating in the Middle East.

CASE STUDY: 'SONY AND DELL HELL – PREVENTION IS BETTER THAN CURE

On 15 August 2006, Dell announced the biggest recall of electrical products in US history. It said it would be recalling 4.1 million of its laptop computer batteries (lithium-ion) because they posed a fire risk. The company had received six complaints since December 2005 about batteries overheating or catching fire. The batteries – made by Sony – were used mostly in computers sold in the United States, but 1 million were said to be outside the United States. The problem occurred when short-circuiting caused batteries to overheat, resulting in a risk of smoke and/or fire. Dell offered customers free replacements and launched a website – www.dellbatteryprogram.com – to assist in this, which was generally regarded as a successful idea.

By the day after the announcement, Dell had received over 100,000 phone calls and 23 million visits to the website. The vice-president of Dell's product group, Alex Gurzen, said the firm wanted to 'put customer safety first despite this being a small handful of incidents'. Dell spokesman Ira Williams also emphasized the small scale of the problem, saying: 'It happens in rare cases but we opted to take this broad action immediately.' Michael Dell, the company's founder, resolutely said Dell would continue using Sony batteries. A Sony spokesman said the same problem did not occur in Sony computers, only with certain types of non-Sony computers. The Japanese company said that it would pay some of the costs involved in Dell's recall.

Two days after the announcement, the US Consumer Product Safety Commission (CPSC) launched an investigation into whether other brands could be affected. Citing legal reasons, Sony refused to name the other brands it supplied. Computer manufacturers Fujitsu and Lenovo Group said they used Sony batteries, but they did not initially recall their products. However, Dell's crisis soon developed into an issue for the whole computer manufacturing industry, resulting in a domino effect of product recalls in the space of two months by Apple, Matsushita, Toshiba, Fujitsu and Hitachi.

The issue also took the unusual turn of spreading across sectors when Qantas said in late August that passengers would only be allowed to run their laptops from the in-seat power supplies with their laptop batteries removed. Korean Air then announced the same measures in September, with Virgin following suit later that month. Virgin has only a limited amount of seats with power supplies, and so the episode caused considerable inconvenience to its customers.

More than two months after the recall announcement, on 23 October, Sony's senior management apologized for the recall of the batteries, which by that stage had reached 9.6 million. Yutaka Nakagawa, Sony's corporate executive officer, said: 'We would like to take this opportunity to apologize for the worries.' He added that there would be no resignations among the company's bosses.

In November, the Portable Battery Working Group was set up by computer firms to implement safety standards for laptop batteries. In December, Japanese firm Matsushita made the decision to mass-produce heat-proof batteries. The firm had been producing them for almost a year, but decided to step up to mass production.

This was by no means the first incident of mass battery recall. In 2000, Dell recalled 27,000 batteries produced by Sanyo after a manufacturing defect caused overheating. A fortnight later, Compaq ordered the return of 55,000 batteries manufactured by Sony that also overheated. A year later, Dell recalled 284,000 Panasonic-made batteries. Apple and Hewlett-Packard have also had to recall hundreds of thousands of computer batteries in 2005 and 2006 owing to overheating.

Media coverage

Since this was primarily an issue for the computer industry, it is little surprise that bloggers were exchanging their opinions immediately after the recall announcement, flagging up similar problems and using the opportunity to document further grievances.

The Inquirer said: 'Dell wants to pass the buck and blame Sony for its public relations nightmare.' Engadget (www.engadget.com) said: 'While we are a little wary of one Dell exec's statement that they're "getting ahead of the issue", which in our opinion would have actually been issuing this recall four months ago, we're glad they're finally taking care of business before someone actually gets hurt.' Slashdot (www.slashdot.org) said: 'Curiously, there is nothing yet on Dell Support's product recall page about this latest recall.' Talking about Dell's customer relations, the Register (www.theregister.co.uk) said: 'Fire-breathing laptops are the last thing you want when you're a company spending hundreds of millions of dollars to repair a fractured relationship with consumers.' (Dell had encountered customer service problems in 2005.)

A *Guardian* comment piece the day after the recall said:

> The outside world has been laughing at the company's expense for almost two months. The pictures have been around the world by e-mail and become a cult hit. The fact that the punchline is the largest product recall in the history of the consumer electronics industry somehow makes the story funnier… But can it really think its brand has not been damaged? Dell is the world's largest manufacturer of PCs, but its products are positioned at the cheap 'n' cheerful end of the market. There is nothing cheerful about a laptop that can seriously singe your lap… The exercise in damage limitation may depend on the quality of the recall service. Dell was unable yesterday to say how long it would take for customers to receive replacement batteries. That does not inspire confidence.

Professors at the London Business School highlighted in the *Financial Times* that 'the internet has added a new layer of visibility, speed and culpability to mass product failures and ensuing product recalls'.

Conclusion

Sony estimated that the recall of its Dell and Apple batteries would cost between US$172 million and US$258 million. A day after the recall announcement, Sony's share price had fallen by 2 per cent at one point before closing 1.2 per cent down on the day. By mid-October, Sony's share price had plunged 10 per cent (impacted by the delayed launch of the PlayStation 3). Analysts then predicted the battery exchange would cost up to US$500 million and affect 10 million computers.

In late October, Sony reduced its profit forecast for 2006 and set aside US$429 million to cover the costs of the incident. It cut its pre-tax profit forecast for the year ending 31 March 2007 by 53 per cent.

However, the incident did not appear to hurt Dell's bottom line as much as Sony's. Indeed, Dell announced that its profits for the three months to November were US$677 million, which led its shares to rise by more than 10 per cent.

Nevertheless, analysts IDC published a report in December that found that 15 per cent of corporate laptop buyers and consumers had altered their buying plans after the battery incident.

It is interesting that the incident has become known as 'Dell Hell' when it was Sony's products that seemed to be the root of the problem. Putting aside the fact that Dell was the company using the largest volume of Sony batteries, it is perhaps unfortunate for Dell that its name could create such a catchy headline and that it was a Dell laptop that was involved in the most conspicuous incident of battery malfunction – when a laptop reportedly exploded mid-conference in Osaka, Japan.

THE IMPORTANCE OF EARLY ACTION

The principal goal of issue identification is to place initial priorities on emerging issues. They can be classified by type (social, economic, political, technological), response source (industry, corporation, subsidiary, department), geography, span of control and salience (immediacy, prominence). Factors such as degree of impact and also the probability that the issue will mature within a reasonably predictable period of time also need to be considered.

Using the Chase/Jones Issues Management Process Model, once emerging issues have been identified and prioritized, the *issue analysis* stage begins. The aim here is to determine the origin of the issue, which is often difficult as few emerge neatly from one source. The authors recommend that existing qualitative and quantitative research should be examined *before* committing to new research and that experience – past and present, internal and external to the organization – should be tapped into. Analysing the present situation will determine the current *intensity* of the issue. Applied research about the relationship of the issue to the corporation should be targeted towards opinion leaders and media gatekeepers. This initial research and analysis stage will help to identify what influential individuals and groups are saying about the issues and provide management with a clear idea of their *origin* and *evolution*.

Needless to say, in practice we have found great reluctance to spend money on this type of research as part of the benchmarking and planning process. Where possible, we try to develop arguments in terms of impact on financial performance and risk to maintaining an organization's licence to operate. These are often more powerful messages in the boardroom than damage to credibility and reputation!

A review of the company's present position (if it has one) and its strengths and weaknesses in positioning itself to take a role in shaping the issue will help to give focus for the action planning stage.

The third stage, called rather cumbersomely *issue change strategy options*, involves making basic decisions about organizational response. The Chase/Jones model cites three options to deal with the change:

Reactive change strategy refers to an organization's unwillingness to change with the emphasis on continuing past behaviour, for example by attempting to postpone the inevitability of public policy decisions. This reluctance to change rarely leaves room for compromise on legislative matters.

Adaptive change strategy suggests an openness to change and a recognition of its inevitability. This approach relies on planning to anticipate change and offering constructive dialogue to find a form of compromise or accommodation.

Dynamic response strategy anticipates and attempts to shape the direction of public policy decisions by determining how the campaigning over the issue will be played out. This approach allows the organization to become a leading advocate of change.

After choosing one of these approaches to responding to each issue the organization should decide on policy to support the selected change, which is the fourth stage – *issue action programming*. This requires coordination of resources to provide the maximum support for reaching goals and objectives.

CASE STUDY: RIBENA FOUND WANTING
Never underestimate stakeholder concerns

In 2004, two New Zealand secondary school students completed a science project comparing the Vitamin C content of their favourite drink, Ribena, against other leading brands of fruit drinks and testing the sentence 'The blackcurrants in Ribena contain four times the Vitamin C of oranges' printed on the packaging of Ribena's ready-to-drink products.

Vitamin C is naturally occurring in juices but can be added to products to boost the Vitamin C content. Vitamin C will degrade over time and, to compensate, many companies put higher levels of Vitamin C in their products to allow for a longer shelf life.

Armed with this knowledge, the schoolgirls were amazed to discover the Ribena ready-to-drink products had very little Vitamin C content at all, let alone four times the content of other drinks. They took their findings to GlaxoSmithKline, which said 'It's the blackcurrants that have it [Vitamin C].'

Not content with GlaxoSmithKline's semantics argument, the girls took their findings further – approaching the Advertising Standards Authority, consumer television programme *Fair Go* and the Commerce Commission – which took the secondary school students' findings very seriously. As a result, GlaxoSmithKline was charged with 88 counts of false advertising between March 2002 and March 2005.

In December 2006, GlaxoSmithKline found itself in court facing a fine of up to NZ $3 million. The following March, the company pleaded guilty to 15 charges of breaching fair trading laws and was fined NZ $217,500 and ordered to pay for corrective advertising (a further NZ $100,000). The outcome was fiercely debated in the media, with some commentators arguing that GlaxoSmithKline had effectively walked away from the incident with a 'smack on the hand', while others took a more objective approach, predicting a fallout on the Ribena brand and sales. Indeed, in April the *New Zeland Herald* reported that Ribena sales had slumped following the court case (down 12 per cent from the same period the year before).

Needless to say, GlaxoSmithKline went into damage control mode following the court case. As ordered by the courts, it ran a series of half-page newspaper ads in national newspapers under the title of 'Ribena: keeping you informed' – giving the impression the company regularly made contact with its consumers to keep them up to date with matters (which the media gleefully pointed out it hadn't).

The advertisements would have been an ideal vehicle for making a public apology. However, the final wording agreed by GlaxoSmithKline and the Commerce Commission (after fierce debate) focused more on GlaxoSmithKline's desire to prove its point that its products did contain Vitamin C ('Our syrup concentrate has always been and continues to be a rich source of Vitamin C'). The closest the company got to apologizing was in the statement: 'We also made the claim "that blackcurrants in Ribena contain four times the Vitamin C of oranges." This may have misled you to believe that Ribena contains four times the level of Vitamin C than in the same quantity of orange juice. That was never our intention and is incorrect. We are sincerely sorry for any confusion caused.'

The advertisements featured a repentant-looking GlaxoSmithKline consumer healthcare New Zealand general manager Paul Rose, the 'author' of the advertisement. He was later referred to in the media as the 'scapegoat' of the Ribena fiasco.

The ads referred consumers to a website that provided more information about the case and how GlaxoSmithKline was rectifying the situation, including reformulating the drink and setting up 'more accurate testing' methods. This was the only online reference to the case – neither GlaxoSmithKline's New Zealand website nor its global counterpart's or other international Ribena branded websites made mention of the incident.

At the same time, GlaxoSmithKline sent letters out to all stakeholders across its consumer healthcare and pharmaceuticals divisions (including medical practitioners around New Zealand) reiterating the comments from the advertising material.

The company also filmed new television commercials with Paul Rose walking through local blackcurrant orchards and discussing the fruit's Vitamin C content.

Overall, between March and May, GlaxoSmithKline spent (full advertising retail value) NZ $652,278 on Ribena product advertising. Television spend in May leapt NZ $215,075 on the March spend to NZ $315,960, while press advertising increased from zero spend in March to NZ $98,617 in May. But, as Mr Rose reported in a newspaper article after the television ads had aired, 'Cost is not the issue. We want to rebuild customer confidence in the brand, and we will spend what we need to do that.'

Media coverage of the case continued throughout March to August in New Zealand and Australia across metropolitan newspapers, business and trade publications, radio and television. While the coverage initially focused on the court case, the media went on to focus on the fallout effect of the case and surrounding issues – reviewing how companies handle crises in general, the impetus for food labelling, and the public's trust in corporate giants.

Interestingly, the media coverage surrounding the case was largely contained to Australasia, with the exception of one article in London's *Daily Telegraph* (written by a Sydney correspondent), in which a GlaxoSmithKline spokesperson was quoted as saying that the problem arose in Australia and New Zealand because the product was 'left on the shelves for too long, causing the Vitamin C to degrade... our testing equipment in New Zealand and Australia was not sensitive enough to pick up the fact that the Vitamin C was degrading.' She went on to reassure UK consumers that 'there was no such problem with Ribena sold in Britain'.

Aside from this statement, other international Ribena coverage during the period focused solely on northern hemisphere-related product issues, including the effects of climate change on growing blackcurrants and introduction of new strains of the fruit and pressure mounting on GlaxoSmithKline to sell off its Ribena and Lucozade brands. This could be attributed to GlaxoSmithKline's international head office choosing not to publicly acknowledge an otherwise 'regional' problem.

In effect, the consumer fallout from the Ribena Vitamin C saga was limited to New Zealand and Australia. But, as we've since found out, these audiences are less than forgiving of the global giant's mistake.

Forgive and forget?

Regester Larkin's partner consultancy in New Zealand, Senate Communications, surveyed a random sample of shoppers (n=50) and retailers (n=10, including large supermarkets and suburban superettes) around New Zealand in August to gauge perceptions of Ribena and GlaxoSmithKline four months after the court case. The results from their conversations showed that the issue is far from forgotten and audiences have yet to forgive Ribena and GlaxoSmithKline for what they perceive as a 'blatant breach of trust'.

Of the shoppers surveyed, 96 per cent had positive feelings toward Ribena prior to the case going public but less than a third said they would buy the ready-to-drink products now, stating '[GlaxoSmithKline] lied to us' and '[Our] view of Ribena and GlaxoSmithKline has been tarnished.' Of note, up until the case went public few of these shoppers had been aware of GlaxoSmithKline as a global corporation or realized it was Ribena's parent company. Those who were aware of GlaxoSmithKline knew of the company solely through its pharmaceutical business.

Interestingly, half the shoppers surveyed still trusted GlaxoSmithKline's claim that the syrup is still a rich source of Vitamin C, but many stated they would still refuse to buy this product.

Asked their opinions of GlaxoSmithKline's response to the court action, 53 per cent of shoppers said they would have liked the general manager to have made an apology at the time – immediately after the case went public – not just in the advertisements weeks later. Of these shoppers, two-thirds thought it would have changed their opinion of the company positively.

Retailers, while somewhat more circumspect about their impressions, also acknowledged failings in GlaxoSmithKline's response. All reported the product had sold averagely to well prior to the court case, despite being a more expensive drink than others on the market. Half noticed an abrupt fall in sales following the court case, with one retailer reporting they had sold just six Ribena drinks in the past month while another said they hadn't sold any for months since the case.

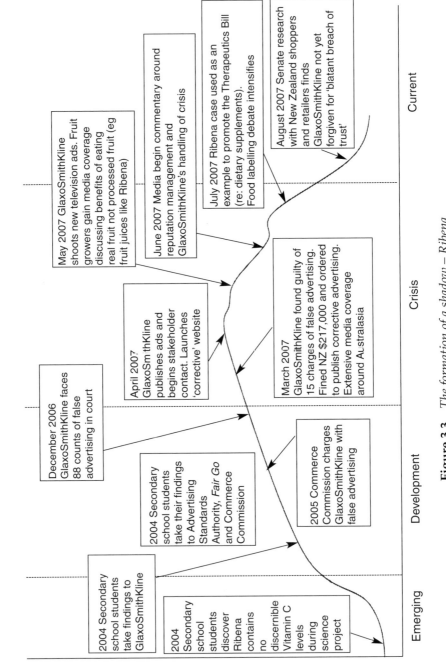

Figure 3.3 *The formation of a shadow – Ribena*

2004 Secondary school students take findings to GlaxoSmithKline

2004 Secondary school students discover Ribena contains no discernible Vitamin C levels during science project

2004 Secondary school students take their findings to Advertising Standards Authority, *Fair Go* and Commerce Commission

2005 Commerce Commission charges GlaxoSmithKline with false advertising

December 2006 GlaxoSmithKline faces 88 counts of false advertising in court

April 2007 GlaxoSmithKline publishes ads and begins stakeholder contact. Launches 'corrective' website

March 2007 GlaxoSmithKline found guilty of 15 charges of false advertising. Fined NZ $217,000 and ordered to publish corrective advertising. Extensive media coverage around Australasia

May 2007 GlaxoSmithKline shoots new television ads. Fruit growers gain media coverage discussing benefits of eating real fruit not processed fruit (eg fruit juices like Ribena)

June 2007 Media begin commentary around reputation management and GlaxoSmithKline's handling of crisis

July 2007 Ribena case used as an example to promote the Therapeutics Bill (re: dietary supplements). Food labelling debate intensifies

August 2007 Senate research with New Zealand shoppers and retailers finds GlaxoSmithKline not yet forgiven for 'blatant breach of trust'

Emerging   Development   Crisis   Current

GlaxoSmithKline's stakeholder response was also discovered to be varied among retailers: some reported that sales representatives had made personal visits to their stores, some reported receiving a memo from GlaxoSmithKline via their store's parent company, and others reported hearing nothing from the company – save for media reports from the general manager and the advertisements. Almost all had found out about the case first through the media.

Seventy per cent of retailers said they would have liked the general manager to have made an apology at the time. Of these, 70 per cent thought it would have changed their opinion of the company positively. However, overall, 80 per cent said their impressions of GlaxoSmithKline had not changed since the case.

Asked whether they thought customers would still trust GlaxoSmithKline's claim that the syrup is still a rich source of Vitamin C, 60 per cent of retailers thought customers would be hesitant and not likely to be completely trusting of the claim given the bad publicity the ready-to-drink product had received.

Building trust

At the time of writing, it's clear the case is still resonating in the public eye and in the media – particularly within New Zealand. With the fallout over its Ribena Vitamin C saga, GlaxoSmithKline has become one of Australasia's 'poster companies' for what can happen after a company crisis. It was a prime example of the dramatic effect poor risk management can have on a company's brand and reputation, and provided a salient lesson about the need to act ethically at all times.

In our opinion, GlaxoSmithKline's court case appears to have effectively destroyed 70 years' worth of consumer trust in its Ribena product overnight. In some cases, a good reputation has been shown to help when a crisis hits. As a corporate entity, GlaxoSmithKline appears to have weathered the storm, aided by its global empire and other ventures. However, in the public eye, the company still has a long way to go to remedy consumer trust in Ribena.

Finally, the requirement for research to evaluate the actual versus intended results of the programme is desirable. We say 'desirable' when it should be 'essential' but, again from practical experience, few companies are willing to do it properly and we have a way to go before enough damning evidence forces better take-up!

It should be remembered that the longer the issue survives, the fewer choices are available and the more it costs (see Figure 3.4).

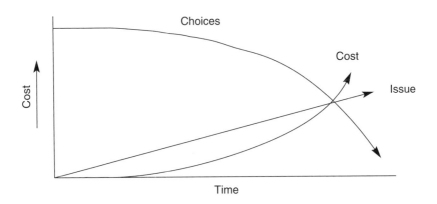

Figure 3.4 *Costs and choices*

SUMMARY

Effective issues management response is based on two key principles: early identification and organized response to influence the public policy process. Issues management is a proactive, anticipatory and planned process designed to influence the development of an issue before it evolves to a stage which requires crisis management. Early action also allows for flexible and creative thinking 'outside the box'.

It is important to remember that issues are constantly being modified and redefined throughout the whole process. Next year's issue is often seeded this year. A brief flurry of media coverage in the UK in 1995 over the potential risk of phthalates – 'gender-bending chemicals' – in infant formula milk preparations could well herald a period of growing public concern over the impact of these synthetic chemicals on human reproduction and the environment in general. The tobacco industry in the United States provides another example, with the rights of smokers evolving into the rights of non-smokers.

Furthermore, defeat on an issue in one area can be seen as success in another. When tobacco companies had to place a warning label on their products, the *loss* in the legislative arena eventually provided a *win* in the judicial arena because when sued, companies were able to argue that consumers had been warned. Exerting an influence on the development of identified issues before they bring negative consequences means that an organization should actively represent its interests in the public policy process, by broadening the debate and informing those groups of importance. This *advocacy* participation in the public policy process is central to issues management (Jones and Chase, 1979).

4

CSR: the new moral code for doing business

You cannot escape the responsibility of tomorrow by evading it today.
Abraham Lincoln

INTRODUCTION

Corporate social responsibility (CSR) is an emerging, as yet poorly defined, process used by some as a fashion statement through glossy reports and websites, and by others as a potential framework for demonstrating a more responsible approach to doing business.

Over the past two decades, the pressure upon business to become accountable and perform a social and environmental role has increased dramatically. Incidents such as the Union Carbide accident in Bhopal, India, in 1984 and the Chernobyl nuclear power station disaster in the Ukraine in 1986 helped put corporate responsibility for environmental hazards on the international agenda. Western industrialized governments responded to such incidents, and established legal and regulatory frameworks for corporate accountability.

Globalization has had an extraordinary impact on its emergence. Throughout the late 1980s and 1990s, the new, knowledge-based economy generated millions of new jobs and a rash of innovative products and services for Western consumers. The offset of this has been to expose a wide range of labour, human rights and environmental abuses, and to create a dysfunction between meeting people's needs, protecting planetary resources and enhancing corporate profits – the perfect trigger for the anti-globalization demonstrations of 1999, 2000 and 2001. The result has been that even companies in sectors with high levels of environmental risk have introduced ways to reform their business by looking and listening.

Globalization has gone hand-in-hand with business short-termism and a total focus on maximizing shareholder value – a strong emphasis on immediate results and a loss of faith in long-term strategic management.

CSR (or sustainable development, which is a closely allied concept) is generally regarded as the opposite of short-termism. It is argued that sustainable development looks at the needs of future generations rather than a focus on short-term delivery with scant regard for the consequences. It appears to run contrary to established market forces and modern business practices. However, there is a growing business imperative to embrace social responsibility, and it is emerging through consequences to the bottom line.

THE GROWING BUSINESS IMPERATIVE

Whether or not organizations are enthusiastic about embracing greater social and environmental accountability, there seems to be a growing business imperative to do so. This can be defined in four categories of commercial penalties and incentives:

1: Socially responsible investment (SRI) and shareholder targeting

SRI and shareholder targeting are developments that are beginning to receive serious attention from financial analysts and institutional investors. Banks, term assurers and asset managers are screening their shareholdings in favour of companies that demonstrate commitment to social and environmental programmes, and against those that engage in activities deemed detrimental to society and the environment. With institutional investors potentially deterred by the 'hassle factor' of picking non-SRI stocks, a company's ability to conform to sustainable development models will potentially have share price implications. The growth of ratings agencies is likely to mean that companies will find their financial position rated on CSR issues as well as conventional criteria, whether they like it or not. It is likely that in the future regulators will make companies hold capital against such risks.

SRI is an investment strategy that takes into account a company's ethical, social and environmental performance as well as its financial performance. SRI has supplanted 'ethical investment' as the criterion for judging responsible business, and has widened to include environmental and social issues. A range of vetted products, including unit trusts and pensions, is now on offer from most large banks and assurance companies.

Today, SRI is a dynamic and rapidly expanding sector of financial services in North America, parts of Europe, and Australia. It is estimated to be worth more than $2 trillion in the United States and around £25 billion in the UK, the largest market in Europe. The Dow Jones Sustainability Group Index has outperformed the Dow Jones Index by 36 per cent over the past five years. In the UK, changes to the Pensions Act now require pension funds to declare how far they take social, environmental and ethical considerations into account when choosing stocks for investment, and other European countries are considering introducing similar legislation.

The initial emphasis of SRI funds was on negative screening – specifically excluding companies engaged in particular types of activity. However, negative screening has partly given way to screening on the basis of companies' positive activities and looking for best practice in what were once seen as controversial industries. Many fund managers now look to invest in companies that make a positive contribution to the economy and to society. A survey of the 23 top European ethical and green unit trusts' adoption criteria revealed that screening under positive measures is rapidly becoming as significant as negative screening:

Table 4.1   *Criteria for negative and positive SRI screening*

Negative criteria	%	Positive criteria	%
Alcohol	74	Community involvement	70
Animal testing	96	Employee welfare/rights	70
Armaments	100	Environmental management	65
Environmental damage	91	Environmental policy	74
Gambling services	83	Environmental products	65
Nuclear power	96	Environmental reporting	65
Oppressive regimes	74	Packaging reduction	61
Pornography	91	Sustainable forestry	61
Tobacco production	100		

Source: Regester Larkin

Strict screening can exclude whole sectors, such as chemicals, from investment, but some new funds are adopting a 'best of sector' or 'light green' approach, and investing in (mostly larger) companies shunned by traditional ethical funds. This has enabled companies in the energy, automotive and agrochemicals sectors to warrant inclusion in some funds. For example, car manufacturer Volkswagen, chemicals company BASF and mining company Rio Tinto are included as sector leaders in the Dow Jones Sustainability Index.

Harnessing the importance of SRI through shareholder activism is now considered by some environmental groups to be a much more significant tool than consumer boycotts. In 1999 concerned investors in the United States introduced more than 200 resolutions on a wide range of issues relating to environmental health and corporate governance matters. In one case, Home Depot, a large lumber and hardware store, announced it would stop selling forest products from environmentally sensitive areas and would give preference to timber certified as sustainably produced, just three months after 12 per cent of its shareholders asked the company to stop selling wood from old-growth forests.

Organizations like Friends of the Earth and Amnesty International are now consulted by fund managers, partly to clarify screening for ethical funds, but also to ensure that future pressures on companies' behaviour are adequately appreciated in financial-led investment decisions. This has developed particularly since the response in Europe to genetically modified products, which led to the near collapse of Monsanto and its subsequent acquisition by Pharmacia Upjohn. Monsanto had previously been strongly commended on Wall Street because of its rapid expansion in the United States. However, NGO pressure in Europe became so intense that it began to affect the US share price. Campaigners targeted all stakeholders, including shareholders. This led Deutsche Asset Management to recommend that institutional investors should sell Monsanto shares quickly. The resulting drop in share price made the company easy prey for takeover at the end of 1999. In spite of being one of the most innovative companies in the agrochemical and biotechnology sectors, the Monsanto brand never recovered from the legacy of this attack.

2: Regulation, reporting and liability

The last 10 or so years have seen an astonishing proliferation in corporate codes of conduct, often linked to reporting initiatives. New voluntary governance and reporting standards such as AA 1000, the Global Reporting Initiative, FTSE4Good and ISO 14001 are adding pressure to the need for greater transparency, better integrated internal issue management controls and a much wider commitment to corporate governance.

The 'old world economy' companies (oil, minerals, automotive, industrial) were the first to embrace CSR reporting. Ford Motor Company developed a number of metrics designed to measure and work towards reducing fuel consumption and emissions, and committed itself to report progress. In addition, the banking sector is now reporting on assets under 'green' management (UBS), the pharmaceutical industry on animals used in research (Novartis) and manufacturing emissions (Roche), and the technology sector on end-of-life recycling (Fujitsu) and lead-free components (Sony).

However, some exponents fall into the category of 'greenwash' – PR smokescreens designed to delay or deter regulatory measures. Nike has a code of conduct based on the International Labour Organization core conventions, but this counts for little to those who see Nike paying demonstrably inadequate wages to workers in their global supply chain. Nike, along with others such as Reebok, Liz Claiborne, Sara Lee and The Gap, established the Apparel Industry Partnership with a view to developing an agreed code and approach to certifiable external verification, but

Table 4.2 *A more inclusive framework for reporting*

Old system	New system
Shareholder focus	Stakeholder focus
Paper based	Internet based
Standardized information	Customized information
Company-controlled information on performance and prospects	Information available from a variety of sources
Periodic reporting	Continuous reporting
Distribution of information	Dialogue
Financial statements	Broader range of performance measures (not just financial)
Past performance	Greater emphasis on future prospects
Historical cost	Substantial value-based information
Audit of accounts	Assurance of underlying system
Nationally oriented	Globally oriented
Essentially static system	Continuously changing model
Preparer-led regulations	Satisfying marketing demands

these companies were widely seen by critics to be conducting a PR exercise. And the idea of a gambling and leisure group, a cigarette manufacturer, a fast food retailer, an alcohol supplier or an arms dealer producing CSR reports appears completely counter-intuitive to many. Others yet are simply determined to keep their heads down, trying not to draw attention to themselves.

Regulation (often enforced through financial instruments), reporting and liability not only have a bottom-line impact, but take the initiative away from organizations in determining how broad social and environmental goals can be achieved. A greater emphasis on transparency and information access is now expected by stakeholders, and regulators are writing these requirements into the rule books. Pioneers of social responsibility reporting are already actively engaged in setting out reporting standards in an effort to retain the initiative ahead of proposed regulation.

If companies do not act in a socially responsible manner, they are likely to face, and lose, expensive lawsuits. For example, the tobacco and asbestos industries lost class action lawsuits following the allegedly inadequate action the industries took to minimize the health risks of their products. Today, legal action is targeting the mobile phone and electricity industries, which are facing potentially tougher, precautionary regulation and the threat of lawsuits in the United States concerning alleged health effects of electromagnetic frequency emissions from power lines, base stations and handsets.

3: Competitive advantage

As demands for environmental and social responsibility in business have developed, they have also become more mature. Concerned consumers look at the corporate face behind the brand, and this influences purchasing decisions. At the same time, there is public acceptance that not every company can be the perfect eco-friendly business. Society needs products like oil and chemicals – but there is demand for companies in these sectors to reduce their negative environmental and social 'footprint'. Consequently, there is an emerging emphasis on CSR best practice and leadership within sectors of industry, opening the way for individual companies to gain competitive advantages.

4: Reputation opportunity costs

The opportunity costs of damage to reputation – loss of existing investment and innovation in marketing; difficulty with recruitment and staff retention; advertising that is undercut by public perception – merit serious consideration. The need to safeguard reputation is already implied in the substantial budgets dedicated to marketing, compliance, recruitment, public affairs and communications. As society becomes less tolerant of companies that do not conform to social and environmental standards, the risks to reputation are much greater. Even more importantly, however, 'doing the right thing' by adopting and integrating a values system into the organization actually does generate financial value. People want to bring their own values to work, as employees, and to have relationships with companies – as customers, suppliers or investors – that relate to their own behaviour, expectations and methods of working.

CSR is concerned with many aspects of a company's impact, from sourcing to service delivery or product disposal, and can affect a host of cost-based as well as reputational aspects of a business. The commercial and reputation risk management case for CSR is demonstrated in the risk to shareholder value from poor management of supply chain issues, inadequate environmental management, human rights abuses and poor treatment of employees, suppliers or customers. Human capital has become more important than physical capital, and so the threat to important relationships has become critical. Concerned investors will apply pres-

Table 4.3 *CSR impacts*

Negative impacts	
Aspect of CSR	**Impact on**
Concern with social and economic impacts	Operating efficiency
Human rights	Innovation Operating efficiency
Positive impacts	
Aspect of CSR	**Impact on**
Ethics, value and principles	Risk profile Brand value and reputation
Focus on environmental process	Risk profile Access to capital Operating efficiency Shareholder value
Community action	Brand value and reputation
Workplace conditions	Human and intellectual capital Operating efficiency Revenue

Source: Buried Treasure – Uncovering the business case for corporate sustainability, 2001

sure to those that are not managing such risks and reward those that are.

The proliferation of financial and regulatory instruments in support of sustainable development is starting to engineer market forces in some countries to the extent that companies need to take a serious look at adoption. Failure to do so risks criticism for lagging behind and a detrimental impact on reputation. A perception of moving slowly in response to new societal and consumer trends and demands can now be damaging in the financial markets.

WHAT CONSTITUTES GOOD SOCIALLY RESPONSIBLE CORPORATE BEHAVIOUR

In response to growing public interest in what constitutes acceptable corporate behaviour, the 1999 Millennium Poll, supported by the Conference Board and the Prince of Wales Business Leaders Forum, polled 25,000 people in 23 countries to gather information about society's expectations. Some of the key findings included:

- People in 13 out of 23 countries think their country should focus more on social and environmental goals than on economic goals in the first decade of the new century.
- In forming impressions of companies, people around the world focus on corporate behaviour and social responsibility ahead of either brand reputation or financial factors.
- Two in three people polled wanted companies to go beyond their historical role of making a profit. In addition to paying taxes, employing people and obeying the law, they want companies to contribute to broader societal goals.
- Actively contributing to charities and community projects doesn't satisfy people's expectations of corporate social responsibility.
- Half the population in the countries surveyed are paying attention to the social behaviour of companies.
- Over one in five consumers report either rewarding or punishing companies in the past year based on their perceived social performance, and almost as many again considered doing so.
- Opinion leader analysis indicates that public pressures on companies to play broader roles in society will likely increase significantly over the next few years.

Friends of the Earth set out guidance for companies seeking to make the CSR transformation under three themes – eco-innovation, social accountability and political responsibility:

- *Innovate for sustainability*: seek out new practices, new products and services, and new technologies that meet people's needs and improve quality of life on minimal material and energy use. This means improving product efficiency and durability, taking responsibility for products over their full lifecycle, and finding ways to replace products with locally delivered services.

- *Prioritize resource productivity*: make 'bottom-line' savings by turning management attention, research and development from labour saving to resource saving through waste avoidance, recycling, reuse and adopting the principles of industrial ecology. Set targets in line with environmental space limits or factor-10 objectives (methods used to quantify the changes in environmental resource use necessary to deliver sustainability; both suggest cuts by up to 90 per cent in economies like the United States and Europe).

- *Spread best practice through supply chains*: ensure that suppliers and subcontractors adopt the same high environmental and social standards as the company – to help spread good practice to small- and medium-sized enterprises.

- *Promote sustainable consumption*: use product development, marketing and advertising strategies to support 'sufficiency' rather than encouraging over-consumption and the spread of products that replace sustainable practices such as breast-feeding.

- *Invest in people*: adopt high, non-discriminatory labour standards and family-friendly working practices, and invest in the knowledge and skills of the workforce, to enhance their quality of life and their productivity.

- *Account to all stakeholders*: report comprehensively and transparently on environmental and social impacts – with independent verification. Respond accountably to the demands and interests of employees, customers, communities and other stakeholders – not just to investors.

- *Play fair in politics*: use lobbying power and influence transparently, in favour of a high level playing field for fair competition with high environmental and social standards. Support green tax reform and effective regulation for environmental protection and corporate accountability, including legal and criminal liability for defaulting companies and their directors.

NEW BUSINESS VALUES

Ethics and values – the basis for good behaviour – are increasingly regarded as the building blocks of sustainable development or corporate social responsibility. The definition of this has evolved to embrace eco-efficiency, business ethics, investment strategies, human rights and a wider social agenda.

The early adopters were PR people who saw value in better communication around environmental impact, and environmental engineers, thinking in terms of inputs, outputs and impacts, who started to recognize that by cleaning up emissions and reducing toxic waste streams, a better overall business solution could be achieved. The debate, however, has shifted from public relations to competitive advantage through good business practice, and reaches from the factory fence into the boardroom.

The development and implementation of CSR policies should not simply be viewed as an additional burden on costs. The fact that companies are coming under increased pressure to be acceptable winners in a wider social context creates opportunities for 'early adopters' to demonstrate best practice and achieve competitive advantage. The companies that have already put down CSR navigation markers are being called 'forward looking' and accredited with 'visionary management' by management peer groups and business commentators.

Consumer pressure, fuelling regulatory pressure, helps to explain why we are seeing more companies revisiting or establishing their business principles to create standards and values that integrate and bind an organization together. Business for Social Responsibility suggests that the reasons why organizations are doing this include:

- A wish to create a corporate culture 'touchstone', with business principles creating the glue or moral backbone of the organization.
- The provision of a focus for evolving internal conversations, with an initial 'straw man' version drawn from existing policies, codes and principles being used to stimulate internal debate and engagement.
- A means to embed values throughout the organization, with the ability to integrate them into strategic planning, decision-making processes, business practices, management systems, employee performance assessment and succession planning.

Issues raised in the CSR discussion have provided a useful starting point for some companies to restate the business case for longer-term strategic planning and investment in reputation. The relaunch of BP in 2000, under the banner 'Beyond Petroleum', is an example of utilizing social and environmental issues on the sustainable development agenda to set out forward-looking priorities that put BP firmly within the sphere of new, cleaner technologies and potential future markets. However, actions always speak louder than words, as BP was soon to discover to its cost.

CASE STUDY: BP's FALL FROM GRACE

Despite reporting huge profits for the year, 2006 was a terrible year for BP. A fatal explosion, two oil spills, price manipulation and workplace bullying have dragged the once-favourable reputation of the oil company through the mud. This case study documents the three major incidents that have undermined stakeholder confidence: the Texas City Refinery explosion, the Prudhoe Bay oil spill and price manipulation allegations.

Texas City Refinery explosion

BP's Texas City Refinery in Texas City is the second-largest oil refinery in Texas and the third-largest in the United States. It processes around 450,000 barrels of crude oil per day – 3 per cent of the domestic oil supply in the United States and one-third of BP's output across the country. On Wednesday 23 March, a cloud of volatile hydrocarbon vapour ignited after it had escaped from an octane unit, killing 15 people and injuring over 170.

The refinery had a chequered safety record leading up to the explosion. In March 2004, it was evacuated after an explosion, costing the company US$63,000 in fines, and in September 2004 two workers died and one was injured when they were scalded by superheated water that escaped from a high-pressure pipe. Texas City was also the scene of the United States' worst industrial explosion in 1947, when a ship carrying ammonium nitrate exploded in the harbour, killing at least 576 people.

After the explosion, several BP spokespeople were available for comment. The following is a selection of the most prolifically quoted employees:

- The refinery site director, Don Parus, said: 'The explosion has caused injuries to multiple BP workers, and it is with deep sadness that I must report that there have been fatalities. We believe 14 people lost their lives as a result of the fire. It's a sad day for BP... We have not had time to investigate causes, and we will not speculate. But at this time terrorism is not a primary focus of our concern.'
- Annie Smith, a spokeswoman, said: 'This will have a huge impact on the plant. But it won't shut it down. There will be a long and intensive investigation to determine the cause of the explosion. But we don't believe it to be an act of terrorism. So that leaves something in the operation of the plant.'
- Spokesman Hugh Depland ruled out the idea that terrorism was to blame after the FBI confirmed their agents had concluded work at the facility. He said: 'We have no reason to believe this was anything caused by an outside agent.'
- BP spokesman Bill Stephens said of the investigation: 'We're going to be very thorough on this one. I can't tell you exactly when we will finish this investigation, but no stone will go unturned.' He also said: 'Bringing units up and down can be a tricky business, but we approach everything we do as potentially dangerous, and that's why we have rigorous policies and procedures in place. That's why this situation is so sad and puzzling to us all.'
- Ross Pillari, BP's US president, said: 'It's clear we have a lot of work to do in the coming days to make sure exactly what happened, and we're going to do that.'
- Lord Browne, the company's chairman at the time, said it was the 'worst tragedy I've known during my 38 years with the company. All of us have

been profoundly affected. All of us want to know what happened... I came to Texas City to assure people the full resources of BP will be there to help the bereaved and the injured... I spent the morning with the men and women that operate and maintain the refinery. I have heard many harrowing stories but the team is in very strong spirits.' Lord Browne also promised BP's 'best people' would be deployed immediately to investigate the cause of the explosion and said the company would 'cooperate fully with government officials responsible for examining the circumstances of this terrible explosion and fire'. Asked if the explosion was an explosion waiting to happen, Lord Browne said: 'I don't believe it was. There is no stone left unturned in making sure all events are investigated and remediation is done after the event. There is no limit to the amount of action we have undertaken. It is a very safe plant. If there is more to be done we will do it.'

By 16 May 2005, BP had completed an interim report into the explosion, which concluded that managers had failed to supervise the isomerization unit, operators were absent at crucial periods and they had failed to take corrective action early enough. It also said that the refinery working environment 'had eroded to one characterized by resistance to change, and lacking of trust, motivation and a sense of purpose'.

Ross Pillari said after the conclusion of the report: 'The mistakes made during the start-up of this unit were surprising and deeply disturbing. We regret that our mistakes have caused so much suffering.' He added: 'The failure of unit managers to provide appropriate leadership and of hourly workers to follow written procedures are among the root causes of this incident. We cannot ignore these failures.' However, BP later retracted this statement, and acknowledged that complacency among the management was an important factor. In June 2005, a sacked employee filed a slander lawsuit against BP, alleging that the company had wrongly blamed him and five other colleagues for the refinery explosion. BP refused to comment, saying that it did not comment on personnel matters. (BP settled the suit in September 2006 for an undisclosed amount.)

It was BP's stated intention to offer 'fair compensation' to the families of the deceased and injured without the need for litigation. Initially, BP allocated US$700 million to compensate the victims of the explosion. This was raised to US$1.2 billion in July 2006.

In December 2005, the US Department of Labor referred the Texas City case to the Department of Justice, raising the possibility of BP facing criminal charges in the United States. The referral came after a US Occupational Safety and Health Administration investigation, which found more than 300 violations of health and safety standards at the refinery. During this month, BP announced that it would spend US$1 billion on the Texas City Refinery over the following five years.

In September 2006, the company announced a complete review of its global operations to take place over 5 to 10 years. The next month, a judge ruled that Lord Browne should testify over the explosion, requiring him to give six hours of his time to lawyers. The Chemical Safety Board (CSB) then concluded that BP knew of 'significant safety problems' well before the explosion. Carolyn Merritt,

CSB chairwoman, said: 'BP implemented a 25 per cent cut on fixed costs from 1998 to 2000 that adversely impacted maintenance expenditures and infrastructure at the refinery.' BP spokesman Ronnie Chapman said in response that the CSB investigation findings were generally consistent with those of BP's. But he said: 'The BP Texas City fatal investigation team did not identify previous budget decisions or lack of expenditure as a critical factor, or immediate cause of the explosion.' He added that maintenance spending at the refinery had increased by 40 per cent over the previous five years.

Also in September 2006, BP settled its final lawsuit just before a jury were to be sworn in for what would have been the first civil case resulting from the explosion.

The Baker Panel report, led by former US Secretary of State James A Baker, was released in January 2007 and found 'material deficiencies' in BP's safety procedures at its US oil refineries. The report said that BP emphasized personal safety but not process safety, and that the problem existed at all five of the firm's refineries in the United States. It said: 'BP mistakenly interpreted improving personal injury rates as an indication of acceptable process safety performance at its US refineries. The panel found instances of a lack of operating discipline, toleration of serious deviations from safe operating practices, and apparent complacency toward serious safety risks at each refinery.'

In March 2007, the CSB concluded that cost cutting, worker fatigue and a failure by all levels of BP management to address safety issues contributed to the 2005 explosion. However, BP said it did not agree with 'many of the findings and conclusions' of the report. It said in a statement: 'BP will give full and careful consideration to CSB's recommendations, in conjunction with the many activities already underway to improve process safety management. BP and its employees are ready, willing and able to achieve the goal of becoming an industry leader in process safety management.'

Prudhoe Bay oil spill, Alaska

The site of BP drilling in Alaska, the North Slope, has been subject to much debate. The Bush administration has long wished to open up the Arctic National Wildlife Refuge for drilling, a move which has repeatedly been blocked by Congress.

BP's Alaska troubles started in March 2005 when the Alaska Department of Environmental Conservation (ADEC) found that BP had failed to follow regulations requiring it to report the release of drilling fluids in excess of 55 gallons.

On 2 March 2006, a worker for BP Exploration (Alaska) discovered a large oil spill at Prudhoe Bay. At least 6,350 barrels had spilled (more than 250,000 gallons of crude oil), making it the largest spill to date on Alaska's North Slope region – an area predominantly used by caribou herds. The US Department of Transportation gave authorization for the transit lines to be inspected for corrosion. In July, BP Alaska workers told the *Financial Times* that wells were leaking oil or diesel insulating agent at the Prudhoe Bay oilfield. Consequently, BP shut down 12 wells indefinitely while the allegations were investigated. In August, BP confirmed corrosion that required 16 to 22 miles of replacement pipes.

In June 2006, it was revealed that BP would be under investigation from the grand jury after the oil spill, which could lead to criminal charges. BP responded by saying that it would provide information showing that it had acted properly.

To add to BP's woes, in August 2006 some of its shareholders took legal action against the company for knowingly allowing one of the company's 'prized assets' to decay.

Then, in September 2006, a congressmen accused BP of 'unacceptable' neglect of pipelines in Alaska at a congressional hearing. Joe Barton, the Republican chairman of the House Energy and Commerce Committee, said: 'Years of neglecting to inspect two of the most vital oil pipelines in this country is simply unacceptable.' Robert Malone, one of the two BP executives testifying, said the company had 'fallen short of the high standards we hold for ourselves'. Richard Woollam, the former head of corrosion management at Prudhoe Bay, used the Fifth Amendment to avoid testifying and possibly incriminating himself. This angered BP, with a spokesperson saying: 'We encouraged Mr Woollam to cooperate with the committee and are disappointed by his decision.'

It was also during September that BP was blamed for a much smaller spill of refined products in Long Beach, California. Local government officials criticized BP for not announcing the spill quickly enough.

The *Financial Times* proved to be problematic for BP again in September when it reported that BP investors had requested meetings with the firm's directors, seeking to establish if the Texas City and North Slope incidents were part of a systematic problem.

To compound BP's reputation crisis, it emerged that the company had launched an investigation into allegations of bullying and worker intimidation at its North Slope operations since 2000. And in October 2006 the governor of Alaska questioned whether BP had misled him over the condition of its pipelines.

Price manipulation allegations

BP's reputation crisis took another big hit in 2006 when it was alleged that the company manipulated propane prices in 2004. Regulators claimed that BP Products North America artificially forced up prices by buying huge stocks of propane and withholding them from the market. The Commodities Futures Trading Commission (CFTC) alleged that manipulation was carried out 'with the knowledge, advice and consent of senior management'. It said that BP bought stocks until it controlled almost 90 per cent of the market. Just before the allegations, BP dismissed several employees for failing 'to adhere to BP policies governing trading activities'. BP denied the charges, saying: 'Market manipulation did not occur. We are prepared to make and to prove that case in the courts.'

Prosecutors produced recordings of BP traders reportedly saying: 'What we stand to gain is not just that we'd make money out of it. But we would know from thereafter that we could control the market at will.'

Then in September 2006 a new lawsuit was lodged against BP, claiming that it had manipulated crude oil prices by refusing to allow traders access to US storage facilities. The suit was filed by oil futures trader Richard Hershey, who said that he had suffered damages caused by BP's refusal to open its oil storage facilities in Cushing, Oklahoma, resulting in BP controlling 30 per cent of the Cushing facilities. According to the *Independent*, it is widely believed that these allegations were intended to step up the pressure over the propane charges.

Press coverage

The day after the Texas City Refinery explosion, *The Times* said: 'So far, BP has handled the emergency openly and well. It will need to show that it does not compromise safety to save investment and that Texas City is not the company's true face.' It also said: 'The loss of so many lives at a facility that only a year ago was fined for breaking safety rules after a (non-lethal) explosion will not be good for BP's reputation.'

The *Financial Times* said that BP 'will need more than sympathetic words and free meals for the families hit by the blast to repair its tarnished reputation'. But it was complimentary to Lord Browne: 'In moving swiftly, Lord Browne has avoided the negative fall-out that hit ExxonMobil when its tanker ran aground in Alaska, creating the largest oil spill in the US. Many bristled at the perceived arrogant tone of ExxonMobil, whose chairman left subordinates to deal with the crisis. In contrast, Lord Browne has been suitably humble.'

The *Wall Street Journal* also speculated on the potential reputation damage for BP: 'In a sign of how seriously the company was taking the incident, Lord Browne flew to Texas City yesterday and pledged to "leave nothing undone in our effort to determine the cause of the tragedy." The ultimate toll on BP's reputation could depend on the findings of continuing investigations.'

Several papers were swift to highlight previous health and safety discrepancies at the Texas City Refinery. The *Houston Chronicle* pointed out: 'The explosion Wednesday at the BP oil refinery in Texas City and another in March 2004 are among a long history of incendiary incidents, some deadly, that have cost the facility's owners millions of dollars in fines and lawsuits.' The *Houston Chronicle* also reported that federal health and safety regulators frequently 'caved in' by reducing fines and downgrading their findings.

After the successive incidents, the *Financial Times* questioned if BP's reputation of the 'responsible corporation' was warranted. Craig Smith of the London Business School commended BP for its early foresight on climate change action, but said: 'Yet for all this attention to climate change, BP appears to have been caught unawares by unacceptable levels of corrosion in its Prudhoe Bay pipelines that could result in more elementary environmental problems – oil spills. This is in spite of earlier reports from whistleblowers of leaks and inadequate maintenance at the facilities.' He went on: 'For all the question marks over its reputation, BP's sustainability strategy remains sound. *What we are seeing is not a failure of strategy but of execution*' (emphasis added). Smith concluded by offering some reputation advice:

> Over the Prudhoe Bay facilities, the company failed to take pre-emptive action, but since its problems became public, has taken some of the right

steps by acting decisively. Fundamentally, however, only by redoubling its efforts to ensure its operations throughout the world are sound will BP minimize the risk of the reputational blows it has suffered in the past 18 months.

The *Independent* said that 2006 'has truly been the annus horribilis' for BP. It was sympathetic to a degree: 'Even if it had not put a foot wrong, this would have been a difficult period for a major energy company seeking to put the accident behind it.' But it continued: 'So much for the "Beyond Petroleum" slogans launched by the eco-friendly behemoth.' It added that the allegations of price manipulation 'seemed to confirm every public suspicion about the behaviour of profit-laden oil companies'.

Then came the final bombshell. On 1 May 2007, Lord Browne resigned as BP's chief executive 'with immediate effect'. He said he stepped down to save BP from embarrassment after the *Mail on Sunday* won a court case to print details of his private life. He also accepted that statements made in legal documents about a four-year relationship with Jeff Chevalier had been 'untruthful'. In a statement he said: 'In my 41 years with BP I have kept my private life separate from my business life. I have always regarded my sexuality as a personal matter, to be kept private.' It was also alleged that Lord Browne had abused company assets for the benefit of Chevalier – an allegation he strongly denied. *The Mail on Sunday* said it was Lord Browne who had 'made his private life a public issue' by lying in court.

According to John Elkington, author of *The Chrysalis Economy: How citizen CEOs and corporations can fuse values and value creation* (2001), sustainable business success in this century will depend on stewardship of the following six values:

- *Ultra-transparency* – assuming everything is public through to the ethics of privacy.
- *Open governance* – to bridge the gap between global capitalism and global governance systems.
- *Equal opportunity* – between today's generations and tomorrow's.
- *Multiple capitals* – human, social and natural.
- *Real diversity* – as reflected in the immense variety of our present ecosystems.
- *Shared learning* – invention and innovation.

Effective environmental and social stewardship makes business sense. In a rapidly changing world where issues are readily highlighted but solutions are sometimes harder to discern, it is difficult to know where to go and how far to travel. Good stewardship isn't just about adhering to policies.

Actions		Benefits			
Business principles					**Business products**
Build sustainable development issues on core values	Embed sustainable development in decision making	Maximize value of business levers	Enhances reputation as organization of first choice	Attracts resources	Creates wealth
Natural capital	Management framework	Reduce costs	Shareholders	Capital	Shareholder value
Economic prosperity		Create options	Employees	Talent	Wealth for society
Social capital		Gain customers	Customers		
		Reduce risk	Society		
			Business partners		

Figure 4.1 *Shell's view of the business case for sustainable development*

Source: Shell International, 2000

Shell highlights the importance of greater engagement and transparency, exploring new ways to assure performance, focusing on reliability of health, safety and environmental data management systems, and providing a clearer indication of what is verified and how. (See Figure 4.1.)

So a combination of legal, regulatory and moral pressure is leading to a changed perception of the goals of business, and growing acceptance of the idea that responsible business entails social and environmental performance and reporting. Some corporations have found opportunities within this changing landscape: to develop reputations as leaders of best practice in product stewardship and environmental reporting; to overcome, as BP, Ford, DuPont and Toyota are attempting to do, the legacy of damaging reputational crises through improved stakeholder communication and engagement; and, like Ikea, the world's largest furniture store, to seize competitive advantage by offering alternatives to questioned practices which are helping to position the company as a credible socially responsible investment. But the jury is likely to be out for some time. Nike's admission in its first corporate responsibility report that it 'blew it' by employing children in Third World countries certainly isn't convincing Oxfam's NikeWatch or the Clean Clothes Campaign.

CSR BEST PRACTICE POLICY DEVELOPMENT AND MANAGEMENT

The Association of British Insurers (2001) has stipulated the checklist in Figure 4.2 for CSR best practice within an organization. From our experience of working with a number of companies across the CSR delivery chain, we believe the principles of socially responsible policy development and management are intrinsically aligned to a successful issues management programme. The four-phased approach we recommend (see Figure 4.3) is mutually supportive, with each stage feeding into the other three.

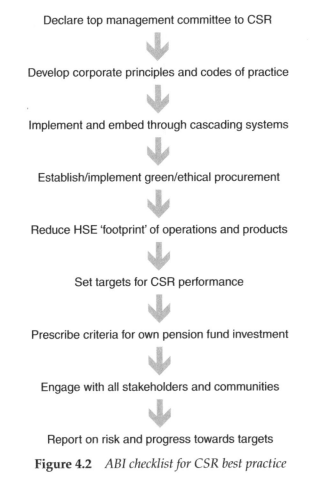

Declare top management committee to CSR

Develop corporate principles and codes of practice

Implement and embed through cascading systems

Establish/implement green/ethical procurement

Reduce HSE 'footprint' of operations and products

Set targets for CSR performance

Prescribe criteria for own pension fund investment

Engage with all stakeholders and communities

Report on risk and progress towards targets

Figure 4.2   *ABI checklist for CSR best practice*

Phase 1: Assessing and planning

Establishing leadership and commitment:

- Identify the business case for and key benefits of a sustainable strategy.
- Secure senior management commitment.
- Appoint a board-level sponsor(s) (executive or non-executive, but allow for an independent audit and assessment function).
- Develop and obtain approval for a framework for management.
- Review existing compliance and governance through internal and external auditing.
- Review business principles and values.

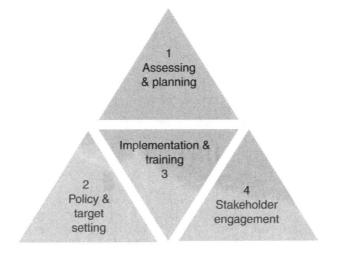

Figure 4.3   *A four-phase approach for CSR*

Phase 2: Policy and target setting

Addressing feedback and policy review:

- Assess feedback; complete a gap/risk analysis associated with policies, procedures, compliance.
- Validate or revise business principles and values.
- Define/agree policy framework: a) against compliance; b) against appropriate accreditation scheme(s) or internal audit procedure.
- Agree strategy, priorities and actions required for implementation.

Phase 3: Implementing policy and training

Consider the most appropriate ways of securing understanding and buy-in across the organization, for example:

- Management workshops to explain purpose, benefits, generate involvement, validate approaches and roll-out (including target setting, KPIs and communication toolkit).
- A 'train the trainers' scheme to facilitate outreach.
- A seminar programme and supporting intranet or printed toolkit for middle management/functional teams to outline benefits, policies, targets and programme for internal and external communications implementation.
- Identify a 'CSR ambassador network' to promulgate rationale, process and solicit employee ideas and initiatives that reflect creativity and innovation in support of business and reputation performance goals.

Phase 4: Stakeholder engagement

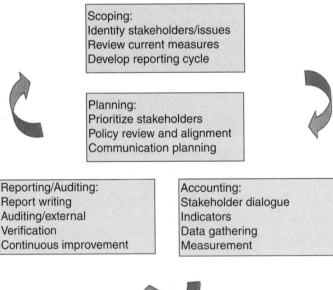

Figure 4.4   *Stakeholder engagement*

- Scope, plan, account and report.
- Integrate with compliance and risk management processes.
- Prepare and develop for accreditation requirements.
- Agree process for external reporting and validation.
- Commit to continuous refinement and improvement.

Above all else, CSR must be embedded into the DNA of an organization. As Andrew Griffin argues in *New Strategies for Reputation Management*, some CSR initiatives are laudable; others are laughable. They are all done, however, under an umbrella that has been put up by others. The term itself suggests that companies are not intrinsically socially responsible, requiring instead a programme of activities and promises to make them palatable to the world. It is not surprising, therefore, that CSR is often managed reactively, defensively and on the territory of others – so much so that it is in danger of becoming a Trojan horse for anti-corporate campaigners to attack the very existence of successful companies.

SUMMARY

CSR does offer a route for creating more flexible and anticipatory reputation risk management processes by sensitizing the business to risks associated with unfamiliar patterns of social change. It is also a means to influence stakeholders which can help to shift the risk burden from one of passive response to one of more active engagement and management.

CSR supports reputation risk management strategies by:

- managing short-term risk by acquiring quality information through dialogue;
- accessing valuable marketplace and social trends data;
- moving towards consensus and away from conflict through better stakeholder engagement;
- influencing views and behaviour inside and outside the organization, with associated performance benefits;
- enhancing value through socially responsible investment.

(*Source*: adapted from Zadek, 2001)

The evidence base is growing, and shows that successful companies are those that can operate in relative harmony with the needs, aspirations, and most importantly values of their stakeholders. When this works well, it can enhance reputation, performance and shareholder value. However, it isn't simply enough to articulate corporate values in an annual report or code of conduct. Nor is it about making financial 'contributions', which will always be interpreted as '£100 towards the new scout hut'. Ethics and values must form an integral part of corporate culture and that must apply consistently across all operations, locally and internationally, to become a living and breathing organism.

Mark Goyder, Director of think tank Tomorrow's Company, insists that CSR must be embedded into the DNA of an organization. As one business leader has said, 'It is one thing to produce a set of universal principles, quite another to ensure they are implemented practically and sensitively across different cultures.' However, he continued, 'our commitment to contribute to sustainable development holds the keys to our long-term business success'. So values must be considered as an intangible business asset, talked about across the business as a source of competitive advantage, as a basis for good corporate reputation and as a reinforcer of effective risk management. Good business and social responsibility will inevitably move forward hand in hand.

5

An issue ignored is a crisis ensured

In the kingdom of the blind the one-eyed man is king.

Desiderius Erasmus

CASE STUDY: DECOMMISSIONING THE BRENT SPAR – IMPLICATIONS FOR A GLOBAL INDUSTRY

In 1995, Shell UK, a leading oil producer, decided to dispose of the Brent Spar, a redundant North Sea floating storage and tanker loading buoy, in Atlantic deep water. The company undertook and independently commissioned numerous environmental and risk assessment studies, the principal findings of which were released for public consultation. Shell also scrupulously observed all national and international legal and regulatory requirements.

Shell was eventually forced to choose what it and others widely regarded as the second-best environmental option, taking the Spar onshore for break-up, because of intense pressure exerted by Greenpeace and some European governments.

The pressure was not characterized by any significant scientific evidence refuting Shell's case – many leading independent scientific experts supported Shell's recommendations. The consortium of Shell, the operator and Esso, a subsidiary of Exxon, was defeated by a single-issue pressure group which skilfully secured the support of influential politicians and administrators in Europe by shaping public opinion. As a result, the oil industry may face an expensive and environmentally questionable requirement to return all North Sea installations to shore when redundant, contradicting existing international disposal agreements.

The rationale for deep water disposal

The Brent Spar was commissioned in 1976. It was a vertically floating buoy, 141 metres high and fixed to the sea bed. The buoy consisted of oil storage tanks at the bottom, capable of holding 300,000 barrels of crude oil, 12 buoyancy tanks towards the middle and a topside containing offshore tanker loading equipment and accommodation for 30 people.

Rising maintenance costs prompted a review in 1991 to conclude that the work necessary to refurbish the facility, to extend its operational life, could cost over £90 million. The buoy would also have to be out of commission for about three years during the work. Given the age of the structure, the presence of a pipeline system for the export of crude oil from the field and the cost of refurbishment, the Spar was taken out of commission in September 1991.

Thirteen methods of abandoning or re-using the Spar were put forward for consideration and six were identified as viable options. These included horizontal or vertical dismantling and onshore disposal, in-field disposal and deep water disposal. Of these, horizontal dismantling and deep water disposal were considered in detail.

The assessments were designed to determine the Best Practicable Environmental Option (BPEO), taking into account factors such as technical feasibility, risks to workforce health and safety, environmental impact, costs and public acceptability. Shell also had to take into account likely additional stress to the structure when upended and the fact that two main storage tanks had been accidentally ruptured some 25 years earlier and repaired only to maintain structural integrity and not on-going use.

In October 1991, undamaged crude oil storage tanks were emptied, process pipe work was flushed through with sea water, buoyancy tanks were emptied, all valves were shut to prevent flooding and loose equipment removed. An analysis showed that an estimated 100 tonnes of oily sludge contained about 9.2 tonnes of oil and a number of heavy metals, with the remainder composed of a mixture of sand and scale. The walls of the storage tanks were, reportedly, coated with an estimated 41.3 tonnes of hydrocarbons in the form of a thin layer of oil and wax. Shell said that scale is commonly found in oil processing facilities and that it may be contaminated by small amounts of naturally occurring radioactive salts from the oil reservoir. The company believed that its impact was minimal with no implications for health or the food chain.

The BPEO demonstrated that the most appropriate action was to dispose of the Spar at an authorized deep water disposal site, as it was the option of least technical risk, minimized workforce exposure to accidents, would have a small but insignificant impact on the environment and was economically the most attractive. Onshore disposal would be a much more technically complex and hazardous operation in safety and occupational health risk terms. Shell summarized its position in a press release in June 1995:

> Extensive studies and an independent report confirmed deep water disposal of the Spar as the simplest operation, posing low risk to health, safety and the environment. It would not be environmentally hazardous and would have a negligible effect on the deep sea environment.

Organizations involved in the 30 studies included the University of Aberdeen, Global Maritime, Metocean, McDermott Engineering, Smith Engineering, Aker, Heerema and Amec.

The decision was taken after consultation with the Scottish Office and other UK government departments, and was endorsed by the UK Department of Trade and Industry. The proposed disposal was in accordance with all relevant UK and international laws and conventions and approvals were received on 17 February 1995.

The Greenpeace allegations

In late May 1995, Shell exchanged correspondence with Greenpeace. A letter from Uta Bellion, chairman of Greenpeace International, addressed to Cor Herkstroter, chairman of the Committee of Managing Directors of the Royal Dutch/Shell group, commenting on Shell UK's 'appalling plans to dump the Brent Spar', claimed that it was:

> laden with over 100 tonnes of toxic sludge and more than 30 tonnes of radioactive scale. It contains a lethal cocktail including lead, arsenic, mercury, and PCBs which, if allowed to enter the marine environment, would present a considerable threat.

Allegedly, the dumping was 'wholly inconsistent with the best international practice in disposing of oil installations' and that in the Gulf of Mexico, where 'dumping of redundant oil installations is prohibited', Shell practises 'far less environmentally damaging methods of disposal'. Shell UK was charged with showing 'utter contempt' in its treatment of the environment. Greenpeace claimed the credit for publicizing Shell's disposal plans and that the decision to dump the Spar was based on economic, not environmental criteria.

In response, Dr Chris Fay, chairman and Chief Executive of Shell UK, replying on behalf of Cor Herkstroter, described the 'widely-publicised assertions repeated in your letter' as 'misinformed and unjustifiably alarmist'. He continued:

> You claim that Shell UK has rejected the best available solution, putting economic performance before the environment, because of the alleged laxity of UK regulatory standards. Neither could be further from the truth.

The UK regulatory regime was among the most scrupulous in the world. The letter stated:

> On every count, the procedures, principles and standards which underlie the Brent Spar disposal plan authorised by the British Government represent current best international oil industry practice in respect of the care, rigour and independence of the analysis of the options, the responsible balancing of environmental, safety and health considerations and the extent and openness of consultations with interested parties, including fishermen and environmentalists, which preceded the Government's approval of the disposal plan.

Dr Fay stressed that Shell UK was not predisposed to the offshore disposal of redundant installations simply to save costs. UK government policy, consistent with best international practice, took into account the individual characteristics and circumstances of each disposal on a case-by-case basis. He continued: 'The responsible option in this case, on environmental, safety and health considerations, is carefully managed deep water disposal'. However, he added that the balanced case-by-case approach could lead to onshore recovery and scrapping for many subsequent disposals of redundant British installations.

Shell denied totally that Greenpeace activity had ensured that the disposal plan had become public knowledge, not least because discussions with interested parties had started in 1994. Fay's letter stated:

> We understand that all the governments which are parties to the Oslo Convention governing international standards for the protection of the marine environment were notified months ago of the proposed disposal plan for the Brent Spar.

The Greenpeace comment that Shell UK was prepared to treat the environment with contempt highlighted the contrast between, as Dr Fay put it, 'those of us who are engaged in the painstaking process of seeking responsible balanced solutions and those, like yourselves, who focus only on the problems'.

The chain reaction begins

The emerging issue of the Brent Spar quickly established a momentum of its own when, on 30 April 1995, Greenpeace activists occupied the Spar amid considerable media interest. In less than a month, from 30 April to 23 May, the UK government had issued a licence for deep water disposal, the German government had lodged a formal protest to its UK counterpart – in spite of making no comment during the earlier compulsory consultation process – and, finally, the activists were removed from the Spar amid one of the most visually striking and intense international broadcast stories of the year. Public interest in this so-called 'David and Goliath' debate, now amplified by a global print and electronic media, quickly brought about top level political resistance as the issued moved cross-border.

At the Esbjerg North Sea Conference in early June, several European countries called for all defunct oil installations to be disposed of onshore, leaving the UK and Norway isolated in arguing for a case-by-case approach.

On 10 June, Shell UK started to tow the Spar to an approved deep Atlantic site – 6,000 feet deep and about 150 miles off the west coast of Scotland. At the same time public perception, through widespread editorial fuelled by Greenpeace, was of a location much closer to the mainland with the potential to create enormous environmental damage to the marine ecology.

Public opinion in continental northern Europe became increasingly vociferous in its opposition to Shell's action and by mid-June, eager to demonstrate his green credentials during elections in Germany, Chancellor Kohl protested about the disposal plans to Prime Minister Major at the G7 Summit in Nova Scotia. In a very short period of time a potential issue that was not widely considered to be of particular importance in the UK had escalated to become one of international public scrutiny and militant action.

In Germany, a boycott of Shell products and picketing of Shell forecourts started and within days some 200 service stations were damaged, with two facilities fire-bombed and one raked with bullets. On 20 June, John Major defended Shell's position on decommissioning the Brent Spar in the House of Commons, only to discover afterwards that in The Hague, the parent company of Shell UK had already decided to abort the decommissioning plan in the face of intense public opposition. As the success of the Greenpeace campaign was acknowledged across the world, Shell was condemned by UK government ministers and the media for its U-turn and the Prime Minister referred to the company as 'wimps'. Michael Heseltine, then UK President of the Board of Trade, said that it was a total embarrassment for Shell and that the company 'should have kept its nerve and done what they believed was right'.

In a press release issued on 20 June, Shell UK effectively confirmed that it was succumbing to pressure. Admitting that the new decision was not taken on a reassessment of the technical factors, the company said that it still believed the deep water disposal of the Brent Spar was the best practicable environmental option.

The *Financial Times* concluded in an editorial on the subject:

> If democracy means the successful exploitation of popular anxieties by a militant minority, then so be it. However, Shell's rout is hardly a victory for rational policy-making, let alone for the environment.

In the aftermath of the Brent Spar incident, commentators have argued that Shell's failure to successfully present its case to a wide audience base not only damaged a reputation for commercial enterprise and environmental vigilance built over many years but created serious financial consequences for the company (for example, through voluntary relinquishment of tax relief) and for the oil industry as a whole if offshore disposal were to be disallowed. The impact of greater public scrutiny, not least surrounding the environmental and social credibility of Shell's operations in Nigeria, has further implications for the business.

Could the surrender have been averted?

The answer has to be 'Yes' and here are our maxims for an effective response.

1. Manage the response

Managing the response to an emerging issue as it gains momentum through the lifecycle curve needs clearly defined roles and responsibilities and the committed time and focused attention of senior management. Without this focus at the absolute top of the organization, reputation and performance are quickly threatened.

In a BBC *Newsnight* interview on 20 June, following Shell's announcement to abandon deep water disposal, the interviewer, Jeremy Paxman, challenged Dr Chris Fay over the company's management competence in handling the issue and argued that a company shouldn't fail with the full might of government behind it. In response Dr Fay said: 'Am I expected to react every day to the misinformation that the media takes in and spend all my time arguing against that misinformation while the media doesn't seem to want to take hold of the total story?' Clearly, responding to every potential issue isn't feasible nor is it good management practice. However, when key issues do emerge, it is critical for the chief executive to decide at the earliest possible stage when to get directly involved and what resources need to be allocated to manage the task. In the case of Brent Spar, the chief executive did not make these decisions early enough.

Because of the consequences of failing to manage and respond to public opinion, senior management must have appropriate systems and resources in place to be able to focus – full-time if necessary – on the management of the issue.

2. Understand the public view

The increasing demands of public scrutiny place new pressures on organizations to be alert, aware and ready to shape or respond to potential public debate. It is often about harnessing and managing emotion.

Shell assumed that because it had followed all the international regulatory agreements and had secured the cooperation of the British and other governments (at least initially) there was no need to seek approval from a wider audience. Indeed, Dr Fay quite reasonably stated that it was 'the first example where governments have openly protested against an option which has been carried out in a lawful and proper manner'.

The speed and amplification techniques of a modern, global media and the growth and sophistication of single-issue campaign groups make them extremely capable in reaching and relating to public emotion. These factors create a new imperative for institutions and corporations to monitor and assess public perception and behaviour on any matter that could affect, either directly or indirectly, operational performance.

3. Make the case – clear and simple

Shell had difficulty explaining detailed scientific analysis succinctly, meaningfully and swiftly. By the time that some allegations were refuted more were made. In contrast, images of Greenpeace members aboard the Brent Spar being attacked by plumes of water fired from nearby vessels made instant news and more interesting broadcast viewing than scientific experts 'dryly' assessing the merits of the proposed decommissioning plan.

As we described in Chapter 1, there is growing evidence of the public's ability to challenge reassurances about risk made by government and industry. Reliance solely on the availability of scientific or technical data without communicating clear messages that distil key findings in a manner that responds to potential public concern about a particular risk is simply not enough to prevent or win the debate. Furthermore, research into memory loss indicates that we forget two-thirds of what we absorb in a day and 98 per cent in a month. Clear message points repeated over time help to make sense of complex issues for most of us.

The avoidance of complex language and statistics is essential. Instead, the use of analogies to emphasize the low degree of potential risk to the environment, coupled with basic facts, message points and illustrations are effective mechanisms for making a clear and compelling case. This approach can be used, for example, to demonstrate the remoteness and depth of the disposal location, the potential for marine life to colonize the structure over time and the health and safety benefits of offshore disposal.

This type of approach isn't about talking down to people but it is about focusing on a few key points, and constantly and consistently communicating those points to secure understanding and, ultimately, support from the majority of those either interested or directly involved.

4. Find out who you are up against and how they are likely to behave

Shell appeared to have no knowledge of the planned campaign by Greenpeace and was seemingly taken by surprise when correspondence started to fly and activists attempted to occupy the Spar.

*The whole point of an early warning system is to monitor, anticipate and assess the likely origin and evolution of potential issues. This involves gathering information on the agendas and activities of **all** relevant audiences, however peripheral in the beginning. In the case of issues relating to public health, safety and environmental protection it is essential that organizations pay particular attention to special interest groups. Building a profile of the working methods and organization of such groups through examining the characteristics, style and approach to campaigning, membership recruitment, funding, promotional activities and current agenda setting, will provide valuable intelligence for planning purposes.*

5. Work with the media

Shell seemed unable to counter the powerful visual icons offered by a very media-aware, single-issue pressure group. Conveying detailed environmental analysis in a 'sound bite' context is a tough challenge but possible to do through some of the techniques described earlier. This needs to be coupled with a clear understanding of the working practices and demands of the media. Shell failed to make this distinction and put its faith in sound science rather than sound bites. There was a clear opportunity to communicate the low potential risk of offshore disposal, the complexity in health and safety terms of onshore disposal and the fact that, for example, many of the heavy metals contained in the Spar are produced in much higher volumes by nature.

Shell was not slow to disseminate material to the media but the latter showed little sustained interest in the story until Greenpeace first occupied the Spar on 30 April. It is inevitable that because of our increasing scepticism and lack of trust in big things, ie corporations and institutions, sections of the media may be biased in favour of campaign groups. In particular, the concept of a 'David and Goliath' combat provides mouthwatering potential for sensational editorial. There is also a tendency by the media to call for and critically scrutinize a company's arguments and supporting data to a much greater degree than that of a pressure group.

Some analysts criticized Shell for not taking a more positive stance with the media earlier. However, the company could argue with some justification that seeking a higher profile might have attracted disproportionate attention to a complex issue. The right balance is often difficult to determine until it is too late.

Finally, as the issue was developing, a perception evolved that Shell representatives were seldom seen or heard on radio or television. Producers turned to other 'experts', which helped to inject some independence into the story but implied, however unjustly, that Shell was keeping a low profile.

The need for regular availability of no more than two or three designated spokespeople for communication with the media is essential.

6. Sing from the same hymn sheet

Faced with managing an issue, a company must never appear divided. *Perceptions matter.* The perception was that Shell did not speak with one voice. When public outrage developed in Germany, the local company attempted to distance itself from its UK counterpart, claiming that it had no influence there. One comment attributed to the German chief executive was that the first he knew about the proposed deep water disposal plan was when he saw the Brent Spar on television! Later, according to a press report, Shell Germany apologized to the public for paying more attention to scientists and authorities than to customers' wishes.

Similarly, Shell in the Netherlands did not want to be seen supporting London, and a senior Shell executive in Austria was quoted as saying that the sinking of the Brent Spar was intolerable.

Although sometimes difficult to institute across international and highly decentralized organization structures, it is imperative that policy guidelines are introduced and adhered to in such a way that there is always a single, consistently communicated position on an issue, with authorized spokespeople assigned to represent that position.

7. Remember – issues transcend borders and politics

Issues that involve an international industry and regulatory environment rarely stay local. Transmission of information and opinion through a host of newly available electronic media cannot be geographically constrained.

Similarly, changing political systems and agendas demands constant review and assessment no matter how removed from equivalent national institutions. Shell in London acknowledged that it was astonished by the depth of German feeling on environmental issues relating to oceans.

Why? Any international organization should be tuned into policy making in all the markets in which it operates, particularly in those that could be affected by a potential change or development like the Brent Spar.

This also applies to monitoring the methods of working and campaign activities of special interest groups. Shell decided that it would not discuss issues with Greenpeace until the illegal occupation of the Spar was ended. However reasonable such a stance may have been, it was a turning point.

> *Talking to an organization may give it added status, but it can help to publicly demonstrate a commitment to listen and potentially negotiate a resolution of conflict.*
>
> *Appropriate early warning systems and internal information networks, which can operate across borders, are essential ingredients to the effective strategic planning and issues management functions within the organization.*

Conclusion

The *Financial Times* noted:

> In hindsight, Shell failed to detect the extent of public concern in continental Europe or to win adequate support for its argument that the best place for the Brent Spar was in a deep trench in the Atlantic. As a result, years of careful cultivation by Shell of an environmentally friendly image have been thrown away.

It is always easy to criticize corporate response with the benefit of hindsight and it is important to note how rigorously Shell followed every procedure with regard to agreed international regulatory policy and environmental best practice.

Shell, alongside other large companies, could be forgiven for questioning the validity of international agreements sponsored in the framework of the law. If governments accept the rules, ignore the deadline for comment on projects devised in strict accordance with the requirements and then reverse their stance because of local protest, where does that place the credibility of such agreements?

Ruminating on the consequences of Shell's decision to do a U-turn on the planned disposal, Shell UK's director of public affairs wrote:

> Businesses will now have to include in their planning not just the views and rational arguments of all concerned – whether opponents or supporters – but will also have to come to grips with an area of deep seated emotions, subconscious instincts and symbolic gestures.

The Brent Spar issue is summarized in Figure 5.1.

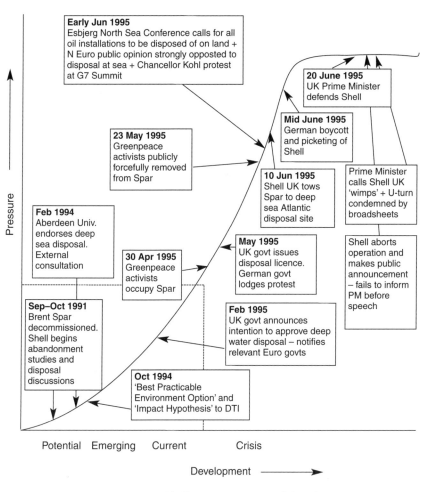

Pressure

Early Jun 1995
Esbjerg North Sea Conference calls for all
oil installations to be disposed of on land +
N Euro public opinion strongly opposed to
disposal at sea + Chancellor Kohl protest
at G7 Summit

20 June 1995
UK Prime Minister
defends Shell

Mid June 1995
German boycott
and picketing of
Shell

23 May 1995
Greenpeace
activists publicly
forcefully removed
from Spar

Prime Minister
calls Shell UK
'wimps' + U-turn
condemned by
broadsheets

10 Jun 1995
Shell UK tows
Spar to deep
sea Atlantic
disposal site

Feb 1994
Aberdeen Univ.
endorses deep
sea disposal.
External
consultation

30 Apr 1995
Greenpeace
activists
occupy Spar

May 1995
UK govt issues
disposal licence.
German govt
lodges protest

Shell aborts
operation and
makes public
announcement
– fails to inform
PM before
speech

Sep–Oct 1991
Brent Spar
decommissioned.
Shell begins
abandonment
studies and
disposal
discussions

Feb 1995
UK govt announces
intention to approve deep
water disposal – notifies
relevant Euro govts

Oct 1994
'Best Practicable
Environment Option' and
'Impact Hypothesis' to DTI

Potential   Emerging   Current   Crisis

Development ⟶

Figure 5.1   *Shell Brent Spar issue lifecycle*

CASE STUDY: THE STORY OF BERNARD MATTHEWS, HIS TURKEYS AND AVIAN FLU

Bernard Matthews is a name famous in the UK as much for his Suffolk pronunciation in television commercials of the word 'beautiful' ('bootiful') as for his vast turkey products empire.

While headline writers must have been rubbing their hands with glee during the 2007 Bernard Matthews bird flu crisis, the company itself was probably fearing the worst. Headlines including 'Not so bootiful' and '500 Bernard staff to get the bootiful' came thick and fast during February as Bernard Matthews attempted to address public concern about the safety of its products after a strain of the H5N1 virus was discovered at one if its farms in Suffolk.

On 1 February 2007, British vets were called to a Bernard Matthews farm in Suffolk where it was suspected that bird flu was responsible for the deaths of 2,600 turkeys. On 3 February the European Commission confirmed that the H5N1 strain of bird flu was responsible, and a day later the culling of birds on the farm began.

In operational terms, the company, working with the various government agencies, acted swiftly to contain the outbreak: 160,000 turkeys were culled and the site was completely disinfected within 72 hours. However, it is the way in which it handled the communications during this time that may lead to longer-term damage to its reputation.

Rather than work to immediately reassure the public about the safety of its products, the company appeared as if it were fighting to show that it was not to blame. It emphasized the problems were caused by an outbreak of the virus in Hungary and that this had nothing to do with its factory in Suffolk. It seemingly failed to grasp the scale of the panic that surrounds a still unknown subject like bird flu, and the media were fuelled by a perceived unwillingness to cooperate and to disseminate information quickly.

The negative press that surfaced suggests that the company failed to convince either the media or its customers that it was being completely forthcoming with the whole truth, and the media started digging further as a result, prolonging the story. Supermarket sales of branded Bernard Matthews products halved.

There were also mixed messages about staff lay-offs and the effect on company sales. This led to confusion and reinforced the perception that the company was trying to hide the facts.

Matters were compounded further by the fact that Bernard Matthews himself – a familiar face in UK advertising campaigns – wasn't put forward to speak to the media until 15 February, two weeks after the initial outbreak. When Matthews did speak out, he rightly apologized, but insisted that it was not the company's fault. Critics pointed out though that, for a brand that relies so heavily on Bernard Matthews's personal touch, his silence up to this point had been deafening.

The case was ultimately damaging for the company because it failed to convince its customers that it was doing all it could to protect them. Despite the fact that it managed to shut down its operation and cull its birds quickly, hesitation in its communications proved costly.

Also, whether the company had been lax in safety procedures or not (Bernard Matthews denied this strongly at the time and continued to do so), headlines such as the *Guardian's* 'String of flaws found at Bernard Matthews plant – firm was twice warned of lapses by meat inspectors' left a nasty taste in the consumer's mouth. Although reputation can be won back over time, it is much more difficult to do so if consumers feel that the company in question didn't do everything it could to ensure their safety.

The fact that Bernard Matthews was already emerging from a difficult couple of years didn't help matters. Jamie Oliver (a UK 'celebrity chef') had declared war on the company's 'turkey twizzlers', and the product became a symbol of derision for those campaigning for healthier food in schools. Also, two Bernard Matthews employees were convicted in 2006 after cases of ill treatment of turkeys at one of its sites. The two events on their own were not significant enough to cause long-term damage to the company's reputation (although profits did decline in 2006). However, they probably worked to compound the bird flu issue further. YouGov's Brand Index Survey, which measures consumers' attitudes to over a thousand brands in the UK, at one point during the crisis had Bernard Matthews at its lowest ever approval rating – second from bottom on its list.

The consequences for Bernard Matthews were significant. Sales reportedly dropped 40 per cent in the period following the scare, and just over 200 staff were ultimately laid off. The scare also had implications for the industry as a whole, and supermarkets reported declining sales of all poultry during the period.

The wider picture

It will generally be understood by the public that a company suffering from the effects of bird flu may have had little to do with it themselves and sometimes accidents happen or bad luck strikes. However, on such emotive issues like health, consumers will always be extra cautious and extremely sensitive. The company in question needs to be seen to be doing everything it can to protect its customers and put safety before profits.

The Bernard Matthews case came at a time when bird flu in the UK was on the radar for consumers and businesses alike. Most businesses have taken at least tentative steps to look at the possible scenarios surrounding bird flu. Some have invested more time and resources than others (most obviously those who stand to lose more in financial terms). The UK pharmaceutical, bioscience and food sectors have run large-scale simulations and established task forces to look at potential impacts and response options associated with a pandemic. The Bank of England, alongside the Financial Services Authority and the Treasury, also ran the largest ever industry-wide crisis simulation for the financial services sector, focusing on the potential effects of the virus hitting the financial heart of London.

All companies, however, no matter what sector they operate in, should be prepared for a potential crisis such as bird flu affecting their business. They also need to look at the bigger picture, testing every possible scenario – including their communications. The Bernard Matthews example shows that, even if a company does get it right and deals with the immediate threat in operational terms, if it does not do enough to allay the fears of its consumers it has ultimately failed and its reputation may suffer. Faced with similar situations companies should strive to be up front and quick in their media response and particularly responsive in demonstrating care and concern with staff and customers – in essence, to tell it all, tell it fast and tell it truthfully.

Also, as an aside, if a company whose sole business is dealing with poultry, and which would therefore have looked at the issue of bird flu in depth, can be caught off guard, it illustrates just how much preparation needs to be done by others to manage the issue effectively.

Conclusion

There is nothing to say that Bernard Matthews cannot win back its hard-earned reputation. Its loyal customer base will always be attracted to the company's offering of affordable and accessible products and will still buy into the concept that it is a family-run, British institution. The company has since taken out full-page adverts declaring that its turkeys are absolutely safe. However, the case proved, once again, that companies need to have their reputation risk radars constantly tuned in readiness for the requirement to manage change – positive and negative – and to ensure a state of readiness to communicate the right messages at the right time to the right audiences.

CASE STUDY: DRUG PRICING IN SOUTH AFRICA – THE BUSINESS PERSPECTIVE IS NOT THE ONLY PERSPECTIVE

Protection of patents and prices has been a constant challenge for the pharmaceutical industry, particularly concerning the costs of essential drugs, such as HIV/AIDS medication. The issue came to the fore in October 1997, when the South African government introduced the Medicines Control Act to make all medicines more affordable. The government was concerned that over 4.5 million people in South Africa were infected with the HIV virus, and the vast majority of those infected did not have access to effective treatment.

In February 1998, 39 pharmaceutical companies, coordinated by the Pharmaceutical Manufacturers Association of South Africa (PMA), responded to the Medicines Control Act by bringing a lawsuit against the South African government to prevent the implementation of the Act. The argument was that patents, and therefore drug prices, must be protected for research and development purposes. The US government and European Community were initially sympathetic to the pharmaceutical industry's position.

From September 1998, the case was suspended while the pharmaceutical companies negotiated with the South African government to stop the Act. These negotiations were unsuccessful, however, and the case was resumed in March 2001. However by, this time the political, public and media reaction was very different. The pharmaceutical industry had failed to anticipate how the issue was to develop.

In 1998 the South African AIDS advocacy group, Treatment Action Campaign (TAC), was formed and began to mobilize global support against the pharmaceutical companies. TAC worked within South Africa to politicize the AIDS problem as a poverty issue, and used the established networks of the European and US AIDS campaigners to raise the profile of the campaign.

The international NGOs Oxfam and Médicins Sans Frontières (MSF) also latched on to the drug pricing issue, helping to make the case more visible, and an international issue as opposed to a local one. MSF and Oxfam both have valuable political and campaign group networks, and used their websites to convey the latest information on the campaign. The NGOs publicly condemned the 'profiteering' practices of the industry while emphasizing the terrible consequences of AIDS. Emotive news reports in Europe and the United States showed young African children dying from AIDS after being passed the disease from their mothers.

The public profile of the AIDS pandemic in the developing world rose dramatically during this period, coinciding with a series of new initiatives in the developing world to address the problems of AIDS in poorer countries. By the time the court case was resumed in March 2001, the AIDS pandemic topped the agenda of the United Nations, World Health Organization (WHO) and the Group 7 countries.

The trial became a subject of industry, government and media debate in Europe and the United States. The pharmaceutical companies continued with the case in spite of rising pressure, intensifying protests (Glaxo SmithKline was nicknamed 'Global Serial Killers') and boycotts. MSF and Oxfam posted a 'Drop the Case' petition on their websites and in the six-week period after the court case was resumed, over 250,000 people from 130 countries signed it, including various members of governments and celebrities.

The issue escalated to such an extent that in April 2001, two of the largest pharmaceutical companies, GlaxoSmithKline and Merck, asked Kofi Annan, the UN Secretary General, to help negotiate a settlement. A joint working party to govern the Act was established and the court case was dropped. The settlement allowed the South African government to implement the Medicines Control Act if the government agreed to abide by the World Trade Organization's Trade-Related Intellectual Property Rights Agreement (TRIPS). This was widely reported as a climb-down by the industry, and as a victory against the pharmaceutical companies' profiteering.

The pharmaceutical industry clearly took too long to acknowledge public concern. The issue ignited a discussion in Europe and the United States about the cost of drugs in the developed and developing world. The pricing policies of Bayer were also called into question after the

September 11 terrorist attacks increased international demand for the smallpox vaccine, Cipro.

The pharmaceutical industry also made the mistake of dealing with the issue of drug pricing in South Africa from a strictly business point of view. When dealing with emotive issues such as AIDS, it is a huge mistake not to show care and humanity. Furthermore, the industry should have assessed the significance of the issue as it developed. The terrible consequences of AIDS were publicized more and more by NGOs and the media as the case developed, removing any sympathies that the international community may initially have had.

Before the South African drug pricing case arose, the pharmaceutical industry did not have a particularly good social and environmental record. Therefore when the issue escalated, the industry did not have credit to draw from its reputation bank.

The rise of socially responsible investment (SRI) has now placed considerable pressure on the pharmaceutical industry in particular. Following the WHO guidelines, institutional investors are placing increasing demands on companies' behaviour towards diseases of the developing world. The industry picture is that market prices in the developing world do not support the average $500 million research and development costs of new drugs. However, large pharmaceutical companies' R&D has long since overtaken academic research in the discovery of new medicines. The power to affect change rests with them – but the perception remains that they are profit-driven over finding cures.

AIDS, malaria and tuberculosis are the world's biggest killer diseases – accounting for 6 million deaths per year (30 per cent of the worldwide total) with the highest rates in the poorest countries – yet little is done to resolve this by those with the power to do so. Massive pressure is now being brought through institutional investors to change this. It is not a time for the industry to make charitable gestures dressed up in CSR greenwash. This is not a contribution to the scout hut. The pharmaceutical industry has to embed developing world diseases drug discovery into its R&D business. Opportunities exist in managing this issue, not least in the potential size of markets opening up in India and China, but it requires effective and considered reputation management.

If the industry wants to stop its drug pricing policies from being called into question in the future and be in a credible position to defend associated business risks such as black market trading and intellectual property rights, it clearly needs to establish a more caring and responsible image.

CASE STUDY: BUSINESS RESPONSE TO CLIMATE CHANGE – WAL MART, EXXON, VIRGIN

Climate change and business

Climate change truly is a global issue. It is complex even for the most discerning climatologists. Climate data show that Earth is experiencing a warming period, which is linked to the release of carbon dioxide (CO_2). It is widely accepted that CO_2 released by humans is the cause of global warming.

Although it has become the perception that people are the problem, recent consumer surveys tend to highlight high degrees of personal apathy in terms of changing behaviours to reduce carbon footprints. And so, much like the food industry is being made scapegoat for the obesity issue, big business is carrying the burden of blame for climate change.

When the Kyoto Protocol was opened for signature in 1997, industry in participant countries became worried by the cost implications associated with implementing mandatory emissions limitations, compounded by three of the four biggest global polluters – the United States, China and India – declining to sign the treaty. Companies in the public eye, however, are working to meet public expectations, while less receptive organizations are beginning to come under some pressure from investors and financial markets to change aspects of the way they operate.

Many big businesses are embarking on a number of schemes designed to meet public expectation. For example, WWF has joined forces with 12 corporations to create 'Climate Savers', which requires them to meet tough greenhouse gas reduction targets. Another high-profile climate conglomeration is the UK's Corporate Leaders Group on Climate Change, which aims to lobby the government to show 'stronger leadership' on climate change. Members, including Shell, Standard Chartered Bank, Unilever and Vodafone, meet regularly to urge the government to adopt stronger policies. Other companies are vying for climate leadership on their own: M&S aims to become carbon neutral; B&Q offers 'climate-friendly' products; Land Rover has promised to offset emissions associated with making its vehicles; BP offers a 'target neutral' initiative for customers; and BSkyB claims to have become the world's first carbon neutral media company.

In the United States, leading energy and utility companies told the Energy and Natural Resources Committee in 2006 that they would welcome or accept mandatory caps on their greenhouse gas emissions. General Electric and Shell were among the companies that called for federal regulations amid concerns that inconsistent rules were being developed throughout the country.

Although there has been a wave of businesses embracing environment and climate change concerns, some companies traditionally refused to embrace the issue of climate change. Two of these are Wal-Mart and ExxonMobil. This case study focuses on these two companies and how profit concern reluctantly appears to have driven climate action – while also looking at Virgin, which quickly seized a leadership opportunity.

111

Wal-Mart

Wal-Mart is the largest retailer in the world. It is the largest grocery seller and toy retailer in the United States. It is also the largest private employer in the United States and Mexico. Wal-Mart has more than 1.8 million employees worldwide, 7,000 stores and wholesale clubs across 14 countries, and a net income of US$12.178 billion. However, its growth and success have been accompanied by criticism from a number of groups, particularly regarding its treatment of employees and its anti-union stance. Other criticisms have been directed at its foreign product sourcing, its treatment of suppliers, the use of public subsidies and its environmental practices. These criticisms found an outlet in November 2005, when a critical documentary film was released called *Wal-Mart: The High Cost of Low Price*.

Since Wal-Mart's conception in 1962, the company has relentlessly pursued profit and become a rampant success. For the most part, caring for the environment has not been an important business concern, and Wal-Mart has kept out of the sustainability debate. Any impact on its bottom line due to negative perception and reputation deficit has been offset by the company's tangible financial results. However, Wal-Mart's share price has not always been commensurate with its high profits. It was perhaps with this in mind that Lee Scott, CEO of Wal-Mart, announced at the end of 2005 a series of startling plans for the business to become more sustainable and environmentally friendly. In 2007 it embarked on these initiatives:

- Investing approximately US$500 million annually in technologies and innovation to reduce greenhouse gases at its stores worldwide by 20 per cent over seven years.
- Designing and opening a retail outlet that is 30 per cent more efficient and will produce 30 per cent fewer greenhouse gas emissions within four years. Wal-Mart says it will favour suppliers who do the same.
- Reducing solid waste from US stores by 25 per cent within three years.
- Increasing truck fleet efficiency by 25 per cent over three years, doubling to 50 per cent within three years.

Lee Scott also has aims to turn the company into one that runs on 100 per cent renewable energy and produces zero waste. He estimates that the above initiatives will lead to savings of US$310 million per year. In an interview with environmental news website *Grist*, Mr Scott said the company's new stance was due to a combination of personal and business motives: 'It just became obvious that sustainability was an issue that was going to be more important than it was last year and the years before... we recognized that Wal-Mart had such a footprint in this world, and that we had a corresponding part to play in sustainability.' He also said that he wished to be a good environmental steward for his granddaughter's sake.

Whatever its motives, Wal-Mart has received wide recognition for its new stance. But it inevitably still draws criticism. For example, its plans for greenhouse gas emission reduction are on a per-store basis and are not countrywide. And of course, as long as the corporation expands, the more greenhouse gases it will emit. *Wake Up Wal-Mart*, a group backed by the United Food and Commercial Workers Union, called it 'a publicity stunt meant to repair a faltering public image'. The editorial and comment columns of newspapers in the UK and the United States seemed to be reasonably quiet on the issue, but in a comment piece about the sustainability of capitalism the *Guardian* said rather sarcastically: 'All hail Wal-Mart for imposing a 20 per cent reduction in its own carbon emissions.'

Analysts say the praise the company has received is not so much down to Wal-Mart finally succumbing to pressure, but the potentially huge knock-on effect its initiatives will create. Wal-Mart has a massive supply chain and is in a unique position of being able to give the clean technologies market a considerable boost. 'Our size enables us to help create markets for clean technologies that exist today, but don't yet have fully established markets', said Mr Scott.

He also believes that Wal-Mart can blaze the trail of democratizing sustainability, explaining: 'In some ways the shift toward sustainable lifestyles has thus far been stratified based on income or education levels.' In February 2007, Wal-Mart announced Sustainability 360, an initiative that moves beyond Wal-Mart's direct environmental impact and engages the company's employees, suppliers, communities and customers.

In 2007 Lee Scott told the *Guardian*: 'This is not an advertising campaign. This is not a publicity campaign. We are not sophisticated enough to greenwash. I mean, we have a hard time getting our true story out. This is about being a better company.' Whatever the motives, Wal-Mart's U-turn has stunned the corporate world and quite possibly galvanized it too.

ExxonMobil

ExxonMobil is the largest publicly traded oil and gas company in the world, and the seventh-largest company in the world. Much like Wal-Mart, ExxonMobil is considered by many as a juggernaut of capitalism, aggressively consuming resources and getting rich from the fat of the land. As with many large multinational companies, ExxonMobil has been subject to criticism for several parts of its business practice. It has been accused of illegal trading in Sudan, bribery in Angola and Kazakhstan, aiding human rights abuses in Indonesia and suppressing gay rights. The company has traditionally been seen as a foe to the environment, particularly in 1989 when the Exxon Valdez tanker spilled 10.8 million gallons of oil in Prince William Sound, Alaska.

In the hydrocarbon industry, ExxonMobil has been the least receptive to the notion that climate change is being caused by human activity.

The company set out its stall early, just as the climate debate was gaining pace. Exxon was firmly against the UN's Kyoto Protocol, with former Chairman Lee Raymond saying as recently as 2005 that Europe needed a 'reality check' over its commitment to the treaty. It has particularly courted controversy by allegedly funding organizations that cast doubt on the mainstream science of climate change. The allegations of the groups involved have varied, but ExxonMobil confirmed recently that it had funded the Competitive Enterprise Initiative (CEI), a free market advocacy group. The group were responsible for an infamous series of advertisements in the United States that challenged orthodox climate change theory. The advertisements themselves made some valid points, but they lost credibility with their end slogan: 'Carbon dioxide: They call it pollution. We call it life.'

In the UK, the *Guardian* has been particularly active in attempting to establish connections between ExxonMobil and what the newspaper views as immoral funding activities. In September 2006, it published a letter from the Royal Society, Britain's prestigious scientific academy, to ExxonMobil asking it to cease its funding to groups that 'misrepresented the science of climate change by outright denial of the evidence'. And again in February 2007 the newspaper alleged that scientists were offered money by a think-tank funded by ExxonMobil to emphasize the shortcomings in the recent report from the UN's Intergovernmental Panel on Climate Change (IPCC). In January, the Union of Concerned Scientists, a US advocacy group, alleged that ExxonMobil had given nearly US$16 million between 1998 and 2005 to 43 advocacy organizations that 'seek to confuse the public on global warming science'.

Public concern with the company's attitude is prevalent. Several monitoring groups have been set up, including Expose Exxon, Campaign ExxonMobil and Exxon Secrets. The latter was set up by Greenpeace and lists well over 100 organizations that it claims have been given money by the oil company. Additionally, a minor film production was released entitled *Out of Balance: ExxonMobil's Impact on Climate Change*, which sought to document the company's influence on governments and the media. In December 2006, ExxonMobil came top of the list in the Worst EU Lobby Awards 2006, organized by Corporate Europe Observatory, Friends of the Earth Europe, LobbyControl and Spinwatch.

And so ExxonMobil's stance on climate change was, or is, never likely to gain mainstream support. This may be part of the reason why the company discreetly indicated a softening of its views. Wal-Mart's entrance to the climate change debate was accompanied by fireworks and astonishment; ExxonMobil nipped in the back door, hoping not to be noticed. The announcement didn't come from chairman and CEO Rex Tillerson, but from the vice-president of public affairs, Kenneth Cohen. In January 2007 he was widely reported as saying: 'We know enough now – or society knows now – that the risk is serious and action should be taken.' He confirmed that ExxonMobil had 'quietly' started meeting with leaders of various environmental groups. Regarding the company's position on climate change, Cohen told *Fortune* magazine: 'We should be putting ourselves on a path, as a society, to reduce emissions in ways that are cost-effective and sustainable.' He also said that government policy had a role to play in emissions legislation, saying that his company wanted to be part of the discussion.

In February 2007, Rex Tillerson confirmed ExxonMobil's shift by saying that nations should work towards having a global policy on climate change. He said: 'It is prudent to develop and implement sensible strategies that address these risks while not reducing our ability to progress other global priorities, such as economic development, poverty eradication and public health.' However, in the same speech he offered a robust defence of the oil industry, saying that there is no clear alternative to oil and gas in the near future. He said: 'I'm no expert on biofuels. I don't know much about farming and I don't know much about moonshine. There is really nothing [Exxon] can bring to that whole [biofuels] issue. We don't see a direct role for ourselves with today's technology.'

But ExxonMobil has always been criticized for its perceived contempt for the environment. Much like Wal-Mart's change of stance, ExxonMobil's softer attitude is most likely due to economic imperatives. While Wal-Mart overtly said that it stands to make more money if it is more environmentally efficient, ExxonMobil has said its new empathy comes from an acknowledgement that the scientific data on climate change is now acceptable. It is likely that the company would prefer to be central to any future – and likely – federal legislation on greenhouse gas emissions. It is also possible that ExxonMobil is simply fed up with continuously struggling with its image. Rex Tillerson told Wall Street fund managers in January 2007: 'We recognize that we need to soften our public image. It is something we are working on.' He also said that ExxonMobil was 'inaccurately and unfairly' depicted as a climate change sceptic and reportedly told the *Guardian* that it was determined not to change its position. It is suggested that another reason for Exxon's change of heart is that it is fed up not being able to communicate the good things it is doing, which include:

- working with the manufacturers of automobiles and commercial industrial engines on research and development;
- supporting the Global Climate and Energy Project (GCEP) at Stanford University, with a charge to accelerate the development of commercially viable energy technologies that can lower greenhouse gas emissions on a global scale;
- mitigating greenhouse gas emissions through efficiency and best practices, with steps taken to improve energy efficiency at ExxonMobil facilities since 1999;
- partnering with the US Environmental Protection Agency and Department of Energy to reduce greenhouse gas emissions in its aim to save more than 6 billion gallons of fuel annually in the US freight transport system;
- partnering with the European Commission to study carbon capture and storage (CCS).

ExxonMobil's recent talk on climate change does not represent a U-turn in its beliefs, but more of a gradual acceptance that the issue of climate change could ultimately damage the company's profitability. This is perhaps why the UK and US media reported the story rather than commenting on it as being an environmental epiphany. While ExxonMobil's move has been welcomed, there seem to be few expectations that the company will take a more positive or pioneering role in averting climate change.

The examples of Wal-Mart and ExxonMobil highlight how two juggernauts of world business are dealing with the issue of climate change – by looking to protect and enhance their bottom line.

Virgin

Sir Richard Branson was a global warming sceptic until around 2005. But after an apparently dramatic conversion, Virgin made tentative moves into the debate, which signalled its acknowledgement of the need for action. The company had a rough ride when, in March 2006, environmentalists accused Virgin Atlantic of double standards for 'offsetting' carbon emissions from its limousines by planting trees. Environmental pressure group Transport 2000 said that such offsetting would be insignificant given the large fleet of Virgin aircraft.

However, in late September 2006 at the Clinton Global Initiative (an annual conference hosted by Bill Clinton), Branson said that Virgin would be investing US$3 billion (£1.6 billion) to fight global warming over the next 10 years. The money used to fund this will come from the profits of his travel companies, such as Virgin Atlantic and Virgin Trains. It will be invested in renewable energy technologies via his investment unit Virgin Fuels. One confirmed recipient is Californian company Cilion, which plans to make bioethanol from corn. Branson said: 'We must rapidly wean ourselves off our dependence on coal and fossil fuels.' He added that transport and energy companies should be at the forefront of developing 'environmentally friendly business strategies'. He also announced the investment during a US television appearance with former vice-president and environment campaigner Al Gore.

A week later, Branson called on the aviation industry to work together to beat climate change. He claimed that a quarter of the 2 per cent of carbon dioxide that aeroplanes emit could be cut if the industry took simple steps. Branson wrote to airlines, airport operators and engine manufacturers to urge swifter action. He suggested a 'starting grid' system at airports that would require aeroplanes to only switch their engines on much closer to take-off. Additionally, he said that a slower and smoother landing would reduce fuel consumption. Branson also suggested that a single European air traffic control system would optimize the use of airspace. And perhaps most surprisingly he insisted on government intervention should the industry not get its act together.

However, Virgin faced opposition from parts of the airline industry. British Airways refused to join the initiative, saying the global airline trade association IATA should take the lead in addressing climate change. Ryanair's Michael O'Leary dismissed it as a 'PR stunt', saying that Virgin's profits from its transport businesses would not match the £1.6 billion offered. EasyJet gave its backing to Branson, saying he was the right man to lead action on emissions. Friends of the Earth said that growth of emissions resulting from airport expansion would outweigh Virgin's suggestions.

In February 2007, Branson again appeared with Al Gore to announce a $25 million (£12.8 million) prize for the scientists who could invent a way of extracting greenhouse gases from the atmosphere. He claimed it to be the largest prize ever offered and compared it to the competition to devise a way of measuring latitude. Branson denied that being in charge of an airline excluded him from the climate change debate, saying that if he closed the airline another would just take its place. He went on to express his admiration for the Gaia theory that suggests the world is a single organism. The theory was developed by scientist and long-term environmentalist James Lovelock, one of the people who will judge Virgin's prize. He added: 'Today we have a threat. Still we have to convince many people that the threat is urgent and real and there is no super-hero. We have only our own ingenuity and we have no hope of a meaningful solution unless we find a way to work together.'

On the whole, Virgin's initiatives have been reasonably well received. Michael Dempsey, business reporter for BBC News, said that Virgin's planned investment of $3 billion was 'much more than green philanthropy', saying: 'It seems there is a compelling commercial logic behind Sir Richard's drive for new fuels.' Dempsey said that Branson was looking beyond the short-term perspective of oil and gas and was setting up a prominent role for Virgin long after his own retirement. The *Guardian* said that Virgin's moves were 'commendable' but said that greater corporate cooperation was necessary to beat climate change. *The Times* made reference to Virgin's planned investments when it said that investing money on clean technologies was where the 'smart money' was going. The *Independent* commended parts of Virgin's initiatives but criticized Virgin's plans for space tourism, which the newspaper said would create carbon footprints much larger than those produced by aviation. It said:

> Sir Richard says that he wants to make a difference. He says he wants to use his influence and wealth to leave a better world for our children and our children's children. The prize he is announcing today to capture and store man-made CO2 is a commendable gesture in that direction. But how does he square that with his desire to turn us all into an army of carbon-crazed space cadets?

As with Wal-Mart and ExxonMobil, the public profile of Virgin as a business means that any action it takes on climate change will have an impact in the business world. Once again Virgin has demonstrated an ability to capture the headlines and project its brand. It remains to be seen where and when the real impact of any of these companies will be felt.

CASE STUDY: *CELEBRITY BIG BROTHER* 2007

Channel 4 began broadcasting in 1982, joining the two established BBC chan-nels and ITV, the only commercial broadcaster at the time. It was originally a subsidiary of the Independent Broadcasting Authority (IBA), which was abol-ished in 1993. Since then, it has been owned and operated by Channel 4 Television Corporation. Although the channel is commercially self-funded, it is publicly owned because Channel 4 Television Corporation is a public body. And so it has a remit of public service obligations that it must perform, which is amended periodically after regulation from Ofcom. The Communications Act 2003 says:

> The public service remit for Channel 4 is the provision of a broad range of high quality and diverse programming which, in particular:

- demonstrates innovation, experiment and creativity in the form and content of programmes;
- appeals to the tastes and interests of a culturally diverse society;
- makes a significant contribution to meeting the need for the licensed public service channels to include programmes of an educational nature and other programmes of educative value; and
- exhibits a distinctive character.

The channel has been hoping to receive a government subsidy to replace the free broadcasting space it received upon its conception, which will become redundant when the UK goes digital in 2012.

Issue development

The issue began when Shilpa Shetty was referred to as 'the Indian' by a fellow housemate who found it difficult to pronounce her name. After the next episode, Ofcom received over 200 complaints of alleged racist bullying by three housemates – a tiny proportion of the viewers of the show, which peaked at 8.2 million viewers. Channel 4 dismissed the incidents as 'girly rivalry'. The number of complaints quickly escalated to 8,000, with the incidents gaining prominence owing to an early day motion (EDM) tabled by Labour MP Keith Vaz, calling on Channel 4 'to take urgent action to remind housemates that racist behaviour is unacceptable'. The motion galvanized political interest, with the then Prime Minister, Tony Blair, agreeing 'entirely with the principles' of the EDM and the then Culture Secretary, Tessa Jowell, describing the incident as 'racism being presented as entertainment'.

The entry of the debate into the House of Commons gave the media the opportunity to develop the story significantly. This credibility meant that the programme was no longer the preserve of the tabloids, but entered the comment and editorial columns of the broadsheets. The escalation coincided with Gordon Brown's trip to India, where effigies were burnt of the programme's producers. The incident was creeping towards a diplomatic incident for the British government, when India's minister for external affairs said the incident had caused 'indignation'. There were few doubts as to how the incident was perceived in India – the *Hindustan Times* carried the front-page headline 'Racist attacks trigger outrage'.

Throughout the escalation, Channel 4 denied the incidents had been racist, insisting contestants' differences were rooted in culture and class. *Big Brother*'s producers, Endemol, also sidestepped the allegations of racism. In the space of three days, the number of complaints rose to almost 20,000. Channel 4 chairman Luke Johnson was caught flat-footed when he spoke to *BBC Today*. He declined the invitation to defend the show on several occasions, instead referring stakeholders to the company's formal statement, of which he had no copy himself. On the same day, Channel 4's chief executive, Andy Duncan, made an appearance at a press conference dressed casually, where he read a press statement line for line, giving the appearance that he was terrified to go off script. The day was rounded off with the programme's main sponsor, the Carphone Warehouse, suspending its sponsorship – evidently

Channel 4's performance was totally at odds with the expectations of its sponsor.

The national press was equally appalled, suggesting that Channel 4 was calculating and selective in the name of profit. The *Daily Express* carried the headline 'Desperate C4 defend "cash cow"', while the *Sun* branded the show a 'National Disgrace'. *The Times* said Channel 4 had 'either been complicit in promoting racial bullying to boost ratings, or worse, cynically contrived a cast list to elicit a row'. The *Independent* called for a change in attitudes, 'and that means not just Jade Goody [one of the housemates] and her companions, but the television channel which profits from broadcasting her excesses'.

Shilpa Shetty won the programme with 63 per cent of the votes. Her eloquent and dignified handling of the incident removed some of the heat from Channel 4, which faced an Ofcom inquiry into the series.

Outcome

On 24 May 2007, Ofcom ruled that Channel 4 had breached the Ofcom code of conduct during the series. The watchdog said Channel 4 had made 'serious editorial misjudgements' in the handling of the row, singling out three incidents:

- derogatory remarks about Shetty's Indian cooking;
- one contestant telling Shetty to 'f*** off home'; and
- one contestant referring to Shetty as 'Shilpa Poppadom'.

Statutory sanctions were imposed on Channel 4, obliging it to broadcast statements of Ofcom's findings on three separate occasions at the start of the subsequent series of *Big Brother*. Channel 4 and Endemol apologized and accepted Ofcom's ruling. Chairman Luke Johnson said the sanction imposed was 'proportionate given Ofcom's ruling that the breaches were not deliberate and that the channel did not act recklessly'.

Channel 4 also conducted its own review and announced it would:

- appoint its first viewers' editor and launch a right-to-reply programme;
- introduce a new written intervention policy that explains how the show will tackle seriously offensive language or behaviour; and
- appoint a senior welfare officer whose sole task is to observe housemates and to advise producers of any concerns.

Keith Vaz MP called for Andy Duncan to apologize to Shilpa Shetty and to step down. The Commission for Racial Equality said it would keep a close eye on the subsequent series of *Big Brother* to ensure that 'such disgraceful behaviour' would not be repeated. In the subsequent series of *Big Brother*, Channel 4 reacted promptly when it immediately ejected a housemate for using racist language. Andy Duncan, chief executive of Channel 4, said the word used was 'unacceptable'.

On 14 June, Ofcom reviewed Channel 4's finances and said that the channel would have to explain its case for demanding extra public support in the future

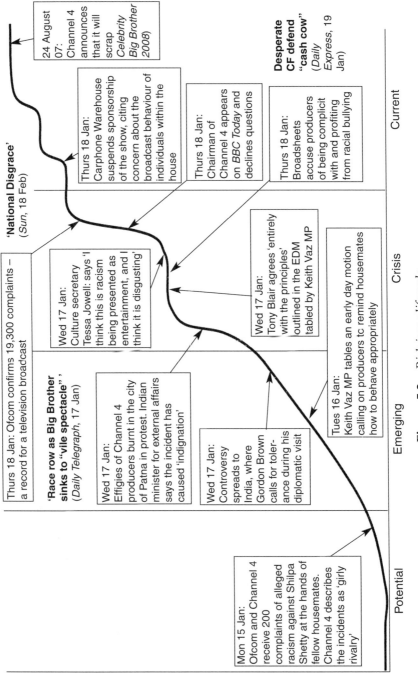

Figure 5.2 *Risk issue lifecycle*

Thurs 18 Jan: Ofcom confirms 19,300 complaints – a record for a television broadcast

'National Disgrace' (*Sun*, 18 Feb)

24 August 07: Channel 4 announces that it will scrap *Celebrity Big Brother 2008*)

'Race row as Big Brother sinks to "vile spectacle"' (*Daily Telegraph*, 17 Jan)

Thurs 18 Jan: Carphone Warehouse suspends sponsorship of the show, citing concern about the broadcast behaviour of individuals within the house

Wed 17 Jan: Culture secretary Tessa Jowell: says 'I think this is racism being presented as entertainment, and I think it is disgusting'

Wed 17 Jan: Effigies of Channel 4 producers burnt in the city of Patna in protest. Indian minister for external affairs says the incident has caused 'indignation'

Wed 17 Jan: Controversy spreads to India, where Gordon Brown calls for tolerance during his diplomatic visit

Thurs 18 Jan: Chairman of Channel 4 appears on *BBC Today* and declines questions

Wed 17 Jan: Tony Blair agrees 'entirely with the principles' outlined in the EDM tabled by Keith Vaz MP

Thurs 18 Jan: Broadsheets accuse producers of being complicit with and profiting from racial bullying

Tues 16 Jan: Keith Vaz MP tables an early day motion calling on producers to remind housemates how to behave appropriately

Desperate CF defend "cash cow" (*Daily Express*, 19 Jan)

Mon 15 Jan: Ofcom and Channel 4 receive 200 complaints of alleged racism against Shilpa Shetty at the hands of fellow housemates. Channel 4 describes the incidents as 'girly rivalry'

Potential   Emerging   Crisis   Current

PRESSURE

and that its finances were under no 'immediate pressure'. In particular, Ofcom dismissed Channel 4's request for assistance in the form of tax breaks and free access to the digital broadcasting spectrum. However, it did say that discussions should begin about 'potential intervention in the long term', conceding that the channel might not be able to fulfil its public service purpose in the future. Ofcom also said Channel 4's remit needed to be 'improved', saying the board should review the channel's programming to remain true to its public service principles. Ofcom said the review had not been influenced by recent controversies. The issue of public funding is crucial to Channel 4, especially since its profits fell by 70 per cent in 2006. It has been reported that Gordon Brown is keen on privatizing Channel 4.

Ultimately, Channel 4 decided not to go ahead with the programme in 2008. Head of programmes Julian Bellamy said the race row had meant the programme was so high-profile that 'it feels like it has never been away this year'. He denied that the race row had made it difficult to sign up new celebrities. He added: 'If we wanted to take the easy path… we'd probably do two series of *Celebrity Big Brother* if ratings were all we were after. These are the decisions of a public service broadcaster in search of the new and the exciting.' He denied that the race row had deterred celebrities from taking part in the next series.

The racism incident on *Celebrity Big Brother* has undoubtedly been a catalyst for public antipathy and distrust in the UK broadcasting industry. Since *Celebrity Big Brother*, UK terrestrial channels have been involved in consecutive controversies, including: phone-in competition scandals across all channels; the BBC's misrepresentation of the Queen; Channel 4 broadcasting photographs of Princess Diana's last moments; and allegations from police that Channel 4 had 'distorted' a programme on Islamic fundamentalism.

Key lessons

- Channel 4 addressed if the individual incidents constituted racism, claiming they were class and culture clashes. Even if this assertion was technically correct, it was a different perception to the one held by many viewers. A more robust articulate defence of Channel 4's position without technicalities might have allayed stakeholder concerns.
- It failed to take control of the issue in its early stages, which allowed the issue to rapidly escalate into a crisis.
- Broadcasting the alleged racist incidents without the channel's acknowledgement of them made Channel 4 appear complicit in racism.
- Entry of any issue into parliament gives a story considerable momentum and broadens media interest.
- The organization's media strategy was largely reactive and at times lacking in preparation.

The development of this issue underlines the importance of:

- ensuring the organization's perception of an event (or events) is the same as that of its key stakeholders;

- close monitoring of potential issues, even if they seem insignificant to begin with;
- early action on an issue, not least to demonstrate understanding of its sensitivity;
- acknowledging people's genuine concerns;
- preparing thoroughly for media interviews:
  - ensuring coherent and consistent messages;
  - presenting and communicating appropriately.

6

Implementing an issues management programme

Not everything that is faced can be changed, but nothing can be changed until it is faced.

James Baldwin

A similar, complementary process to the issues management model described in Chapter 3 can be defined for the role of management decision making at each phase and is shown in Figure 6.1. The *awareness* phase maps on to the first stage in the issues lifecycle – *potential issue*. Here, the emphasis in the management team is on listening and learning. Those involved need to be alert, open, low-key, inquisitive and challenging. Full use should be made of background information, research and ensuring monitoring infrastructures are in place.

The *exploration* phase indicates an increased urgency over the importance of the issue. Specific responsibilities need to be assigned, organizational awareness is raised and the analysis and opinion formation process begins. Based on working with a number of pharmaceutical companies, an example structure and allocation of responsibilities is shown in Figure 6.2. Typically, in this type of organization, representation should come

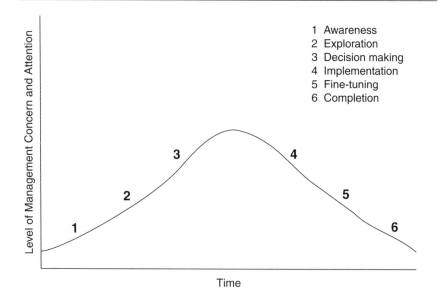

Figure 6.1 *The management process*

from medical, safety, regulatory, planning, legal, marketing and communications functions with authority to take specific action. Characteristics of any task force are:

- seniority to make decisions, allocate resources and direct programme implementation;
- breadth of disciplines represented and appropriate access to information for decision-making purposes;
- easy access for arranging meetings and 'networking' information; flexibility and informality in working methods;
- ability to combine analytical and creative skills with rapid, focused decision making and action;
- minimal paper flow to avoid bureaucracy, slow response and leakage of sensitive information.

Broader awareness of the issue in the company is raised at this stage and the analysis and opinion formation process begins.

At the *decision-making* stage the company has to consider action. The management team must objectively assess and decide upon the alternatives presented while still encouraging broad thinking and creativity in the formulation of an action plan.

The *implementation* phase involves taking the necessary steps to make management decisions work in practice, while *fine-tuning* allows for the

Roles and Responsibilities:

Task Force
(chair and secretariat)

Communications	Marketing/Sales	Medical	Regulatory	Legal/Planning
● media contact and intelligence gathering ● media training ● briefing documentation ● media briefings/workshops ● article drafting and syndication ● crisis communications support	● sales force briefing and training ● product education (doctor/patient) ● competitive analysis ● doctor mailings ● medical meetings management ● sales and marketing support materials	● review/analysis of data ● opinion leader networking ● study definition/commissioning ● data presentation at symposia, medical meetings, workshops, regulatory working groups, etc	● liaison with authorities ● submission of data ● licence approval status/monitoring ● analysis/assessment of approval processes	● impact assessment ● liability implications ● strategy review ● counsel

Figure 6.2 *Example task force for a pharmaceutical company*

measurement and evaluation of current actions and results so that adjustments or enhancements to the action plan can be made.

Completion is the wind-down period which should decrease senior management involvement. Key activities involve appropriate delegation and ensuring implementation of any resulting change management within the organization.

Effective issues management can help to build competitive advantage and sales, particularly in new and emerging markets; it can exploit opportunities or protect corporate policies where there is the potential for major social change. The pressures of market dynamics, competitor activity and resource availability can make it difficult to anticipate, initiate or plan for important issues.

Kerry Tucker and Bill Trumpfheller (1993) have created a five-step plan to help establish an issues management system, which we have found works well in practice.

1. Anticipate issues and establish priorities

This first fundamental step can take many forms, from drawing up a very basic set of assumptions through to a highly elaborate issues anticipation system. Setting up an internal task force, based on the approach outlined in the previous section, is a crucial starting point. Brainstorming sessions and database analysis should focus on responding to questions like:

- What immediate and medium-term competitor, social or regulatory factors do we need to contend with?
- What changes do we anticipate in the marketplace and wider political and social environment over the next 12 months and beyond?
- What factors are likely to affect the way we are working?
- What special events are likely to take place and have an impact on our ability to sustain and develop our markets?

Once these issues are identified, priorities can be set and decisions can be taken on how much time and resource to devote to them.

2. Analyse issues

Develop a formal brief or analysis of the issue, looking at the opportunities and threats against a series of different scenarios. This should cover what could happen if the issue is ignored, and an assessment of how key audiences are likely to be affected by the issue. There should also be a summary of the direction in which the issue is likely to be heading. This will give management a broad view of the issue and its effect on a number of areas such as product marketing positioning, financial performance, corporate reputation and the potential for regulation or even litigation.

3. Recommend an organizational position on the issue

The analysis from the previous step should provide a database to develop a position designed to create support from the greatest majority of individuals and groups affected. The database is built from answers to the following questions:

- Who is affected?
- How do the affected groups or individuals perceive the issue?
- What are their likely positions and behavioural inclinations?
- What information/data can we gather to support our case?

4. Identify groups and opinion leaders who can advance your position

These groups and individuals should emerge from asking:

- Who makes decisions on the issue?
- Who is likely to support our position?
- Who is likely not to?
- Who can we target successfully to make the biggest difference in advancing our position?

If possible, research should be undertaken to validate assumptions made about groups during the analysis stage. Opinion leaders, closely followed by influential industry or employee associations, consumer and other special interest groups and informed media, can be powerful allies in dealing with a range of audiences, and criteria for selecting them include:

- Who do members of our target groups look to for advice on the issue?
- Who will the (customer, consumer) community and the wider public trust on the issue?
- Who has the credibility to best advance our position on the issue?
- Who is likely to be open to our position on the issue?

5. Identify desired behaviours

This is an easy point to overlook, according to the authors. Advancing specific behaviour relating to the company's position drives development of the rest of the planning processing, namely: communications and marketing strategy, goals, objectives, messages, tactics, resource allocation and budgets.

Finally, evaluation of progress needs to be incorporated into plans to ensure that key milestones are met, the course of the issue is charted, and adjustments made if necessary.

Our experience from dealing with current and historic issues across different industry sectors endorses the value of implementing the following types of activity as early as possible, both to gain the initiative and protect against adverse developments.

Task force set-up

- Identify an appropriately experienced/resourced task force to define and manage issue response strategy.
- Maintain a flexible, creative approach to considering competitive counter-measures, regulatory change and positive corporate positioning initiatives.
- Think positively and proactively throughout – it is easy to be drawn into a defensive strategy from the outset and lose the opportunity to secure or regain the advantage of opinion leader, media and public support.

Intelligence gathering and analysis

- Invest in and establish an early warning intelligence gathering network to monitor, collect and review relevant research/data.
- Constantly assess competitor/regulatory activity and refer to similar, practical experience from other companies for guidance on approach.
- Obtain and monitor relevant peer review/specialist publications as early as possible for assessment and action where appropriate; track trade and broader mass media.

Issue champions

- One way of managing resourcing requirements for information gathering and analysis is for each issue to be assigned to an appropriately experienced individual within the organization. These in-house experts – issue champions – should act as authoritative, up-to-the-minute sources of information to assist task forces and other management in the planning and coordination of related activities.

Background briefing materials

- Prepare background information relevant to desired positioning, eg key messages, corporate/product/service back-grounders, Q&A, reference contact and research databases, core presentation kits, etc.

Research databases

- In industry sectors where there is the potential for risk to public health, safety or the environment, it is essential to build and maintain technical and scientific databases of information relating to, for example, the long-term safety of a drug, the rigour of hygiene monitoring systems in food processing, the frequency of routine safety checks and actual incident occurrence at manufacturing facilities, the use of independent expert safety audits and impact assessments to encourage best practice techniques for minimizing the risk of chemical or oil spillage, etc.

Relationship management

Build equity *early* through developing and managing influential relationships with:

- supportive academic and other opinion leaders;
- informed journalists;
- peer review journal editorial boards;
- regulatory authorities;
- industry and employee associations;
- policy units;
- political groups at local, national and international levels;
- local and other special interest groups.

Do this through informal contact and briefings; information distribution; educational programmes and research sponsorships, etc. These groups communicate informally and formally together, so it is important to understand the linkages between them and the potential for common agendas on issues relating to an organization's positioning. Try to assess their perceptions/opinions on potential issues by classifying them into positive/neutral/negative groupings.

Opinion leader development

- Contact and build relationships with potentially supportive opinion leaders who may become influential, independent endorsers of the company's desired positioning.
- Consider the use of tactics such as research and publication sponsorship, invitations to attend symposia, chair or present data at meetings, round-table discussions where appropriate.

Information/education programmes

- Build support at grass roots level through the organization of community meetings, correspondence, roadshows and provision of training/education aids to encourage more effective understanding and interest. Similar activities should be considered for customer and supplier groups.

Regulatory affairs

- Be prepared to proactively respond to potential regulatory questions relating to organizational, product and service performance.
- Prepare responses and develop relevant information updates that can be regularly mailed to appropriate authorities.
- Organize a meetings programme to build relationships and neutralize potential critical reporting.

Media management

- Work with the media (specialist, general at regional/national and international level as appropriate) proactively by establishing contact, ensuring spokespeople are available, issuing press statements, letters to specialist publications, bylined articles, media briefings and workshops.
- Monitor editorial coverage and individual journalists or publications for interest/bias; classify into positive/neutral/negative editorial stance on an ongoing basis and immediately following major announcements.
- Train appropriate spokespeople – corporate, technical and marketing, and supportive independent opinion leaders where possible.

The 'glocal' approach

- Act local but think global… in managing issues. Consider implications for other operating companies, the industry as a whole, to decide whether a coalition approach is likely to be more effective, etc.
- Be aware that as the impact of an issue declines in one market, it can easily cross national borders and quickly activate in other countries where local political or competitor agendas may trigger new threats.

Checklists can help

- A checklist to assist in planning an issues management programme is provided on the following page.

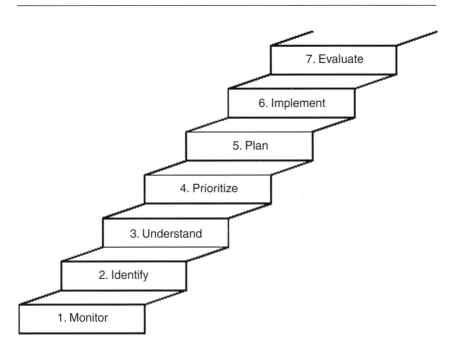

Figure 6.3 *Stepwise diagram*

Table 6.1 *A summary of the seven steps of issue management*

Step 1 – Monitoring	**Step 2 – Identification**
• Analyse the business environment.	• Assess from the business environment those elements that are important.
• Scan and monitor what is being said, written and done by public, media, interest groups, government and other opinion leaders.	• Look for a new pattern emerging from what most people take for granted.
• Consider what may impact on the company or its divisions.	• Identify the issues that impact on the company and are gaining widespread support.
	• What is the type of issue and where is it in its lifecycle?
Step 3 – Prioritization	
• How far-reaching will an issue's impact be (product, sector, company, industry)?	**Step 4 – Analysis**
• Assess what is at stake – Profit? Reputation? Freedom of action?	• Analyse the most important issues in some detail.
• What is the probability of occurrence?	• Determine their probable impact on the company or its divisions as precisely as possible.
• How immediate is the issue?	

Step 5 – Strategy decision
- Create a strategic response and define the content of the message.
- Identify the target groups.
- What are the company's strategic options?
- What resources are needed?
- What specific actions should be taken? By whom? When? With whom?
- Develop issue management communication plan – consider timing.

Step 7 – Evaluation
- Assess results.
- Evaluate the success of policies and programmes to determine future strategies.
- Capture learnings from failures and successes.

- Establish issue support teams if appropriate.
- Identify/rank stakeholders.

Step 6 – Implementation
- Implement the policies and programmes approved by management.
- Communicate the response effectively with each target group in a credible form.
- Advocate the company position to prevent negative impacts and encourage actions with beneficial effects.

EXAMPLES OF ISSUE MANAGEMENT MODELS AND PROCESSES

There are many different company models for the practice of issue management principles. There is no one-size-fits-all approach; in fact, the best practice is often to mirror the organizational processes elsewhere in the organization to ensure that issue management procedures are successfully embedded in a company culture. The following three example models have been well and truly inculcated into the DNA of their respective organizations (one for as long as 20 years), and address three key areas of issue management: the issue manager ('champion'), the issues management process, and the involvement of senior management. (*Source: Corporate Public Issues and their Management,* January 2004.)

Memorial Health: the role of the issue manager

Issue management is most often launched and championed by a single individual within an organization, preferably a full-time equivalent position. This person learns the fundamentals of issues management, observes how others approach the discipline, and then recommends the appropriate process and initial participants. The champion, or 'steward', selects an initial issue to address, and with ratification from senior management, activates the issue management process.

The process steward's maintenance responsibilities include:

- Identify emerging issues.
- Monitor prospective issues.
- Help set issue priorities.
- Help set accountabilities and 'issue owners'.
- Ensure appropriate resource allocation.
- Create issue consistency by identifying and eliminating conflicts among issue plans.
- Provide a 'one-stop-shop' macro overview of issues across the organization.
- Deliver and collect issue intelligence.

The issue process steward responsibilities model at Memorial Health was developed nearly 20 years ago and remains pertinent today. It is summarized in Figure 6.4.

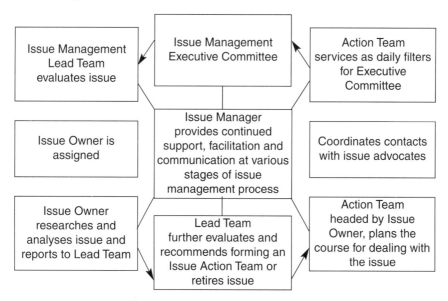

Figure 6.4 *Memorial Health issue management model*

Weyerhaeuser Company issues management process

Some people process information verbally. Others prefer a visual point of reference. The reality is that everyone suffers the constraint of limited time, so to create an awareness and understanding of how issue management works at a company it is useful to be able to map the process. That way, the individuals who have key roles and responsibilities on any given issue can easily see the intended end product and their role in achieving it. Senior management can also more easily grant resource allocation and evaluate progress against issue goals.

At paper and wood products firm Weyerhaeuser, where issue management has been continuously practised since the 1970s, the process finds a balance between being simple and comprehensive. See Figure 6.5.

DaimlerChrysler Group: weekly issue management process flow

The most senior officers of a company are responsible for being sure they are fully apprised of the results of the issue management process. They are also responsible for providing the necessary resources to achieve those results. DaimlerChrysler's weekly global issues call concludes with a key issue briefing that is sent to the board of management. Through this process, top management is regularly supplied with fresh and relevant insights on the issues that have merited task force assignments, as well as those that are likely to build steam and may therefore require resources for a more thorough treatment. See Figure 6.6.

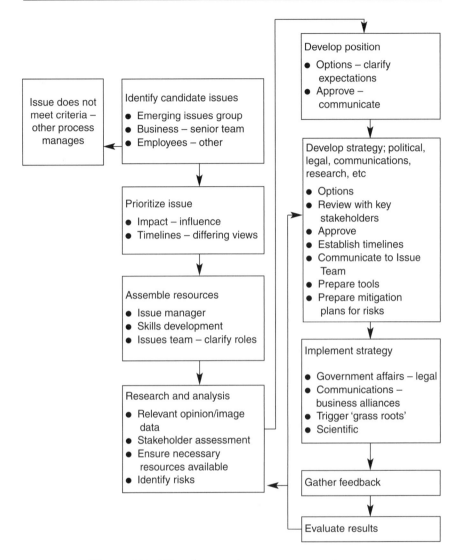

Figure 6.5 *Weyerhaeuser issues management process*

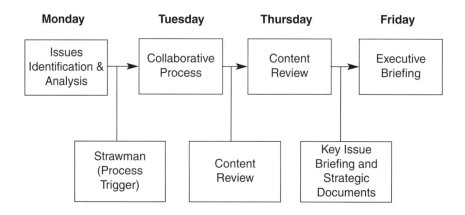

Figure 6.6 *DaimlerChrysler issues management process*

SUMMARY

While there is never a single generic approach that will work for every issue, this type of framework will help to anticipate, identify and plan a response to potential issues in a methodical and innovative way. Information should always be carefully focused, and briefing papers should have specific objectives that concentrate on realistic outcomes. Defining action in the context of potential bottom-line implications is a good discipline for maintaining this focus.

Part 2

Crisis Management

7

So it hits the fan – now what?

If you can keep your head when all about you are losing theirs, it's just possible you haven't grasped the situation.

Jean Kerr, humorist

In business as in life, crises come in as many varieties as the common cold. The spectrum is so wide it is impossible to list each type. Product-related crises alone range from outright failures as in the case of the over-heating laptop batteries, which resulted in millions of them being withdrawn from the market by Dell in 2006, to unanticipated side effects illustrated by cases of asbestosis and thalidomide. Accidental or deliberate contamination experienced by Lucozade, Perrier, Tylenol, and more recently Cadbury and enforced obsolescence as in the case of PCBs are yet two more categories.

However, it is major crises such as aeroplane and ferry disasters involving tragic loss of life which lead to greatest public interest. It is this type of crisis which leads to the most visible and measurable erosion of public confidence. The public perception of the risk of such events – fuelled by the disproportionate amount of negative publicity – is often out of kilter with the statistical evidence. For example, in the United States it would take two 747 crashes per week to equal the number of people killed on US highways in the same period, but automobile crashes rarely make the headlines in the way aeroplane crashes do.

Advancing technology, which the public has often come to believe to be foolproof, forms yet another category. This category includes the 1967 Apollo spacecraft fire in which three astronauts died, the 1979 'incident' at the Three Mile Island nuclear reactor, the 1986 Challenger space shuttle tragedy, and Chernobyl in April of the same year. In 2000 the world was stunned to learn of the fatal Concorde crash.

CASE STUDY: CADBURY SALMONELLA OUTBREAK

In July 2007, Cadbury was fined £1 million for food and hygiene offences relating to a salmonella outbreak that made 42 people ill, with three requiring hospital treatment. The outbreak occurred between January and March 2006. It originated from a leaking pipe at the company's Herefordshire plant. The company recalled more than a million products in the UK.

Cadbury admitted nine charges brought against it by the Birmingham and Herefordshire councils (the former enforces health and safety laws at Cadbury's Bourneville plant). In December 2006, Cadbury said the cost of dealing with the contamination would reach £30 million.

The judge said he did not believe Cadbury had changed its quality-testing systems (which resulted in the contamination) in order to cut costs. Instead, he said it was a 'serious case of negligence'.

Cadbury apologized and spoke of its 'sincere regrets' to the people affected. A spokesman said:

Quality has always been at the heart of our business, but the process we followed in the UK in this instance has been shown to be unacceptable. We have apologized for this and do so again today. In particular, we offer our sincere regrets and apologies to anyone who was made ill as a result of this failure. We have spent over £20 million in changing our procedures to prevent this ever happening again.

CASE STUDY: THE ASIAN TSUNAMI AND THE TRAVEL INDUSTRY

On 26 December 2004 the world witnessed the worst natural disaster in living memory. At around 1 am (GMT) a massive undersea earthquake occurred just off the coast of Indonesia. The quake, the most powerful for 40 years, triggered a series of deadly tidal waves, which fanned out across the Indian Ocean. An estimated 280,000 people in coastal areas from Somalia to Sumatra were killed and many millions left homeless or destitute.

Coastal areas in the northern Indonesian province of Aceh, the closest inhabited area to the quake epicentre, took the full force of the tsunami. The nearby

Indian-controlled Andaman and Nicobar islands were also hit. Waves measuring 10 metres in height slammed into towns and villages without warning. Initial reports from Aceh did not even hint at the monstrous scale of disaster, speaking of unexplained flash floods damaging bridges and roads.

Tourists enjoying the delights of southern Thailand's beach resorts saw a wall of water approaching at high speed. As the tsunami swept in, foreign holiday-makers and locals alike were trapped. Many drowned in hotel rooms, others were dragged out to sea. The deadly waves lost little of their power as they raced across the Indian Ocean, so when they reached eastern Sri Lanka, just a couple of hours later, they crashed into coastal areas with overwhelming force. As the tsunami moved inshore, reducing buildings to rubble, it also hit a passenger train. The carriages were packed with more than 1,500 people, most of whom drowned as the train was ripped off the tracks.

The low-lying Maldives are just four metres above sea level and as the deadly waves continued their rampage across the Indian Ocean they flooded the archipelago. Locals and tourists, many of them newlyweds enjoying their honeymoons, were left clinging to palm trees to try to avoid being swept away. Between six and seven hours after the earthquake occurred, the waves it triggered arrived on Africa's east coast. Surging seas destroyed homes and poisoned water supplies. Worst affected there was Somalia, where fishing boats were engulfed by the waves and crews lost.

The scale of the Asian tsunami disaster shocked the world and instigated an unprecedented relief effort. Government aid to the affected countries reached US$3.5 billion and was matched by massive public donations across the world as funds were raised to assist the survivors and the devastated region. It was a terrible tragedy that touched every nation. The immediacy of the disaster as news of the tsunami broke was amplified in many Western countries by the sheer numbers of nationals present in those popular tourist destinations at that time of year. As the story unfolded in the UK, significant attention was turned towards the thousands of British tourists on holiday in the region. The scale and complexity of the disaster presented an unprecedented challenge to travel companies and the industry at large.

How did the travel industry react?

Travel companies are among the best-equipped and most prepared organizations to handle a crisis. The example of Thomas Cook in this book bears testament to the importance placed by tour operators on successful and responsible crisis management and the commitment made to ensuring procedures are in place and well tested. The reputation of the company is of pre-eminent importance in an industry that hinges on the care it shows its customers. On the occasions of tragic accidents, how the company acts and is seen to act is vital. However, the tsunami disaster presented an unusual scenario; one unlike anything the tour operators would likely have considered in their preparedness planning.

This event was not an incident that exclusively involved one operator: it was a natural disaster on an unimaginable scale that left no company unaffected. Rather than one company having to manage its own crisis, the tsunami was indiscriminate and the vast majority of the travel industry in the UK was impli-cated.

As each travel company involved swung its individual operational recovery plans into action to locate and address the needs of its customers, the question of communicating around the crisis was a different matter. The tsunami was a catastrophe that impacted no one company in isolation; it had involved thou-sands of British holidaymakers and it was an entire travel industry that was responsible for their well-being. The industry needed to unite, with one voice communicating the efforts being taken across the travel industry.

Being able to talk with one voice was something that the travel industry was well placed to achieve. Even without having a premeditated plan of action for such an eventuality, the industry was able to draw on its trade associations and the way it organizes itself in other areas.

The Association of British Travel Agents (ABTA) quickly assumed the role of spokesperson and the Federation of Tour Operators (FTO), which represents the large tour operator groups such as First Choice, Tui, Kuoni and MyTravel, co-ordinated a consistent operational response. Utilizing structures already in place, the industry was able to move dynamically to manage the crisis operations and communications.

Coordinating the response

More than 10,000 British tourists were stranded in the areas affected by the tsunami. While many, particularly in Thailand, were independent travellers and backpackers, the majority were on package holidays with tour operators. Consequently, they benefited from the support that the tour operators were able to provide both on the ground and in coordinating disaster recovery plans from the UK.

As news of the consequences of the tsunami broke, the entire travel industry quickly became focused on common goals to:

- locate and identify all holidaymakers;
- ensure that all concerned relatives and friends are kept abreast of the latest information;
- arrange the rapid repatriation of tourists back to the UK and provide for the needs of those choosing to remain on holiday; and
- contact all tourists due to fly out to the affected areas with information on what to do, including the offer of full refunds or alternatives for cancelled holidays.

The FTO is blessed by having a relatively small number of member companies while at the same time representing a very large volume of the travel industry. Because of this it was able to make decisions very quickly to help a large number of holidaymakers. The FTO became the liaison with the Foreign and Common-wealth Office (FCO), which was coordinating the search for and identification of British nationals as well as the relative information helpline in the UK. With specific advice from the FCO on the state of different areas in the affected region, the FTO was able to formulate operational plans for the recovery of stranded tourists very quickly. The focus was, and had to be, the welfare of those and future travellers, regardless of monetary cost to the industry. But the industry also needed to be *seen* to be doing this. ABTA represents the widest membership in the industry and it became responsible for communicating via the media and reassuring the public.

In much the same way as the attack on the World Trade Center presented uncharted territory for the news media, so did the Asian tsunami disaster. A rapidly evolving scenario, with poor communications links to the directly affected areas yet continual updates in information, combined with widespread shock and emotional reactions to the events from the public, left the media to plough a route through a minefield fraught with sensitive hurdles.

The initial reaction of the rolling 24-hour media in particular reflected that of the wider public – shock, and an inability to comprehend the sheer magnitude of the disaster that had unfurled. However, increasingly the media began to ask the question, 'how could this disaster have been averted?' As sources of blame began to be explored it was important that the travel industry protected its reputation.

The first ABTA knew about the disaster was at 4.30 am on 26 December when Keith Betton, the head of corporate affairs, was woken at home by the BBC. Within 30 minutes contact had been made with the Foreign and Commonwealth Office to establish their understanding of the situation. After this several early radio interviews were given to provide an initial reaction. By 8.30 am the first live TV interviews were being given as the public woke up on Boxing Day to the news. At this point a number of travel pundits were already being used by the media to predict doom for the industry, so ABTA interviewees were made readily available to put things in perspective. An early challenge was to predict the number of Britons in the affected area and some were putting that at nearly 100,000. ABTA moved quickly to place a more accurate estimate of between 10,000 and 20,000 – the true figure was quickly disseminated and became widely used by all the media.

The key messages on the first day were sympathy for those caught up in the tragedy, support for the FCO efforts, and an assurance that tour operators were doing everything possible to help those tourists affected. Over 125 media calls were handled and 16 national broadcast interviews were given over the course of that day.

On the second day ABTA provided live studio interviews to the BBC *Today* programme, BBC Breakfast, BBC News 24, Sky News and Talk Sport – all before 9.30 am. These were the crucial outlets and an estimated 10 million people were reached with this breakfast update on what the industry was doing to bring home holidaymakers. In total around 100 media calls were handled on day two. In addition, a special edition of the association's member update *ABTA Today* was e-mailed to all member companies giving them details of how to download the latest advice and news from the ABTA website. Even though it was still a bank holiday, travel agencies were being opened to handle requests for information from the public – it was vital to have the consistent communication of the information contained on the ABTA site. The media were also encouraged to use the latter as their official source of information.

On the third day, stories of the first returning passengers were being reported. These were generally positive towards the rescue effort, although the Foreign and Commonwealth Office came in for criticism for the inability of the helpline to handle the sheer quantity of calls from the public. ABTA chose to support the FCO as a demonstration of the different factors involved all sharing a common goal – the welfare of those involved in the disaster and concern for their relatives and friends.

The financial markets re-opened following the Christmas break on 29 December and a new business angle from the media was added to the mix. What were the short- and long-term implications for the travel industry? At this stage individual tour operators such as First Choice were in a position to communicate specifically on their own business implications, while ABTA continued to address the broader efforts of the travel industry regarding the disaster recovery.

Much of the media coverage was happy to point out that package holiday-makers had a distinct advantage with the support of their tour operators and the 'duty of care' for their customers. While independent travellers were effectively on their own, the repatriation efforts of tour operators were non-discriminatory. The media warmly embraced the fact that the 'rescue flights' by the tour operators were collecting all stranded tourists regardless of who they booked with or if they were independent travellers.

The reputation of an industry enhanced

As Keith Betton commented, 'One would never hope for such a disaster in order to show the travel industry in a good light, yet it is a brutal fact that events such as these throw the industry into the spotlight.' It is an obvious consequence of the devastation to the region that there will be a short-term impact on tourism and that this will impact the travel industry. However the compassionate, committed and united approach taken by the travel industry in the UK was widely and positively received. An interesting reflection of that is how the share prices of the big tour operators were unaffected when the markets re-opened. It is a resilient industry and the goodwill generated by the behaviour of its members in such a disaster will continue to benefit it in the future.

BUSINESS CRISES

Business crises are often created by mismanagement of the company – injudicious expansion or diversification. Fraudulent behaviour has led to the demise of some major businesses in recent years of which Barings, Enron and Arthur Andersen are key examples. Increasingly, business crises are the result of the failure to have in place an issues management system which enables companies to spot greater forces at work, such as the underlying economic tides of the 1980s boom and the early 1990s recession which the late billionaire Sir James Goldsmith of Cavenham Foods did and George Walker of Brent Walker did not.

But the business tribulations of recent years are hardly unique. In 1637, speculation in Dutch tulip bulbs peaked at today's equivalent of more than £500 per bulb and the market collapsed under its own weight, presenting financial nightmares to speculators and their backers.

In 1861, the infant Pony Express in the United States met its sudden demise when Western Union inaugurated the first transcontinental telegraph. In 1906, the San Francisco earthquake devastated the city and its banking community – except for A P Giannini, whose small Bank of America continued making loans during the crisis and went on to become one of the world's largest banks – showing that sometimes a crisis can be turned into an opportunity. In 1912 the 'unsinkable' *Titanic* sank.

William Shakespeare showed a keen business sense when he wrote:

There is a tide in the affairs of men,
Which, taken at the flood, leads on to fortune:
Omitted, all the voyage of their life
Is bound in shallows and in miseries.

CASE STUDY: SAYONARA CITIBANK

Having your 'licence to operate' withdrawn is one very serious and 'final' consequence of poor issues and crisis management. Perceived occasionally as a drastic measure, governments often baulk at the prospect and prefer to pursue fines or regulation as a means of resolution. Its slim likelihood and the 'pinprick' effect of fines to the bottom line have often led big business into a sense of complacency as far as governance is considered. But complacency is a dangerous state of mind. In 2004, Citibank found this out to its cost.

On 17 September, Japan's regulators ordered Citigroup to close its private banking offices in Japan. The world's biggest bank by stockmarket capitalization was to be shut out of the world's second-biggest market for wealthy clients, where it has around 10,000 such customers and once held high hopes for boosting profits.

In issuing its sanctions against Citibank Japan, the country's Financial Services Agency (FSA) cited improper transactions and a flawed system of controls that allowed abuses to take place. It accused the private bank of selling securities and derivatives at 'unfair' prices to its clients, many of whom appeared to have been rich but unworldly, without explaining the risks. It also claimed that Citibank ignored warnings to teach its salespeople better practices and to keep a closer eye on them. On top of that, the FSA took Citibank to task for letting a client open an account that 'could be suspected of being associated with money laundering' while giving too little thought to what it was doing, and for lending money to clients who used the proceeds to manipulate share markets.

The bank, the FSA went on, had constructed 'a law-evading sales system that disregards the laws and regulations of Japan', and had done so 'in a management environment in which profits are given undue importance by the bank headquarters'. This followed continued failure to improve internal controls, despite regulatory warnings going back three years and a scolding by the FSA in May.

Douglas Peterson, who took over Citigroup's Japanese arm in May of the same year, was faced with the need to overhaul the bank's local practices and rebuild its reputation. Citigroup did not try to play the charges down, and chief executive, Charles O Prince III, issued a memo to employees highlighting 'the serious consequences of failing to comply with regulatory requirements and of violating our business standards'.

Citigroup still runs its century-old retail bank in Japan, which had enjoyed a reputation for convenient service and for financial soundness. It also has a corporate bank, which provides cash management, currency trading and other transactions for business clients, plus it has a securities joint venture with Nikko Cordial. However, all three business were left concerned with the knock-on consequences – that Japanese clients would shy away in response to Citigroup's tarnished reputation. While the Japanese private banking unit probably only contributed 0.5 per cent of Citigroup's profits, it is these wider ramifications that worried analysts.

Merrill Lynch, in a report published the week after the Japanese FSA announcement, warned that Citigroup could have difficulty in growing private-banking markets in other Asian countries, such as China and India – the new 'tiger' economies. It also suggested that the bank might attract scrutiny from regulators outside Japan, noting the FSA's remarks about pressure from head office in New York. The report downgraded the bank's shares to neutral from a buy, with a charge that 'aggressive profit incentives [are] overriding judgement'.

There is a threat that Citigroup's aggressive, profit-driven culture has created a 'monster' beyond the control of management. Financial analyst Howard Mason explained: 'Citi has become so large that it is simply not possible to mandate behaviour. The challenge now is to create a culture to inculcate a shared set of values that guide employee behaviour.' It will take more than a memo to affect a case of 'turning an oil tanker'. Prince's memo stated that 'Citigroup's culture must be synonymous with integrity', but as another analyst said, 'these people grow up with claws and fangs'.

Regulators in the United States, UK and across Europe are circling Citigroup, and there is a real threat to the bank's financial goals. As Mason said, 'It may well be that Citi can't achieve its growth ambitions because it cannot safeguard itself properly from regulatory and reputation risk.' Certainly more than a memo is required.

Finally, in November 2007, Charles O Prince III retired as CEO and Chairman of Citigroup after significant losses related to the turmoil in the credit markets.

Of course, when looking at different corporate crises, hindsight is the best of all management tools. As *Management Today* (1994) has pointed out, a major corporate crisis never fails to provoke – from journalists, investment managers and fellow businessmen – a chorus of exemplary wisdom after the event.

The writing was on the wall months ago, the pundits will claim. You only had to walk down any high street to see it. Surely you could see the board was incompetent, the management deceitful, the auditors complacent, the advisers gutless, the banks irresponsible.

Why didn't 'they' stop George Walker from buying the William Hill chain of betting shops from Grand Metropolitan for £689 million, later pinpointed by Walker himself as the deal that broke the Brent Walker empire? Why didn't the colleagues and advisers who read the draft of Gerald Ratner's 1991 speech to the Institute of Directors stop him from describing his products as 'total crap'?

The answer is that Walker was overwhelmingly persuasive, that the banks were slavishly keen to back him, that analysts were prepared to argue that a chain of betting shops, with their abundant cash flow, represented a brilliant addition to the Brent Walker portfolio, and that no one at the table had a crystal ball.

In Ratner's case, his upmarket audience thought the joke was funny and true. It was the next day's tabloids, notably the *Sun*, which devoted five pages to the story, a story which tore Ratner apart for his mocking insincerity towards the customers who had made him his fortune.

HOW THE MIGHTY FALL

No company, no matter how financially successful, powerful or reputable, is immune to crises. Very often, organizations ignore the warning signals which are so obvious in hindsight. Here are three examples in the 'accident' category.

CASE STUDY: NORTHERN ROCK ON THE ROCKS

The US sub-prime crisis had been building throughout the summer of 2007 in the United States, where mortgage lenders had been lending to customers with poor credit ratings. These mortgages had low initial interest rates, but as US rates began to rise many struggled to repay their debts. As a result, some customers started to default on their loans. About 30 mortgage lenders in the United States folded.

This had implications for the wider financial community. Other banks raised money to lend to borrowers by selling the loans they had already agreed to other financial institutions, such as hedge funds and investment banks. The investment banks repackaged the debts, which they sold on to other investors.

Banks soon became wary of just how much money had been invested in the faltering system by other banks. They then started to hold back funding to each other.

Northern Rock had financed a lot of its growth (about 75 per cent compared to some of its other competitors such as Bradford and Bingley's 50 per cent) in this way. When the inter-bank lending rates became prohibitive, Northern Rock didn't have the cash flow to continue lending to its customers. It was forced to go to the Bank of England, in that bank's capacity as the 'lender of last resort', to bail it out.

Press coverage

● 'Given the Bank of England's firm and principled stance against bailing out banks that have made risky lending decisions, its willingness to lead a rescue of Northern Rock may legitimately raise some eyebrows... Never has the reputation and credibility of Mervyn King, the Bank's governor, dangled from such a thin thread' (Chris Giles, 'Credibility of governor in the spotlight', *Financial Times*, 14 September 2007).

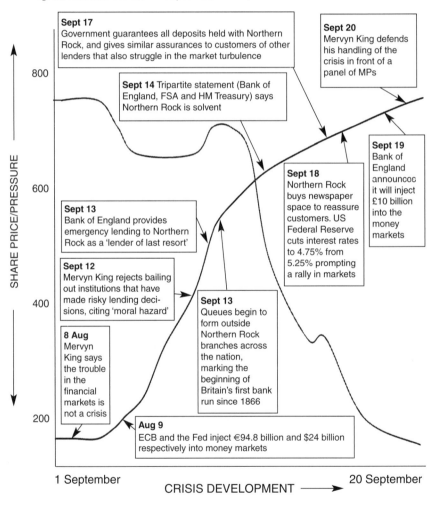

Figure 7.1 *Risk issue lifecycle*

- 'Little more than six months ago, shares in Northern Rock were trading at an all-time high and the chief executive of Britain's fourth largest mortgage lender, Adam Applegarth, was feted by analysts as the banking sector's pin-up boy. Today, Mr Applegarth's reputation lies in tatters and the Northern Rock brand is very likely toast... It is hard to recall a swifter or more dramatic fall from grace' (Jeremy Warner, 'Northern crisis rocks financial system', *Independent*, 15 September 2007).
- 'What is certain is that Northern Rock will struggle to undo the damage done to its reputation. As a brand, it will no longer command the trust that is a pre-requisite for consumers looking for a loan or a mortgage. It will always be seen as the mortgage provider that was bailed out by the Bank of England' (Andrew Murray-Watson, 'A takeover would serve Northern Rock right', *Independent on Sunday*, 16 September 2007).

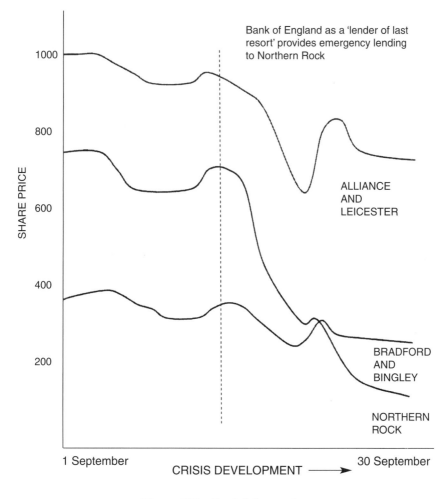

Figure 7.2 *Banks' share price*

- 'So regardless of the fact that this crisis originated in the US mortgage market, the Northern Rock rescue will rattle confidence in the governance of the British economy. It will test the credibility of the Bank of England, the Treasury and the Financial Services Authority. It will undermine the public's already shaky faith in corporate governance and capitalism's capacity to police its own excess. And it threatens to dent the reputation of Gordon Brown, whose chief boast has been a record of stability and prudence' (James Harding, Business Editor, 'An American crisis that could harm an awful lot of reputations here – including Gordon's', *The Times*, 17 September 2007).

Outcome

The Bank of England's governor, Mervyn King, tried to play down the crisis subsequently. He commented: 'Headlines come and go. TV pictures come and go.' Most would argue, however, that pictures of those queuing outside branches of the bank will be etched in the mind for some time to come. The reputations of Northern Rock, the Bank of England and the Financial Services Authority (FSA) have undoubtedly been damaged.

For Northern Rock the crisis was devastating. Its share price collapsed in a matter of days. At the time of writing, the company still exists in its current form, but a takeover seems all but inevitable. A series of UK and international banks including the Royal Bank of Scotland, HSBC and US group Citi were asked to step in. However, owing to the lack of confidence in the markets there have been no takers. The credit crunch meant that banks had no idea how badly competitors had been exposed to the crisis and how much debt they were left with. Lloyds TSB was the closest to making a serious offer, but refused to go through with the deal after the Bank of England could not guarantee a back-up facility to support all of Northern Rock's deposits. At the time of writing the final outcome for Northern Rock is not known.

Even if Northern Rock does continue in its present state, its outlook is bleak. Some commentators reported on the company's and, in particular, the senior executive's 'arrogance' throughout the crisis. Analysts and government officials criticized the company's aggressive growth strategy. Some consumers criticized a slow response and IT systems that buckled under pressure.

The enduring memory however, from the crisis will be queues of people outside Northern Rock branches up and down the country. Pictures of the bank run were beamed around the world and proved to be powerful images. The loss of confidence in the brand and the damage to its reputation will be difficult to rebuild.

The tripartite system

Although the Bank of England, the FSA and the Treasury were meeting on a regular basis and holding frequent calls, the lack of joined-up decision making was evident for all to see.

Despite initial coordination in the early stages, the main parties seemed to try to pass the buck when the media went looking for those responsible. The Bank of England said the FSA should have stepped in sooner to warn Northern Rock over its aggressive and risky growth tactics. The FSA claimed the Bank of England should have offered liquidity into the system earlier as the US Federal Reserve and European Central Bank had done. The Treasury was blamed for only guaranteeing customers' savings after the bank run had taken hold.

The tripartite system as a whole is now under intense scrutiny in terms of structure and governance.

Bank of England

The Bank of England, and in particular the senior executives including the governor, Mervyn King, and the deputy governor, Sir John Gieve, arguably came in for the most criticism during the period, leaving the bank's and personal reputations severely tarnished. One MP said that Sir John appeared to be 'asleep in the back of the shop while the mugging happened at the front'. There were calls for resignations. The bank faced criticism over its leadership, and some analysts felt it was at best indecisive and at worst incompetent.

It drew criticism for not taking action after the Federal Reserve and European Central Bank waded in to bail out the failing markets, and for then making a dramatic U-turn in its decision to inject £10 billion into the system. Mervyn King became the most high-profile 'personality' in the affair, and his face was splashed across newspaper front pages for days. The principles behind his decision to withhold a cash injection into the markets, because it might encourage further risk-taking practices, were broadly understood and welcomed by most commentators. Subsequently, when it became apparent that the decision might be too simplistic and impractical in the 'real world', and King went back on his decision, the criticism was severe.

Financial Services Authority

The FSA was criticized for not spotting, or at least acting on, Northern Rock's situation sooner. The *Guardian* summed up the FSA's job in financial crises as: 'spotting potential fires while the Bank of England wields the hose'.

Many were confident that Northern Rock had left itself too exposed and that the crisis could have been avoided if the FSA, as the regulator, had stepped in sooner. There was also a claim that the Bank of England was not told immediately by the FSA when Northern Rock's potential problem came to light.

The regulator, however, is in a difficult position, and market intervention is clearly not a decision to take lightly. The FSA treads a tightrope between a softly-softly approach and being over-burdensome. Northern Rock had adopted a business strategy that was delivering it excellent growth and was a UK success story.

The FSA, along with the Bank of England, has been called before the Treasury Select Committee to explain its actions.

HM Treasury

The Treasury seemed to take decisive action only after it was too late. It acted to guarantee customers' money, which stopped the queues, but it only did so a few days into the crisis. If it was prepared to take that course of action, why did it not do so immediately and avoid the panic? Many argued that it only acted after the negative images and press coverage took hold, which were playing badly to voters, with the prospect of a General Election looming large.

There was also some criticism of the Prime Minister, Gordon Brown, who, when Chancellor, had introduced the tripartite system that caused such indecision. Brown seemingly distanced himself from the crisis and left it to Alistair Darling, the Chancellor, who was still getting to grips with his new brief.

Key lessons

So what are the main lessons to be learnt from the Northern Rock crisis?

1. *Leadership in a complex stakeholder environment.* Arguably the biggest failing, and ultimately the catalyst in the escalation of the crisis, was a lack of leadership. The consumer was looking for someone to take control, steady the ship and reinstate trust.

   The tripartite system does not readily lend itself to clear decision making. However, the organizations should have coped better. During the Bank of England's evidence session to the Treasury Select Committee, Michael Fallon MP asked Mervyn King, 'Who is really in charge?' King replied, 'What do you mean by in charge?'

   No single organization took the lead and acted with enough conviction or authority to stem the tide of panicked consumers. When the media began to look for those responsible, the organizations began to pass the buck.

   A crisis is not the time for a consensual approach to decision making. There needs to be a single voice and leader to gather the facts, listen to the analysis and make decisions.

   The Northern Rock case is of course complex, but rarely do crises, in the modern day, involve the company and the company alone. A multitude of stakeholders are now involved, and organizations have to become better at implementing crisis plans alongside others.

   When preparing crisis plans, organizations must therefore think through every eventuality and test the worst-case scenario in each situation. You must also only commit to messages you know you are prepared to see through and that will continue to stack up later, possibly under intense scrutiny.
2. *Learning the lessons from past experience.* The cyclical nature of the markets and economy means there are constant corrections and even crashes. Although the extent of Northern Rock's downfall was difficult to predict, many analysts who in the past year or so had been labelled prophets of doom were accurate in their predictions a downturn was on its way.

Northern Rock board members lacked experience of international money markets and had adopted a strategy of aggressive growth that went unchecked by the FSA. This trend is repeated across the City. And it doesn't just apply to the UK but across money markets worldwide.

A recent survey by the University of Nottingham's Financial Services Research Forum claims that, overall, consumers are only moderately trusting of financial services institutions. Financial crises over the past decade have exacerbated the problem, and greed in financial services is becoming an issue in terms of trust and credibility.

CASE STUDY: PIPER ALPHA CATASTROPHE

On the night of 6 July 1988 the oil production platform, Piper Alpha, operated by Occidental Oil in the UK sector of the North Sea, blew up and was completely destroyed. The disaster killed 167 men, 109 of them dying from smoke inhalation. No system existed to lead the men on the platform to safety. Only 61 survived.

A leak of gas condensate, which later exploded, was caused when a pump was activated while, unknown to the control room, it was under repair. A blank flange fitted to a valve was not leak-tight. The initial explosion caused extensive damage and spread fire through the platform. Gas pipelines leading to other platforms in the area ruptured and intensified the blaze.

Lord Cullen, who led and wrote the report on the disaster, concluded Occidental Oil had not provided adequate training to make its work permit system effective; monitoring of the system was inadequate; communication was poor. Action following a 1987 fatality involving a failure of the work permit system had no lasting effect on practice.

The report said Occidental management should have been more aware of the need for a high standard of incident prevention and fire-fighting. They were too easily satisfied that the work permit system was being operated correctly, relying on the absence of feedback of problems as indicating that all was well.

> The management adopted a superficial attitude to the assessment of the risk of major hazard. They failed to ensure emergency training was being provided as intended. The platform personnel and management were not prepared for a major emergency as they should have been. The safety policies and procedures were in place; the practice was deficient.

Occidental Oil's UK assets were subsequently acquired by another oil company and it has vanished as an entity in the UK North Sea.

CASE STUDY: PADDINGTON RAIL DISASTER

Two commuter trains crashed into each other at high speed at 8.11 am on 5 October 1999, killing 30 people and injuring 160. Today, if you went out on to the street and asked people to name the two train companies involved, chances are most people would not remember. Would you?

But ask people to name the company that was vilified by the press after the accident and everyone would say 'Railtrack'. So why did Railtrack get it in the neck when most people can't even remember the names of the train companies – Thames Trains and Great Western Trains?

The answer, we suggest, is that when the accident happened Railtrack had no credit left in its 'reputation bank'. In fact, its account was in the red. There were a number of reasons for this:

- a widely held perception that Railtrack put 'profits before safety' – that the only stakeholders it cared about were its shareholders;
- recommendations after the Clapham and Southall crashes had not been implemented;
- the perception that rail services had deteriorated since privatization;
- Railtrack bosses were 'fat cats' and paid too much.

Because Railtrack had no reputational credit among its stakeholders, other than shareholders, when the accident occurred, it instantly became the villain of the piece. It possessed no reputational credit upon which it could draw, in this worst of all possible circumstances, to help it through.

Needless to say, as soon as the two train companies involved saw that Railtrack was getting all the blame from the media, they both introduced a 'no interview' policy and vanished without trace (not a bad policy in the circumstances).

Immediately after the accident, Railtrack responded well. Its CEO, Gerald Corbett, was on the scene within the hour giving media interviews, but after a few days he got tired of media questioning and handed the role over to other executives in the company. His refusal to appear on *Newsnight* because 'he was too tired' became a headline story in the print media.

In our experience, it is always a mistake to change the spokesperson role in a major crisis because viewers and listeners begin to identify with, and often sympathize with, the spokesperson. Of course it is a tiring, and sometimes irritating, role, but you absolutely cannot give up on it until media appetites are satisfied. As we often say to our clients: 'This is like wrestling a gorilla; you take a break when the gorilla takes a break.'

One of the substitute spokesmen then went on the BBC Radio 4 *Today* programme. In response to a question from interviewer John Humphrys, he angrily stated, 'It's about time we stopped this national *hysteria* about the safety of rail travel.' He used the 'hysteria' word at a time when the front carriages of the two trains were still locked together, some of the bodies had still not been identified, and Paddington station was still closed – inconveniencing thousands of commuters.

What he said was strictly true – rail travel is the safest form of travel after air travel. But he failed to factor in what we call the 'emotional dynamics' of the situation and caused a national outrage through his remarks. Railtrack's share price spiralled even further and the company was forced to issue a public apology later that day.

The company went on to take another extraordinary action. In a major crisis, when the company becomes the focal point of attention from hundreds of reporters, the only sensible way to communicate with them is via news conferences (see page 220), supported by constant updates of a website if possible. Inexplicably, but probably on bad advice, Gerald Corbett chose to visit the offices of the main London-based newspapers to give individual interviews. He began with the *Daily Mirror* because it is the tabloid most widely read by the Railtrack workforce. The workforce by this time were in a highly demoralized state. Passengers were spitting at them and they were threatening to go on strike over safety issues.

However, during the course of the interview, Gerald Corbett got a question he found to be insulting. It went along the lines of, 'Mr Corbett, if the inquiry finds Railtrack to have been negligent, will you resign and do you expect to be prosecuted for corporate manslaughter?' These are perfectly legitimate questions and are perfectly answerable.

But Mr Corbett took umbrage and stormed out of the *Daily Mirror* offices – hotly pursued by *Daily Mirror* photographers. Next day he found himself on the front page under the headline, 'RATTLED! Railtrack boss walks out of interview over "deeply offensive" question'. This triggered a smear campaign by the *Daily Mirror* and the whole one-to-one interview strategy backfired.

Later, the Hatfield tragedy occurred and, under huge pressure from the Prime Minister and Deputy Prime Minister, Corbett had no option but to resign.

What have been the consequences for Railtrack? They began with the company being stripped of its safety role, which was handed over to the government's Health and Safety Executive; £280 million being wiped from the company's value in 10 days because of a collapse in the share price; and deepened loss of stakeholder confidence in the company.

Paddington always seemed to be an accident waiting to happen. As the *Wall Street Journal* wrote at the time of the accident, 'There is no conflict between safety and profit, unless you assume it's good business to kill your customers, smash up your capital stock and expose yourself to tort litigation'.

By May 2001, Railtrack had reported a much-worse-than-expected loss of £534 million for the year. This was the company's first loss since privatization and was largely due to a £733 million payment spent on a rail renewal programme and compensation claims in the wake of the Hatfield crash in October 2000, which claimed four lives. The disruption led to huge compensation payouts to train operating companies.

Finally, in October 2001, the company was declared bankrupt, de-listed from the London Stock Exchange, and today represents one of the UK's most embarrassing corporate failures.

Three brief examples of crises in the 'accident' category but some themes are identifiable: the confusion of image with reality; the belief that because it hasn't happened in the past, it won't happen in the future; the vain hope that because 'the procedures' have been written the accident can't happen and, in each case, a failure to communicate appropriately.

CEOs ARE NOT INFALLIBLE

In the examples of Brent Walker and Ratner, why, instead of shouting 'stop', have the combined forces of non-executive directors, auditors, public relations advisers, investment analysts and journalists been so often complicit in encouraging chief executives to believe in their own infallibility?

These are circumstances which particularly affected – but not exclusively – the kind of entrepreneurial, share-price-driven companies which came to fame in the 1980s. The crises which affected them have tended to be financial rather than operational.

In some famous cases, outright fraud has either temporarily weakened a company (Guinness and Mirror Group) or destroyed it altogether (Barings Bank and Enron); in others, excessive appetite for acquisitions, or exposure to property, has stretched the balance sheet to breaking point. In another 'business' category, clever, well-focused businesses such as GPA (in aircraft leasing) and Tiphook (in containers) were suddenly revealed to have misread the downturn in their own highly specialized markets.

The common thread here is that, in almost every case, there is one person in charge, usually the founder of the business, a natural optimist, risk-taker and autocrat, perhaps with no more than two or three long-standing associates whom he really takes into his confidence.

CASE STUDY: MARKS & SPENCER

Marks & Spencer, under the stewardship of its autocratic former boss, Sir Richard Greenbury, completely failed to spot changes in consumer buying habits of clothing and consumer expectations of a more exciting shopping experience.

Because for a time, indeed for a long time, Marks & Spencer customers all wanted to look the same ('middle class, middle aged and middle England', as someone quipped) it didn't mean they were going to stay like that forever. The problem was compounded by a corporate culture that discouraged entrepreneurial flair and rewarded conformity and sycophancy.

Where was the risk radar screen in St Michael House? Certainly not switched on. Marks & Spencer was not boycotted. It was just abandoned.

To make matters even worse, the company had a policy of no communication with the press under Sir Richard. But if a journalist dared to write a story about the company and got a fact wrong, it has been alleged that Sir Richard would call the hapless journalist personally and blow him (verbally) to kingdom come. Needless to say, when Sir Richard retired and the company was on the skids, there was a legacy of embittered journalists only too happy to sharpen their knives and stick them into the company.

Fortunately, under the stewardship of Stuart Rose, the company has achieved a complete recovery. In 2006, Stuart Rose was awarded 2006 Business Leader of the Year by the World Leadership Forum.

Veteran company doctors have been quoted as saying that if there is one reliable indicator of a company that will eventually run into trouble, it's having a charismatic, high-profile chairman. Tiphook's founder-chairman Robert Montague, suntanned, Ferrari-driving sponsor of the Conservative winter ball, has been cited as a classic example. But this may be an unduly pessimistic view; Richard Branson (Virgin) the late Anita Roddick (The Body Shop) and Alan Sugar (Amstrad) have all bucked this trend.

Nonetheless, a past president of the Society of Insolvency Practitioners has said the most common misjudgement made by companies in incipient financial difficulties is that they are not quick enough to change the person at the top.

The one sure way to buy the company time when it is on the edge of trouble is to appoint a new chief executive. So long as he (or she) can put up a reasonable business plan the banks will almost always give the new CEO six months.

PRODUCT-RELATED CRISES

The contamination scare which prompted the withdrawal of millions of bottles of Lucozade from shops throughout Britain (13 November 1991) is a nightmare of a kind which has come to haunt a growing number of consumer product companies over the past two decades.

In 1990 Perrier was forced to recall every bottle of its popular sparkling water worldwide after some were found to contain traces of benzene. More recently, in June 1998, Coca-Cola faced a contamination scare in Belgium, but appeared to have learnt none of the lessons from the Perrier experience. (See page 159.)

A few years prior to the Perrier incident, Tylenol, a headache pill made by Johnson & Johnson in the United States, was temporarily withdrawn after an extortionist laced capsules with cyanide, killing seven people.

The cost of dealing with such recalls can be huge. Industry experts have estimated that the cost of recalling suspect products from shops is nine times as much as delivering them in the first place.

This pales into insignificance, however, when compared to the costs of lost production and rebuilding public confidence in products once they have been declared safe. Johnson & Johnson is estimated to have spent more than £50 million to recover from the Tylenol crisis, and Perrier twice as much. However, the manner in which each company managed its product crisis was entirely different – as were the consequences.

CASE STUDY: THE TYLENOL TALE

Never in corporate history has an organization in crisis gained as much public and editorial sympathy as Johnson & Johnson did in the United States for its conduct throughout the Tylenol-related poisonings and their aftermath. The day before cyanide-laced Tylenol tablets caused deaths in the Chicago area in September 1982, Tylenol commanded 35 per cent of the US adult over-the-counter analgesic market, accounted for some $450 million of annual sales and contributed over 15 per cent of Johnson & Johnson's overall profits.

At first, just three deaths from cyanide poisoning were associated with the capsules. As the news spread, as many as 250 deaths and illnesses in various parts of the United States were suspected of being part of a widespread pattern. Eventually enquiries from the media alone were logged at over 2,500.

After testing 8 million tablets, Johnson & Johnson found no more than 75 contaminated tablets, all from one batch. The final death toll was seven, all in the Chicago area, but the alarm had been spread nationwide. Surveys showed later that 94 per cent of consumers were aware Tylenol was associated with the poisonings.

Key to the success of the way in which the Tylenol case was handled lay in the assumption of the 'worst possible scenario'. Ironically, the closest thing the company had to a crisis plan was its credo that its first concern must be for the public and its customers – a credo which ultimately saved its reputation.

To its credit, Johnson & Johnson lost little time in recalling millions of bottles of its extra-strength Tylenol capsules. The company reportedly spent half a million dollars warning doctors, hospitals and distributors of the possible dangers. At the same time, the *Wall Street Journal* wrote: 'the company chose to take a large loss rather than expose anyone to further risk. The "anti-corpo-ration" movement may have trouble squaring that with the devil theories it purveys'.

The company also resisted the temptation to relaunch the product as soon as it was known to be safe and the lunatic who contaminated the capsules had been arrested. At the time the US government and local authorities in Chicago and elsewhere were pushing for new drug safety laws. Johnson & Johnson saw a marketing opportunity and took it by edging out its competitors in the $1.2 billion analgesic market. It was the first in the industry, after the recall, to respond to the 'national mandate' for tamper-resistant packaging and new regulations imposed by the US Food and Drug Administration.

Johnson & Johnson later went on to relaunch the product and win the Silver Anvil Award of the Public Relations Society of America for its handling of the crisis. Within five months of the disaster, the company had recovered 70 per cent of its one-third share of this huge market. The company had clearly posi-tioned itself as the champion of the consumer, given meaning to the concept of corporate social responsibility, and demonstrated communication expertise hard to equal since.

The plaudits which Johnson & Johnson received leading to, most importantly, market share recovery, stemmed from its decision to anticipate the worst. The company could have restricted the recall to the Chicago area and saved itself millions of dollars. Had it done so, however, its Tylenol sales would almost certainly have suffered more dramatic losses because of poison-tampering hysteria. Their losses would have been far more difficult to recover because of continued uncertainty and loss of public trust. What was happening to Tylenol users in Chicago was receiving coast-to-coast television coverage in America. (If you had been sitting in your New York apartment, had seen the news about Tylenol, and then developed a headache would you have rushed out to the corner drugstore to purchase a bottle of Tylenol? Most unlikely.)

CASE STUDY: WHAT TOOK THE FIZZ OUT OF PERRIER

In complete contrast to Johnson & Johnson, when Perrier found traces of benzene in its water, it dismissed the problem as 'a little affair which, in a few days, will all be forgotten'. Less than 24 hours later Perrier shares were falling like ten green bottles off the wall as more contaminated samples were discovered around the world.

In the United States the company decided voluntarily to clear millions of bottles from supermarket shelves. The company in France put this down to American wimpishness rather than a real health scare. To some extent the difference in outlook by the two countries was reflected by their marketing techniques. In the United States Perrier advertisements proclaimed 'Perrier is Perfect' while in France advertisements claimed '*Perrier C'est Fou*', ie it is crazy, bubbly and enlivens the spirit.

The company's spokesman in France went on to imply consumers in France were less neurotic than in other countries; they didn't worry about such things. Maybe not, but his remarks were reported in other key markets and the company's apparent lack of concern for its customers caused outrage. Company executives in different countries made conflicting statements and clearly no worldwide strategic recall plan was in place.

Under increasing pressure, four days after the initial discovery of the benzene traces in the United States, Perrier decided to withdraw the product worldwide amid proclamations that 'with this action we have saved the image of Perrier all over the world'. By then, however, the damage to the product's reputation had been done. The company had been seen to procrastinate and be inconsistent in its messages about the seriousness of the problem. It was ridiculed by the media (in this country particularly by the now defunct *Today* newspaper).

People drink bottled water partly because they think it is chic and partly because they believe it to be purer than tap water. It is certainly marketed on a 'platform of purity'. Implementing a worldwide recall of a key product is a huge decision to take because of the financial consequences, especially when the reality of the size of the problem is tiny. However, the company which is not seen to take seriously the genuine concerns of its customers, does so at its peril.

Research undertaken across Europe by MORI for design company Henrion, Ludlow & Schmidt in 1995 found Perrier's corporate identity to have been the second most damaged as a result of corporate error. The most damaged was believed to be Shell's after the Brent Spar debacle. Interestingly, the survey was conducted in the same year as the Brent Spar issue but *five years after* the Perrier recall.

Even after Perrier's chaotic recall the situation might have been recoverable. A brilliant advertising campaign signalled the end of the problem and that Perrier was back. But it was back, inexplicably, in 750 ml bottles instead of the original 1 litre bottles – yet it cost at least the same amount as the original bigger bottle! The inference seemed to be that customers should pay the cost of the company's own negligence. The company never recovered market share and, with its own share price weakened, became easy prey for a predator. Nestlé soon came along and swallowed it up.

CASE STUDY: COCA-COLA

Lessons it might have learnt from history

On 8 and 9 June 1999, more than 230 schoolchildren in Belgium claimed illness after drinking Coca-Cola products. More customer complaints came in during the following days. A further 80 complained of similar symptoms in France. The general symptoms included vomiting, dizziness and headaches. Ultimately, in March 2000, results of an independent investigation by Belgium's High Hygiene Council at the government's request revealed that the vast majority of those people with the symptoms had suffered mass sociogenic illness (MSI), or 'mass hysteria'. What emerged from Belgium was an organization unable to handle public perceptions in a crisis. While Coca-Cola searched for the facts – hard to establish when dealing with MSI – it failed to address the relationship between stakeholders and its own reputation.

On the morning of 8 June, children in Bornem, near Antwerp, who had drunk 200 ml bottles of Coke and Coke Light, complained of the symptoms. The headmaster immediately called Coca-Cola Belgium and the company launched a high-priority investigation into the possible link between the illness and its products. It identified an 'off-spec' batch of the product manufactured in Antwerp most probably caused by defective carbon dioxide. In the afternoon of the same day Coca-Cola issued a product recall for that batch number, and by the end of the following day all the bottles had been removed from shelves. The head of sales for Coca-Cola even visited those in hospital to check after their welfare. So far so good for the world's biggest brand.

However, on the day of the incident Flemish commercial TV station VTM had run the news story during a prime-time bulletin that 37 schoolchildren had fallen ill after drinking *cans* of Coke. The company called the station to ask for a correction to bottles in any subsequent bulletins.

The next day other schoolchildren, and indeed adults, across Flanders said they were suffering as well. These cases, however, referred to cans (produced in Dunkirk), not the batch of bottles from the Antwerp plant. In fact, it later emerged that 49 per cent hadn't actually touched a Coca-Cola product at all and the symptoms were the consequence of MSI. Understandably, Coca-Cola could not find a fault causing these new reported cases.

From 10 June, and mistakenly, the company took an increasingly centralized approach to its communications response – with heavy involvement from its Atlanta headquarters. For four days, Coca-Cola's message remained that it was merely a bad odour that was causing the nausea and other side effects, but there was no risk to public health. As a precaution, the batch of defective product was recalled, but with no evidence of a fault related to the cans, there was no reason for a wider/total recall. However, as a consequence of the company's failure to provide a clear explanation, the Belgian health minister simply ordered Coca-Cola to withdraw all products for which his ministry had received complaints. On Monday 14 June – the day after general elections in which the government suffered defeat for its alleged mishandling of the discovery of the carcinogen dioxin in a range of meats, eggs and various dairy products – he ordered a total recall of all Coca-Cola products.

Cold, scientific news releases were posted on the company's website, which failed to take account of the emotional dynamics of the situation. For those suffering and the wider public, this felt like a dismissive uncaring corporate response, triggering widespread anger and public concern, evidenced by the deluge of calls to Belgian poison centres – 900 calls in one day.

Independently a Belgian professor, and acknowledged authority on these matters, hypothesized in a television interview that it was MSI without having checked the patients first. There was understandable outrage from parents – and the credibility of this hypothesis was immediately undermined. As the facts got out of control, Coca-Cola stopped communicating while desperately looking for an explanation to offer the health minister.

It was only after the Belgian and French governments insisted that the products were withdrawn that the company finally mobilized the chairman and CEO, Douglas Ivestor, for a visit to Europe to help manage the crisis and bring it to a close. Coca-Cola took the right steps by withdrawing the contaminated batch initially, but then lost the high ground when it began arguing against a total product recall.

Its biggest mistake, however, was in failing to empower local Belgian and French managements to take care of their own communications response. Back in Atlanta, the corporate communications people had little idea that the Belgian government – at election time – was in a crisis of its own over criticism for the way it had handled the simultaneous dioxin food health scare. The government was anxious to prove to the electorate that it did take food safety issues seriously, and jumped at the chance of forcing Coca-Cola to withdraw all its products.

In France, the government was equally anxious to show its concern over food safety issues and quickly followed the Belgian lead. The governments looked like the good guys and Coca-Cola was definitely the bad guy.

Not communicating is not an option – if you haven't anything to say, then explain that and the reasons for it, and add when you do expect to have information. While Coca-Cola was frantically trying to identify the causes for the apparent anomalies in the consumption patterns, the Belgian health minister was anxious to hear what went wrong directly from the company, not the media. In that context, Coca-Cola was not open about the fact that it didn't know.

It seems almost inconceivable that the biggest brand in the world, valued at US$50 billion, did not act more promptly and with more regard for the protection of its most precious asset – its brand. The root causes of the wholly inappropriate response lay in what we call the 'head office knows best' syndrome, and an overly internalized perspective on the crisis at hand. Global organizations are like octopi; all the operations are at the end of the 'tentacles', and this is where there is the most potential for things to go wrong. The centre of the octopus must train and empower management at the end of the tentacles to take the right decisions and make the right responses, because they know the local scene best.

The cost of Coca-Cola's mistakes was enormous:

- At the end of 1999 the company announced a 31 per cent drop in profits.
- By losing free media opportunities to reassure the public as the crisis unfolded, Coca-Cola had to launch costly, post-crisis advertising and promotional campaigns.
- Competitors seized the opportunities to fill Coca-Cola's empty shelf space and challenged the company's 49 per cent share of the market.
- The total cost to the company was US$103 million (£66 million) – nearly double the original estimate.
- The majority of media coverage on Coca-Cola following the crisis referred to a company 'struggling to rebuild its reputation'.

These mistakes might easily have been avoided if Coca-Cola had taken a quick look at the Perrier case study.

After the Belgian contamination issue, the new CEO of Coca-Cola reorganized the company away from its centralized structure, and introduced an appropriate balance between local autonomy and global coordination. Coca-Cola now has systems in place to ensure that all offices are equipped to handle crises in their own localities, and can disseminate information internally to enable other markets to manage any consequences in their countries. Moreover, the other key principle now is to manage crises as they are perceived from the outside – perception is reality.

WHO WILL HAVE A CRISIS?

Next week there can't be any crisis. My schedule is already full.
Dr Henry Kissinger while US Secretary of State

Companies could cite a variety of reasons which prevent them from addressing crisis issues before they occur. Some believe their size, location or the type of business they are in will protect them. Others believe issues and crisis management to be a luxury, or believe crisis is an inevitable cost of doing business. (Indeed, a survey conducted a few years ago among prominent US businessmen found they believed a crisis in business was as inevitable as paying taxes and death.)

In our experience, some executives have difficulty admitting to themselves that their companies could face a crisis because in doing so they would have to question the excellence of their company and, in some cases, even their own professionalism.

Others subscribe to the fallacy that well-managed companies simply do not have crises. This trait can affect even the most public relations conscious companies. Indeed, it can affect them more than others. When Nestlé was attacked for selling infant formula in developing countries, where it was often mixed with contaminated water, the company's belief in its own caring, nurturing image made it difficult for senior executives to accept the criticism. There was a prevailing belief that anyone who attacked Nestlé must be a loony or a communist or both.

According to business academic Ian Mitroff, in his book co-authored with Thierry Pauchant, *We're So Big, Nothing Bad Can Happen to Us* (1990), 'how people react to crises provides one of the most powerful windows, if not *the* most powerful window, into the souls of people and their institutions'.

He divides 'crisis-prone' corporations into two types: destructive companies, which believe it is their fundamental right, even their duty, to exploit all human, financial and natural resources for the profit of their shareholders; and tragic companies, which understand the need for change but do not have the emotional or cultural resources to make it happen.

Mitroff cites Exxon Corporation as a 'destructive' company (see Chapter 8) for which little can be done; 'but tragic companies can be helped by outside experts, analysts who can identify problems not apparent to those too close to them and inhibited by fear for their jobs'.

As recently as the early 1990s some companies (especially in the United States) even avoided crisis anticipation because of legal liabilities they might assume in doing so. The concern was that if companies identified potential risk areas and failed to guard against them, they might be more responsible legally than if they had not bothered to investigate in the first place.

There used to be an attitude of what you didn't know wouldn't hurt you. Nowadays, however, the courts say if you didn't know you should have known (see Chapter 10).

In this age of corporate accountability, and for all the reasons we have argued in previous chapters, the truth is that no organization is safe from a crisis and the potentially lasting damage it can cause. It is no longer a question of whether a major crisis will strike; it is only a matter of when, which type and how.

WHAT KIND OF CRISIS WILL HAPPEN?

In research conducted for us at the start of the 1990s by Business Planning & Research International among senior executives from the *Times Top 1,000* companies, the following crises were regarded as most likely to occur:

- environmental pollution;
- product defect;
- unwanted takeover bid;
- sabotage;
- death of senior management member;
- kidnap of senior management member;
- computer breakdown;
- industrial dispute;
- fraud.

More recent research among senior UK company executives, conducted by Infoplan in 1994, showed a shift in belief as to what kinds of crises might occur. The majority of respondents from 250 major British companies thought sabotage, extortion and product defects were the most likely forms of crises (see Figure 7.2). It is interesting to note the underlying current of optimism here that the most likely forms of crises were seen to be events 'done to the organization', ie, sabotage and extortion, rather than any fault caused by management error – a hope which is certainly at odds with slightly more recent findings from the United States.

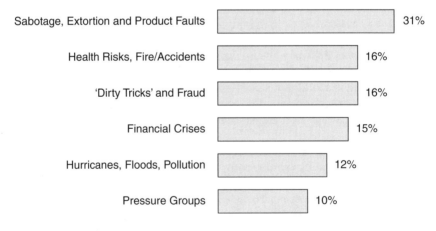

Source: Infoplan International, Japan, 1994

Figure 7.2 *The most likely causes of crises according to respondents*

Research conducted in 1995 by the Kentucky-based Institute for Crisis Management showed that company executives and consultants had been focusing on the wrong kinds of crises. Business crisis stereotypes such as fires and explosions accounted for only 17 per cent of 1995 crisis news stories. The real problems had revolved around white-collar crime, labour disputes and company mismanagement.

The fastest growing categories in the US were class action lawsuits, executive dismissals, hostile takeovers and sexual harassment – all of which had more than doubled since 1990. The news stories on these management crises were small in number compared to white-collar crime, labour disputes and mismanagement but they invariably attracted the media's attention because of the gut-wrenching personal and professional problems which they surfaced (see Figure 7.3).

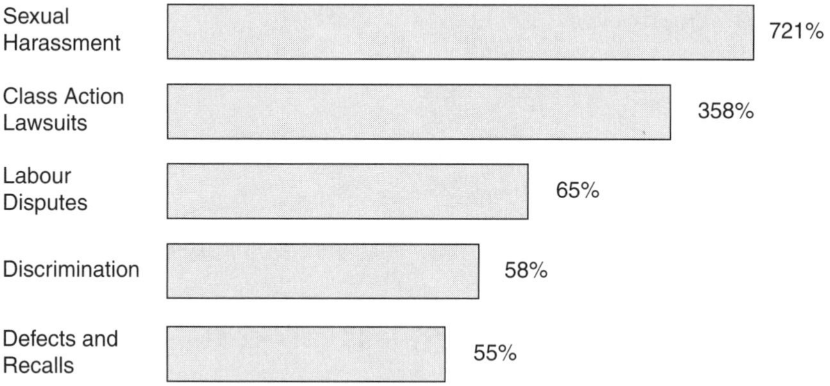

Category		Percentage
Sexual Harassment		721%
Class Action Lawsuits		358%
Labour Disputes		65%
Discrimination		58%
Defects and Recalls		55%

Source: Institute for Crisis Management, Kentucky, USA

Figure 7.3 *Fastest growing business crisis categories 1990–95*

This same research also revealed that executives not employees had been responsible for most crisis news coverage in the 1990s – management decisions were directly or indirectly involved in 78 per cent of 56,000 crisis news stories.

The most crisis-prone US industries in 1995, measured by the number of crisis news stories devoted to them, are shown in Figure 7.4.

For the purposes of the remainder of this book we are going to use our own definition of a crisis:

> an event which causes the company to become the subject of widespread, potentially unfavourable, attention from the international and national media and other groups such as customers, shareholders, employees and their families, politicians, trade unionists and environmental pressure groups who, for one reason or another, have a vested interest in the activities of the organization.

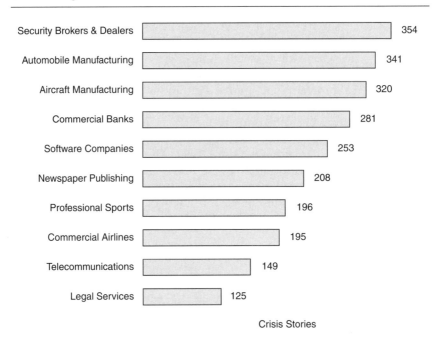

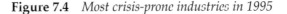

Source: Institute for Crisis Management, Kentucky, USA

Figure 7.4   *Most crisis-prone industries in 1995*

Foot-in-mouth disease: careless talk costs – reputation

Often an organization can find itself slap bang in the middle of a crisis when it has done nothing wrong by deed. Out of the blue, a company can find itself at the centre of outrage and with its reputation in tatters. It can occur without any emergence of an embryonic issue, without any stakeholder or NGO pressure and without any accident. Sometimes all it takes is a careless phrase, a throwaway line or an 'off the record comment'. It is always entirely self-induced, and can occasionally destroy an organization that has actually done nothing wrong. Usually it is the consequence of a company or individual having no empathy for its most important stakeholders – not holding them sacrosanct and being dismissive of them.

The following are just some examples of instances where 'gaffes' by executives have cost their organization:

- In 2003 Barclays Bank boss, Matthew Barrett, said the firm's credit card was too expensive for him. He told astonished MPs at the Treasury Select Committee that he didn't borrow on credit cards as it was 'expensive' and no way to fund 'chronic borrowing'. One MP accused Barclays of 'bare-faced cynicism' for an offer to cardholders that allowed balance transfers from rival cards without incurring any interest – as long as the cardholder spent at least £50 a month on the card. He condemned cash-back offers as 'a bait and trap'.

- Stagecoach chief executive Keith Cochrane compared US bus passengers to riff-raff, in the US magazine *Forbes*, leading to a fall in share price. Stagecoach seems to have a habit of publicly bad-mouthing its customers: colourful chairman Brian Souter once described all northerners as 'beer-drinking, chip-eating, council house-dwelling, Old Labour-voting masses'.

- Retail entrepreneur, and darling of the City, Sir Philip Green was forced to offer an unreserved apology in 2003 to the Irish in a bid to prevent a customer boycott. Attacking the *Guardian*'s financial editor, Paul Murphy, during an investigation into his accounts, Green said: 'He can't read English. Mind you, he is a f***ing Irishman.' Green referred to nationality several times while attempting to prevent the paper writing about his accounts. He was forced to apologize and said he had not meant to offend.

- Another entrepreneurial doyenne, the late Anita Roddick, spoke frankly when she described the Body Shop's anti-ageing cream as 'complete pap' and said that women who worried about their wrinkles would be better off 'spending the money on a good bottle of pinot noir'.

- In 2001 Top Man brand director David Shepherd said a typical customer at their stores was a young hooligan buying a suit for his first court appearance.

- Newcastle United Football Club's chiefs, then Freddy Shepherd and Douglas Hall, branded Geordie women 'dogs' and said club shirts cost £5 to produce and sold for £50. Mass outrage ensued among probably the most loyal and dedicated fans in England, and the club risked disenfranchising one of its most powerful assets.

- Camelot's Dianne Thompson had to live with her suggestion in 2002 that punters would be extraordinarily lucky to win on the National Lottery. 'People have realized it probably won't be you. You would be lucky to win a tenner,' she confessed, and sales of tickets continued to plunge.

- Also in 2002, Sir Keith Whitson of HSBC said he would rather use cheap workers in India or China than his own British call-centre staff. He said the bank could get work done in Asia 'for a fifth of the price by smartly dressed employees who were keen to turn up to work'.

- And finally, the most famous gaffe in British corporate history – Gerald Ratner's description of his firm's products as 'total crap' in 1991. Ratner, whose company that year produced profits of £110 million as Britain's biggest high-street jeweller, made his remarks at the Institute of Directors (IoD). Ratner was reported by the *Financial*

Times as saying, 'We do cut-glass sherry decanters complete with six glasses on a silver-plated tray that your butler can serve you drinks on, all for £4.95. People say "How can you sell this for such a low price?" I say, because it's total crap.' Ratner paid a terrible price for his comments: investors forced him to leave the board of his own company, and the profits soon turned into a loss of £122 million as consumers reacted with disgust. Eventually the Ratner name, which had unofficially become 'mud', was dropped in favour of Signet. The reason? Gerald Ratner made fools of the customers who had made him his fortune – they were so 'stupid' they would pay money for 'crap' products. He lost everything because he wanted to get a laugh from his peer group audience at the IoD.

CASE STUDY: MERCURY ENERGY TURNS OFF THE POWER

Electricity is something we often take for granted, save for when the monthly power bill arrives – or when the power goes out. In May 2007, however, the New Zealand public were made to realize just how crucial electricity had become in their lives, and how much power electricity companies could have over their customers.

On Tuesday 29 May, it was business as usual for a Mercury Energy contractor – visiting the homes of households that had failed to pay their bills and disconnecting their power supply. When he visited the Muliaga household in South Auckland, in his eyes at least, it was no different – the family obviously hadn't heeded disconnection notices and so he was charged with cutting off their power. Only it later transpired this situation was vastly different. With the disconnection, the contractor had in fact turned off power to an oxygen machine, which Mrs Folole Muliaga relied upon to breathe. The mother of four died two and a half hours later (although, as yet, there is no proof to say one event led to the other).

Come morning, the news media were all over Mrs Muliaga's death – a tragedy caused by the senseless disconnection of her power by Mercury Energy. And so began a month of media scrutiny, commentary, criticism from politicians including the prime minister, and a growing shadow over Mercury Energy's reputation. The month ended with the threat of regulatory intervention from the electricity retail sector and a sectoral advertising campaign featuring former iconic All Black rugby player and nephrotic kidney syndrome survivor Jonah Lomu, encouraging medically reliant New Zealanders to register with their electricity provider.

The Mercury Energy saga erupted in a period in which low minimum wages were in the news, with industrial disputes and lockouts, and a growing public awareness of low-income families in debt to loan sharks while utility bills and household expenditure were rising. Against this, there was growing public dissent about multimillion-dollar profits amassed by electricity companies year on year. The Mercury Energy case quickly became framed as a David-versus-

Goliath situation in the public eye, with the low-income Muliaga family up against the 'archetypal corporate with no sense of social responsibility' (Mercury Energy) and, guilty by association, its parent company, Mighty River Power.

One event, many issues, many parties

While the issue began with the death of Mrs Muliaga, the ensuing debate saw different agendas and issues come together from a range of parties – covering all matters from corporate power and social responsibility, regulation of the power industry and private and public sector relations to minimum wage levels, budget advice and financial planning and cultural pressures.

The national regulator was brought into the fray, along with the New Zealand police, Telecom (the main telecommunications company in New Zealand), Auckland's Middlemore Hospital (which had been overseeing Mrs Muliaga's treatment), industry commentators, the prime minister, ministers and members of parliament, and members of the media advocating for compensation and industry change while covering the incident and issues involved.

Mercury Energy is vilified while a nation grieves

The evening Mrs Muliaga died, her nephew Brenden Sheehan phoned a contact at Radio New Zealand and told them of the incident. By morning the story was broadcast nationwide, leading morning radio news and internet reports with 'family spokesperson' Mr Sheehan detailing how the Mercury Energy contractor had been taken inside the house and shown the oxygen machine but that the power was cut off anyway. The situation was compounded by the fact Telecom had also disconnected their phone and thus they were unable to call for help. In these early reports Mr Sheehan described how the family had been left to mourn in the dark – despite repeated attempts to contact Mercury Energy to ask it to turn the power back on.

These passionate, emotive reports continued throughout the day and quickly gained momentum in the media – largely fuelled by Mr Sheehan's comments. A former trade union representative and media officer for the Australian Services Union, Mr Sheehan was articulate and vocal and played the anti-'big business' theme aggressively. His actions and ongoing involvement were a major factor in the case becoming a full-blown crisis for Mercury Energy. Mr Sheehan was later quoted as saying, 'If they didn't have a relative with media skills, it might have been just another Auckland death, another number. It's an amazing story. I bet they [Mercury Energy] are cursing having someone like me around.'

However, Mercury Energy's own actions didn't lend themselves to sympathy. While its general manager was quoted the day after Mrs Muliaga's death as being 'distressed by this tragic event', the company later added that they 'were simply unaware that the loss of electricity to the household was putting a vulnerable customer at risk'. This response was exacerbated the following day when the company announced 'We're in the clear' and that it 'didn't put a foot wrong'. This statement in many ways set the agenda for the subsequent media coverage.

Another aggravating factor was the influence of the New Zealand prime minister, who launched a scathing attack telling Mercury Energy to 'fess up and stop making excuses' and suggested the incident might prompt industry regulation to ensure 'it never happens again'. The prime minister indicated the story had already gone around the world and was portraying a bad image of New Zealand.

Within two days of Mrs Muliaga's death, trade unionists and community activists picketed outside Mercury's headquarters while other retail power companies moved quickly to distance themselves from the incident and halted all disconnection procedures.

Amid the public outcry, Mercury Energy maintained it had followed processes. It was not until four days after Mrs Muliaga's death that Mercury Energy staff visited the family – hours after the prime minister herself had called upon the family to pass on her condolences. After taking cultural advice on board, the CEO and chair of Mighty River Power and the general manager of Mercury Energy visited the Muliagas wearing the traditional Samoan lava-lava and bringing gifts and NZ$10,000 for the family to assist with funeral costs, including flying family over from Samoa (this figure was promptly compared in the media to the Muliagas' NZ$168.40 unpaid power bill).

Another two days passed before Mighty River Power released a public apology, with its chairperson stating, 'No one should ever die because they can't pay a power bill. I am here to say sorry publicly to the family and to apologize to the community for our part in this tragedy.'

The media attention continued throughout June and into July. The political criticism also continued, with the prime minister and several ministers slamming Mercury Energy's conduct and handling of the case. The parliamentary debate led to tougher guidelines being introduced for the sector by the national regulator. While the guidelines were 'voluntary', the regulator received written assurances from the chief executives of all electricity companies that the guidelines would be implemented and compliance would be reported annually. The regulator stated if companies failed to comply with the new guidelines the government might be forced to regulate the sector.

An important turning point for Mercury Energy came in mid-June when it sent its customers a letter apologizing for the incident and providing additional resources for others in a similar situation. This first direct communication preceded an announcement that the company would allow a six-week bill payment deferral on all overdue bills and tightening of their medical-related disconnection policies.

At this point, the focus of the case moved to a discussion around financial hardship, with agencies commending the company's efforts to assist low-income families to pay their bills. The general manager publicly announced the company had made a commitment to learn from the Muliaga tragedy and improve its credit management systems. This was in complete contrast to early media reports in which the company had stated it was 'helping' the Muliagas by disconnecting their power, preventing the family from going further into debt.

A month later the general manager again stated, 'It's not about today; it's about those people who are now saying they are prepared to talk to budget agencies about payment plans.'

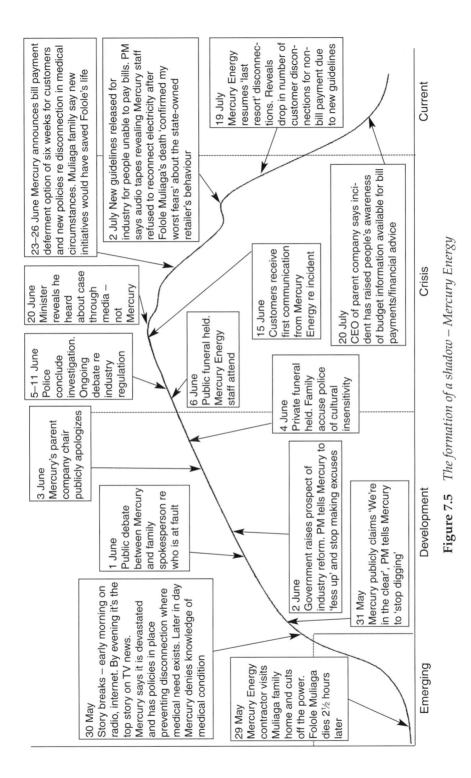

Figure 7.5 *The formation of a shadow – Mercury Energy*

29 May
Mercury Energy contractor visits Muliaga family home and cuts off the power. Folole Muliaga dies 2½ hours later

30 May
Story breaks – early morning on radio, internet. By evening it's the top story on TV news. Mercury says it is devastated and has policies in place preventing disconnection where medical need exists. Later in day Mercury denies knowledge of medical condition

31 May
Mercury publicly claims 'We're in the clear', PM tells Mercury to 'stop digging'

1 June
Public debate between Mercury and family spokesperson re who is at fault

2 June
Government raises prospect of industry reform. PM tells Mercury to 'fess up' and stop making excuses

3 June
Mercury's parent company chair publicly apologizes

4 June
Private funeral held. Family accuse police of cultural insensitivity

5–11 June
Police conclude investigation. Ongoing debate re industry regulation

6 June
Public funeral held. Mercury Energy staff attend

15 June
Customers receive first communication from Mercury Energy re incident

20 June
Minister reveals he heard about case through media – not Mercury

23–26 June Mercury announces bill payment deferment option of six weeks for customers and new policies re disconnection in medical circumstances. Muliaga family say new initiatives would have saved Folole's life

2 July New guidelines released for industry for people unable to pay bills. PM says audio tapes revealing Mercury staff refused to reconnect electricity after Folole Muliaga's death 'confirmed my worst fears' about the state-owned retailer's behaviour

19 July
Mercury Energy resumes 'last resort' disconnections. Reveals drop in number of customer disconnections for non-bill payment due to new guidelines

20 July
CEO of parent company says incident has raised people's awareness of budget information available for bill payments/financial advice

Emerging   Development   Crisis   Current

The outcome

What was interesting about this case was that, despite the virtual media hysteria surrounding the death of Mrs Muliaga and a debate that veered heavily towards total sympathy with the family and condemnation of Mercury Energy, public opinion of the case remained largely balanced. Early on, reader responses to newspaper coverage discussed the family's responsibility, querying why an ambulance wasn't called earlier. Another poll held a month after the story broke found that 40 per cent of respondents still believed responsibility lay with the family, while only 22 per cent thought Mercury Energy was responsible for Mrs Muliaga's death.

However, it was clear Mercury Energy made several errors in its approach to this crisis. The company fumbled its way through the first week of the ordeal, making serious errors in its approach, starting with its public blame-shifting statements, with lack of clear leadership and inviting political criticism. This case exemplifies the need for companies to prepare for crises and have policies and protocols in place to communicate to their stakeholders and the public from the outset of an incident – to tell it all, tell it fast and tell it truthfully and, more importantly, to respond on a human level.

SUMMARY

- Beware the obsequiousness of advisers.
- Don't confuse image with reality.
- Don't believe it can't happen because it hasn't before.
- Don't believe that writing the 'procedures' will prevent it from happening.
- Communicate at all times at all levels.
- Faced with disaster, consider the worst possible scenario.
- Be prepared to demonstrate human concern for what has happened.
- Never underestimate genuine concerns of customers.

8

Perception *is* the reality

Are you going to believe what you see or what I'm telling you?

Groucho Marx

Virtually every crisis contains within itself the seeds of success as well as the roots of failure. Finding, cultivating and harvesting the potential success is the essence of crisis management. The essence of crisis *mis*management is to make a bad situation worse. Many would argue, for example, that President Nixon's cover-up of the Watergate break-in created a bigger crisis than the original transgression would have produced.

Successful management of a crisis situation is about recognizing you have one, taking the appropriate actions to remedy the situation, being *seen* to take them and being *heard* to say the right things. Companies often misclassify a problem, focusing on the technical aspects and ignoring issues of perception – as we have seen with Shell's response to Greenpeace over the disposal of the Brent Spar.

The problem in this stage of crisis management is that perception truly does become reality. In the case of Shell and Brent Spar, as the *Wall Street Journal* reported at the time: 'Shell made a strategic error. In a world of sound bites one image was left with many viewers: a huge multinational oil company was mustering all its might to bully what was portrayed as a brave but determined band'. Whatever the reality of the situation, Shell found itself floundering on the shoals of worldwide media perception.

Ordinary people couldn't get their heads round Shell's scientific and environmental arguments. The company's response focused almost entirely on the print media when television is by far more the most influential, and therefore important, medium. The television pictures showed water cannons being sprayed at the 'brave but determined band'.

Exxon Corporation's handling of the *Valdez* oil spill also taught students of crisis management important lessons in how poor communication can create a perception which does not reflect the reality – lessons we observed and did our best to remember when we were called in to help with the *Braer* disaster off the Shetland Islands in 1993 and the *Sea Empress* disaster in Milford Haven, Wales, in 1996.

A TALE OF THREE SORRY TANKERS

CASE STUDY: *EXXON VALDEZ*

How pouring oil on water created plenty of troubles

On 24 March 1989, at 2100 hours, the 987-foot *Exxon Valdez* oil tanker left the harbour of South Alaska's Valdez and entered Prince William Sound bound for California. The seas were calm and the weather was good. A local pilot, who had guided the super-tanker out of the port, was taken off shortly after 2330 hours. Twenty minutes later the *Exxon Valdez* ploughed into rocks and America's worst oil spill disaster had begun. Ten million gallons of oil spewed out of the vessel into Prince William Sound, a rich natural habitat. The disaster became instant world news.

Exxon, one of the five largest companies in the United States, had been under the leadership of Lawrence G Rawl since 1986. The son of a truck driver, an ex-marine, and with 37 years as an employee of Exxon before becoming chairman, Rawl was known for having a strong dislike of publicity and journalists. He perceived the media as a danger, to be avoided at all costs.

When the media asked for a comment at Exxon's headquarters in Houston several hours after the disaster it was told this was a matter for the Exxon Shipping Company. They could not and did not want to make any further comment. When asked if the chairman would be interviewed on television, the response was that the chairman of the board had no time for that kind of thing.

Later, a spokesperson for Exxon Shipping coolly informed the press that emergency procedures and manuals existed for such events. Meanwhile the entire world was watching televised pictures of these emergency procedures failing as thousands of birds, otters and seals died in the oil slick.

Emergency procedures should apparently have been initiated by the Alyeska Pipeline Company, a consortium of seven oil companies that use the Alaskan pipeline. In the event of disaster, the consortium would be the first to act. But in this case even the most basic steps were not taken, and a ship specially designated for fighting oil pollution was left sitting in the dock for some time.

After more than a week Exxon was still pursuing a policy of 'no comment'. The publicity became so hostile that eventually Frank Iarossi, the director of Exxon Shipping, flew to Valdez to hold a press conference. This ended in a bitter battle with fishermen and journalists. Iarossi retaliated and the one small opportunity to cooperate and communicate with the press was lost. Iarossi's subsequent daily briefings were likened to the press conferences during the Vietnam War: generals who summed up small successes only to be immediately confronted by journalists who had seen completely different things on the battlefields.

Suddenly the chairman, Lawrence Rawl, decided to appear on television. He was interviewed 'live' and watched by millions of extremely angry Americans right across the United States. The first question put to him concerned the latest plan for the clean-up. He hadn't read it. He explained: 'it is not the role of the chairman of a large worldwide corporation to read every technical plan'. His arrogance was blatant.

When asked about the public relations disaster his company was facing – Esso products were being boycotted in the United States by this time – he replied: 'the reason we've got this public relations disaster [admitting he had one] is because of the media's reporting of the situation'. He proceeded to place the blame for his company's problems at the feet of the world's press. He showed no emotion over the enormous environmental disaster and offered no apologies to fishermen whose livelihood had been destroyed.

He didn't bother to go to Alaska to see for himself the damage which had been done until a fortnight after the event. When he did go the media was kept unaware of his visit. The damage to Exxon's reputation was complete.

The consequences for the company and the rest of the industry were dire. It is estimated the spill cost the company – in fines, clean-up expenses and lost market share – at least US$16 billion.

New legislation was imposed on the oil tanker industry requiring all new ocean-going tankers to be built with double hulls. Experts in the shipping industry suggest double hulls are potentially more dangerous than single hulls because of the risk of a build-up of gas between the two hulls. Having seen the *Braer* and *Sea Empress* disasters first hand, it is easy to form the view that four hulls would not have prevented those oil spills. The new legislation appears to be a cosmetic, knee-jerk political reaction by governments that felt they had to be seen to 'police' the wicked oil tanker and oil industries – a perception of wickedness created by Exxon's appalling communication in the aftermath of the *Valdez* spill.

Lessons from *Exxon Valdez*

When a tanker spills millions of gallons of oil into the sea, or an aeroplane falls out of the sky, or a ferry turns over in Zeebrugge harbour, people's first reaction is one of shock. It is difficult to accept that such disasters can still occur in this age of advancing technology and environmental consciousness. But, ultimately, no one expects there to be a zero-risk associated with any industry. Accidents do happen, whether in our private lives or in business.

This initial sense of shock, however, quickly turns to anger if the company at the centre of the crisis is not seen to take the appropriate action and to say the appropriate words. People need to be quickly reassured about certain things, essentially that:

- Everything (hopefully) was in place to try to prevent the accident from happening in the first place.
- Nonetheless, given the nature of the industry the company works in, it had the foresight to anticipate the possibility of such an event occurring and knew what to do to remedy the situation as far as possible, and as quickly as possible. In other words, to have the ability to paint a picture in words of a group of competent, caring people who swung into action really quickly to handle the situation.
- *The company really cares about what has happened.*

Exxon failed miserably on all three counts. In the aftermath of disaster, no action demonstrates more a company's concern for what has happened than the top man or woman being seen to go to the site, to be seen to take personal charge of the aftermath, and to communicate three simple messages:

- This is what has happened.
- This is what we are doing about it.
- This is how we feel about what has happened.

People will still feel aggrieved by what has happened but the anger will be dissipated if the company is seen to do its best in what is likely to be the most difficult of all circumstances. It is people's anger which causes the lasting damage to organizations. It leads to product boycotts, shares being sold and more demanding restrictions and penalties.

CASE STUDY: *BRAER*

Behind the headlines

During the course of 5 January 1993, we watched on the office television the events following the *Braer* oil tanker's grounding on rocks off the Shetland

Islands earlier that day. At 5 pm we received a telephone call from New York. It was the chairman of Ultramar Inc. whose oil formed the cargo of the *Braer.* Could we help?

He told us he was catching the overnight flight to Heathrow and would then fly to Aberdeen where we were to rendezvous the following morning. Michael Regester takes up the story:

I booked myself on the last flight that evening from Heathrow to Aberdeen. The plane was packed with journalists and press photographers all headed for the same destination.

From Aberdeen I called the oil journalist Philip Algar, already on the Islands. Philip had travelled to the Shetland Islands not in his capacity as a journalist but in response to a request from the owners of the *Braer* to act as their media adviser. He brought me up to date with the facts.

The 89,000 dwt tanker, carrying 84,000 tonnes of crude oil from Norway to Quebec, lost engine power early in the morning of 5 January. The owners believe pipes probably damaged an air vent, resulting in sea-water entering the fuel tanks.

The vessel subsequently went aground at Garth's Ness on Shetland. Dreadful weather, with winds up to 100 mph, thwarted salvage attempts. By the end of the week the entire cargo was spilt, causing considerable loss of wildlife and inflicting immediate damage on a part of the local salmon fishing industry.

Ironically, the bad weather responsible for the accident played a major role in dispersing the oil rapidly. Within a few weeks the tourist authority stated: 'everything for the summer visitor season is now back to normal. Indeed, if you missed the news of the *Braer*, and now visited Shetland, there is nothing what-soever to indicate that the islands came close to such a disaster'.

The trouble was, you would have to have been a Martian to have missed the news of the *Braer.* Within 48 hours of the accident there were over 500 journal-ists on the Islands, all based at the tiny Sumburgh airport at the southern end of Shetland. The scenes were amazing. Shetland is not renowned for its overca-pacity of hotels or cars for hire. Journalists were knocking on people's doors, asking: 'How much for a room for a few nights and the use of your car?' The nearest hotel we could obtain rooms at was 60 miles away. The two showers at Sumburgh airport had been rented out as editing suites to the BBC and ITN.

I had booked a private room at Aberdeen airport to brief the Ultramar chairman on the latest situation and organized a charter plane to take us on to the Shetland Islands after his arrival. All commercial flights were booked up for days.

When we are called into crisis situations, often at a moment's notice, it is usually by companies for which we have never worked before. The situation is already highly pressurized by the time we get there and it is important to estab-lish a quick and trusting rapport with the senior people we are dealing with. As I shook hands with the Ultramar chairman and was about to bring him up to date our flight was called. Our take-off slot had been brought forward.

Once on board it was impossible to have a conversation such was the noise from the tiny plane bouncing around in 100 mph winds. Knowing we were likely to be surrounded by the media on arrival at Sumburgh I gave him a copy of the statement I had hoped to discuss with him in Aberdeen. I waited with some anxiety as he read it for this was to be a critical moment in the establishment of our relationship.

One of our golden rules concerns the order in which statements are made in crisis situations. Whether written or spoken they must always cover the following topics in the following order:

- people;
- environment;
- property;
- money.

This is simply because this is the order in which most newspapers and broadcast media will cover the story. But sometimes our clients, not unusually on the advice of lawyers, don't agree and prefer to say something banal like: 'We will issue a statement when we have all the facts.' I need not have worried. The chairman agreed with the statement and proved to be an excellent communicator.

Press conferences were held twice a day for the next few days. When dealing with such large numbers of journalists and television crews this is the only practical way of keeping them up to date (see Chapter 12). Philip Algar and I were keen for our respective clients to be represented at the press conferences organized by the Shetland Islands, in order to present a united team dealing with the situation. This was agreed.

At the first press conference in which we participated, Ultramar's chairman had only about 5 per cent of press questions directed at him. The vast majority were aimed at the owners of the *Braer* and the Shetland Islands Council which was in charge of the clean-up. I therefore suggested we participate in no more press conferences but advised the chairman to remain on the Islands in case ownership of the crude oil became an issue. He should not be seen to be 'running away' from the situation but I didn't want him as a sitting target if there was no interest in the oil's ownership.

Instead, we focused on giving one-to-one interviews for the North American press who had arrived and in assessing for ourselves the amount of damage to the Islands. In crises of this kind it is important to obtain your own record of what has happened – particularly for dealing with future insurance claims and assisting with official investigations (see Chapter 10).

I hired a filmcrew from Aberdeen. They wanted to fly over but we asked them to take the ferry so they could bring a car with them. That solved our own transport problem as well as providing us with the footage we needed. Later, the footage had an additional use when it was turned into a film for Ultramar employees and investors back in the States.

In crisis situations a primary consideration must, of course, be audiences. Who needs to know what and how quickly? While messages to each audience must be consistent it is not always possible to transmit them all at the same time to each audience. In the case of the *Braer* the key immediate audience for Ultramar was its shareholders. After all, everyone in the financial community knew the *Valdez* spill had cost Exxon $16 billion. Ultramar was a tiny organization in comparison. If its shareholders thought they were going to be facing a bill of similar proportions, what was going to happen to the share price? So a first action taken by the company was to get its shares suspended on the New York Stock Exchange until it could assess the company's likely amount of financial liability, and check it had the insurance policies in place to meet the liability. Having done this the situation was explained to shareholders and their advisers and, later that day, trading in the shares was resumed. In the event, they dropped just 25 cents on the previous day's price.

The 'information void'

> The vacuum caused by a failure to communicate is soon filled with rumour, misrepresentation, drivel and poison.
>
> Business academic C Northcote Parkinson

Meanwhile the appalling weather conditions on the Islands were preventing workers from stemming the leaking oil and helicopters from spraying dispersant. In fact, nothing was happening. This absence of activity led to an 'information void' – typical in a crisis situation.

Instead of communicating positive messages about what would be done to minimize the environmental damage once the weather had subsided, virtually nothing was communicated by those responsible for the clean-up.

The void was instantly filled with media reports that the Islands were 'covered with oil', that 'oil was carcinogenic' – you could get leukaemia from breathing the fumes. As a consequence, 'school children were being evacuated', 'sheep were being evacuated' and 'all the salmon fish farms were contaminated'. And so the media pollution went on.

After oil, the two most important industries in the Shetland Islands are the export of salmon to Japan, and tourism. Following the media reports, the Japanese refused to import any more salmon and tourism fell right away. In that year alone, the Shetland Islands Council reported a £1.3 million loss in tourism revenues and forecast a cumulative loss of £18.2 million by 1998. The public perception of the situation had become the reality.

179

These lessons were uppermost in our minds when we were called in by the Wales Tourist Board on 15 February 1996, after the *Sea Empress* hit rocks on its approach to Texaco's refinery in Milford Haven.

CASE STUDY: *SEA EMPRESS* IN DISTRESS

The Wales Tourist Board had a huge challenge on its hands to prevent a similar impact on Welsh tourism. Tourism in Wales generates about £1.4 billion per year and is directly responsible for employment of one in nine of the workforce.

The protracted delay in the salvage operation only fuelled the daily saturation coverage of oiled beaches and birds. Media reports in Germany, Denmark and further afield implied the whole of Wales was affected. The task in hand was to correct these misconceptions and convert the massive exposure of Pembrokeshire in the world media into an advantage.

Our strategy, which won immediate approval from the Wales Tourist Board, had to be aimed at supporting the tourist trade, reassuring holiday makers and persuading the media that every possible effort was being made to clean the affected beaches and restore them to their natural state prior to the tourist season.

Less than a week after the spill the Welsh Tourism Fights Back campaign was under way. Colleague Rosie Clifford devised the theme: 'The Treasure is Still Here – But No Longer a Secret'. This was a reference to the Pembrokeshire coastline being known as the 'secret treasure of Wales'. The theme struck a chord and the 'treasure' frequently appeared in newspaper headlines.

We wanted to minimize the medium- and long-term damage to the tourist industry by capitalizing on the rapid and comprehensive clean-up operation; and to emphasize that only a small area of Wales had suffered. The majority of Pembrokeshire's beaches were unaffected. This would hopefully counteract the predominantly negative and exaggerated image of the extent of environmental pollution propagated by media coverage.

The campaign included:

- a telephone hotline to respond to holiday makers concerned about their bookings; and to monitor public concern;
- organizing over 20 television and radio interviews for the Wales Tourist Board's chief executive, John French – over a critical 48-hour period when the issue was still headline news – to convey agreed messages;
- transmitting positive messages to key UK and overseas markets via British tourism offices overseas;
- consulting with Texaco, owners of the crude oil cargo, tourist operators, accommodation and attraction owners, local authorities and other agencies to ensure consistent messages to key audiences;
- briefing HRH Prince of Wales and the Secretary of State for Wales on the campaign to gain their support.

The words of Wales Tourist Board chief executive John French summed up the passion and rigour with which the potentially damaging information void was filled to best advantage: 'the images which brought us worldwide attention were negative but now more people than ever before know of the beauty that can be found here. We were determined not to let the media's images outlast the pollution itself.'

Positive media coverage immediately began to outweigh the negative. On one day alone – St David's Day – the Wales Tourist Board press office broadcast its reassurance campaign live through 25 local radio stations reaching in excess of an estimated 1 million listeners throughout the UK.

A study jointly published in July 1996 by the Welsh Economy Research Unit, University of Wales, Cardiff Business School and the Welsh Institute of Rural Studies, entitled *The Economic Consequences of the* Sea Empress *Spillage* (1996), concluded:

> the weighted anticipated impact of the spillage on tourism spending in Pembrokeshire in 1996 was an average reduction of 12.9 per cent and slightly less for south west Wales overall. Applying this average impact, supported by actual turnover experience in the early parts of 1996, to the total estimated tourism spend in Pembrokeshire in 1995 of £160 million, gives a gross estimated impact on tourism spending in Pembrokeshire of £160m $\times$ –12.9% = £20.64 million.

From a potential total loss of revenue from tourism expenditure in Pembrokeshire, and severe reduction in expenditure in other parts of Wales, the damage had been limited to 12.9 per cent. For once, the perception had more or less matched the reality.

SUMMARY

- Recognize you have a crisis.
- Be seen to take the appropriate actions.
- Be heard to say the right things.
- Remember television is the most important medium.
- Don't blame the media for your problems; they can be your best friends.
- People's anger leads to product boycotts, fall in share price and more demanding restrictions and penalties.
- Talk about people first, then the environment and property and, finally, money.
- Don't be a sitting target at press conferences.
- Anticipate the 'information void' and be prepared to fill it.
- Remember 'media pollution' can outlast environmental pollution and be more damaging economically.

9

The media in crisis situations

Four hostile newspapers are more feared than a thousand bayonets.

Napoleon Bonaparte

The chairman of Exxon's fear and distrust of the media became a self-fulfilling prophecy for him. Ignoring the media when dealing with issues and crises will always prove to be a catastrophic error of judgement. This may seem obvious but it is a mistake often made by organizations facing a tricky, potentially disastrous, situation.

For example, in the immediate aftermath of the Lockerbie disaster, Pan Am made a conscious decision to minimize communication with the press. The airline believed a policy of non-communication would somehow distance Pan Am's name from the tragic consequences of the disaster.

This was a huge error of judgement. In a situation like this the media will descend on the site of the accident like a plague of locusts which needs to be fed. If it isn't fed by the organization which finds itself, however inadvertently, at the centre of the crisis, it will feed from the hands of others. And become deeply suspicious of the hand which obviously isn't feeding it.

When questioned about the warning of a possible terrorist attack, Pan

Am initially said it was unaware of any warning. It was later revealed that all carriers operating in Europe, including Pan Am, had been informed. A cardinal public relations principle had been breached. Concealing the truth is simply not an option. There are too many eager sources and too many eager reporters. In crisis situations, it is imperative *to tell your own story, to tell it all and to tell it fast.*

So did Pan Am's CEO, Thomas Plaskett, go to Lockerbie, apologize, attend memorial services, atone for responsibility? He did not. The media made mincemeat of the airline. It was already in financial difficulty and the transatlantic route was its only remaining profitable one. Passengers lost confidence in the airline – in its willingness and ability to transport us safely from one side of the Atlantic to the other – and chose other airlines in preference. The boycott proved to be the final nail in the airline's financial coffin. It went bankrupt.

CASE STUDY: HOW AN ORGANIZATION GOT IT RIGHT

The biggest fire in peacetime Europe

At 6.03 am on Sunday 11 December 2005, there was a series of explosions at the Buncefield oil depot, a fuel storage facility at Hemel Hempstead, Hertfordshire. There were no fatalities, but 43 injuries were recorded at the time, with two people needing hospital treatment.

Hertfordshire Oil Storage Limited (HOSL) is a joint venture between Total (60 per cent) and Chevron (40 per cent). BP, Shell and the British Pipeline Agency (BPA) also operated at the Buncefield complex, which is of key strategic importance to the UK. Prior to the explosion, Buncefield handled 8 per cent of overall UK oil supplies into the market. The terminal also acted as a main pipeline transit point to meet 40 per cent of Heathrow Airport's demand for aviation fuel.

A Health and Safety Executive (HSE) and Environment Agency report by the Buncefield Major Incident Investigation Board said that tank number 912 filled beyond its capacity, filling the bund wall with an estimated 300 tonnes of petrol. A vapour cloud spread beyond the boundaries of the site. The resulting fire was the biggest in Europe since the Second World War and was extinguished on 13 December 2005. About 150 firefighters were called to the incident (75 per cent of Hertfordshire's firefighters were utilized, with additional help from 16 other brigades).

Herefordshire Oil Storage Limited (HOSL)

Regester Larkin is on 24/7 emergency call-out to Total UK, one of the joint venture partners of HOSL. Michael Regester was telephoned at 6.10 am with news of the explosion. He takes up the story: 'I immediately switched on the television and saw pictures of the huge fire. Local residents had gone to the boundary fence, filmed the scene on their mobile phones and sent the pictures to the television companies. The new phenomenon of "citizen journalism" was in full swing.'

Other members of the Regester Larkin emergency response team were called and everyone headed for Total UK's headquarters in Watford. Thanks to years of rehearsing the crisis communications plan the teams knew exactly which rooms to set up for the response, knew their roles, and had the response under way in little more than an hour.

During the first 24 hours after the incident, they gave a number of live broadcast interviews and answered hundreds of telephone calls.

The Buncefield incident is a good example of how companies are not alone when managing arises. HOSL recognized this from an early stage and communicated with many other stakeholders including Heathrow Airport, the UK Petroleum Industry Association (UKPIA), Total Group Paris, the Department of Trade and Industry (DTI), Dacorum Borough Council, Hertfordshire County Council, HSE, Environment Agency, Hertfordshire police and Hemel Hempstead Recovery Group.

HOSL recponded swiftly to provide services for those affected by the incident as a gesture of goodwill. This included:

- providing a 'repair and assistance' team to help with emergency property repairs;
- providing a 24/7 counselling service to help provide psychological support for those who needed it. This also remains available;
- additional financial donations to the Salvation Army and the Red Cross in the weeks prior to Christmas to assist them with their work with residents;
- a donation of £250,000 by HOSL to the Dacorum Community Trust Mayor's Recovery Fund.

HOSL also jointly sponsored the Hemel 2020 Regeneration, a key initiative to promote inward investment. It pledged to give £100,000 to Maylands Business over the next two years to fund a development manager who will be tasked with preparing a bid to make Maylands a Business Improvement District (BID).

Emergency services

The emergency services led the immediate response, making many operational decisions, such as which roads to close, etc. Hertfordshire Constabulary did not have the capacity to meet the needs of the incident and so called in the help of forces from around the UK. Police told those in the smoke-affected areas to close all windows and stay indoors, and encouraged those with damaged windows to seek refuge at the homes of friends or families.

The chief fire officer for the Hertfordshire Fire Authority, Roy Wilsher, said his team had carried out their duty heroically. However, Geoff Ellis of the Fire Brigades Union (FBU) said the Hertfordshire unit had been 'woefully prepared for anything but the most minor oil fire at the depot'.

Media

The incident was an international story, and with early rumours of a terrorist attack the incident was given significant media attention. The story was covered by all the major news wires and news publications from around the world, including the Xinhua News Agency, the *Los Angeles Times*, the *Australian*, the *Hindu*, the *Turkish Daily News* and the *Washington Post*. The local weekly newspaper, the *Hemel Gazette*, was tireless in its coverage of the Buncefield incident. On top of reporting, the newspaper took on an assistance role, giving developments on disruption and information to those affected. And, as might be expected from a local newspaper, the *Hemel Gazette* was a useful gauge of public opinion in the area.

Health and Safety Executive (HSE) and Environment Agency

Both agencies turned up at the scene very quickly to begin their investigations. As the catch-all government body for health and safety (it absorbed other bodies such as the Factory Inspectorate and Railway Inspectorate), the HSE reports to the Health and Safety Commission and was under a good deal of pressure to be efficient. Similarly, the Environment Agency (for England and Wales) took over the roles and responsibilities of other bodies: the National Rivers Authority; Her Majesty's Inspectorate of Pollution (HMIP); and the waste regulation authorities in England and Wales. It is answerable to the Secretary of State for the Environment, Food and Rural Affairs.

Heathrow Airport

The Buncefield complex acted as a main pipeline transit point to meet 40 per cent of Heathrow Airport's demand for aviation fuel. The explosions resulted in a shortage, resulting in the British Airport Authority (BAA) bringing in more fuel by road and rail.

UKPIA

The United Kingdom Petroleum Industry Association represents the interests of nine member companies engaged in the UK downstream oil industry. The organization significantly took the heat off the oil companies by being available to supply information about safety and operational regulations at UK facilities. After the incident, UKPIA said no one should try to apportion blame in the early stages. Nick Vandervell, the UKPIA spokesman, said an incident like Buncefield 'had never happened before' and 'The safety record of the UK refining and distribution industry business is better than the other industrial sectors and the wider European industry.'

Mike Penning MP

Hemel Hempstead is a single parliamentary constituency currently represented by Conservative MP Mike Penning, who was also the MP during the time of the explosions. After the incident, he positioned himself as the 'voice of the people', which was helped by his status as a former firefighter.

Dacorum Borough Council

After the incident, the local council provided updates on its website, released press statements, and held press conferences directing people and businesses where to find help. The Mayor's Recovery Fund, run by the Dacorum Community Trust, continues to give grants to people affected by the incident.

Hertfordshire Chamber of Commerce

The Chamber set up helplines for businesses, offering help and advice about insurance companies and solicitors.

Conclusion

The oil companies' speed of response, preparedness and willingness to communicate with all stakeholders involved in the aftermath of the incident did much to protect their own reputation – and that of the industry. The preparation and response structure it used is described in Chapter 12. Had there been the slightest lapse in open and honest communication the outcome for the companies involved – and the industry as a whole – might have been entirely different.

Many smaller businesses, surrounding the depot, were affected by the explosion. Next, we look at what enabled some of the smaller businesses to survive the devastation.

CASE STUDY: HOW SMALLER BUSINESSES SURVIVE CRISIS

At the time of the incident, Hemel Hempstead was home to several large and recognizable businesses. These all came through the incident, largely because of: 1) comprehensive insurance that offset financial losses from work disruption and restricted access to offices; and 2) detailed Business Continuity Plans (BCP), including an alternative operating location.

Businesses that prevailed

A number of companies had operations near the oil storage depot, including Waverley TBS (a subsidiary of Scottish and Newcastle), DSG International (the owner of Dixons and Currys), PC World and Marks & Spencer.

All of these companies are well established and had the resources to return to operations quickly. By having comprehensive insurance and reasonable contingency plans, they were not affected significantly. The Association of British Insurers (ABI) said that such companies would have had denial-of-access cover, which compensates for profit loss if a company cannot access its business. In addition to this, the ABI said some of the businesses would have had business interruption cover, which covers alternative accommodation.

Northgate Information Solutions

Northgate Information Solutions is a specialist supplier of software for human resources. The company employed 400 people at its Hemel Hempstead headquarters (around 3,200 employees in total) and had to relocate them to a deserted building in Dunstable that it owned. Mark Farrington, Northgate's new recovery director, said that this engendered a sense of purpose among employees, which would not have occurred had they been sent home. The company had various continuity plans for different times of the year. Northgate worked with its recovery partner Sungard, which activated the back-up servers.

Kodak

Kodak had offices 200 metres from the depot, which housed some of its customer call centres. The company had a rigorous BCP, because it was crucial that its customer service call centres continued to operate. It relocated staff to its Harrow, west London, office and was ready to operate normally by 8.30 am on the Monday morning. Kodak lost no data in the incident because the company used global systems with data stored centrally that could be accessed from any Kodak offices. Paper documents at the Hemel Hempstead office had been scanned and were easily retrieved.

Steria

Steria is an IT services company that also, ironically, consults on business continuity management (BCM). It employs 400 people and has its main office in Hemel Hempstead (9,300 employees Europe-wide).

Steria's BCP was broken into manageable hour-by-hour segments, rather than the company taking the whole plan head on – this allowed priorities to be changed. The third phase of its BCP focused on communications. Internally, it contacted employees by e-mail and with a cascade phone system from managers. It held internal meetings every two hours for progress updates. Externally, Steria communicated with customers, prospects, analysts and the media. The company's staff all had a role to play in caring for clients during the crisis. Steria also logged any actions for insurance claims. By 12 December, 95 per cent of all 400 staff were operating the business as usual, and few clients noticed any disruption. The company was pleased with the outcome of its actions, but admitted its response could have been better integrated to ensure that all parts of the business were in harmony during the crisis.

A business that struggled to prevail
Colour Quest

Colour Quest was a printing firm that had its factory hit by the Buncefield explosion. The company had the choice of tearing down and rebuilding the factory or moving into temporary accommodation for six months. Its insurance only covered one removal and installation. And so, instead of incurring significant financial loss Colour Quest negotiated a merger with another nearby printing company, Buckingham Colour.

Conclusion

Generally speaking, the businesses that prevailed in the crisis were those with comprehensive insurance, business continuity plans and swift stakeholder engagement. Businesses that struggled to prevail were those that had inadequate insurance coverage, that had only one operating premises and that lacked business continuity plans.

Many businesses had to wait while engineers assessed the safety of damaged buildings, thus complicating the businesses' decisions on whether to refurbish, rebuild or relocate.

When small companies did have the capacity to relocate, they did so close by. Relocation destinations were Hemel Hempstead town centre, St Albans, Radlett, Apsley and Pitstone. The Buncefield Economic and Business Confidence Impact Study concluded that small firms were hit by Buncefield because: they often operated from a single site; had little scope to avoid cost increases; over-relied on key individuals; and relied on local markets.

CASE STUDY: VIRGIN TRAIN CRASH

On the evening of Friday 23 February 2007, a Virgin train travelling from London to Glasgow derailed and crashed at Grayrigg, near Kendal, killing one person and injuring five. The train was travelling at around 95 miles per hour and was carrying about 120 people. Eight out of the nine carriages derailed and slid down an embankment. Virgin Trains immediately suspended services between Lancaster and Lockerbie, providing replacement buses. By Sunday, Network Rail had passed safety checks on 700 points across the country that were similar to the ones suspected of causing the crash. Early speculation was rife that the railway line was to blame, with both Bob Crow, the Rail, Maritime and Transport Union leader, and Sir Richard Branson saying that site investigators had suggested that points failure was to blame. John Armitt, chief executive of Network Rail, which manages the UK railway infrastructure, said immediately after the crash: 'I have to live with the reality that it could be something that has gone wrong on our watch.'

On Monday 26 February, Network Rail announced that the suspected set of points was in fact the cause of the accident. One of the stretcher bars was not in position, two were fractured and bolts were missing. It also said that there was no evidence that the train was a contributing factor. John Armitt said that he would not resign because he did not wish to 'abdicate his responsibilities'. Network Rail stated that a monthly maintenance check of the points was carried out on 3 February, and at least one weekly visual check should have been done since then. Every 13 weeks a major maintenance check takes place, and every year points are dismantled and rebuilt.

The last time an accident occurred due to industry error was the Potters Bar, north of London, crash in May 2002, which evoked similarities with the Virgin crash. At the time of Potters Bar, track maintenance was contracted out to private companies. After the disaster, Network Rail decided to take maintenance back in-house. Louise Christian, the solicitor who represented the families of victims of the Potters Bar crash, called for a public inquiry into the Virgin crash instead of an inquest, to find out 'why the lessons haven't been learnt'.

Train services on the line resumed on 11 March after rail workers had replaced 1,000 yards of track and overhead power lines. Virgin Trains has since said that it contacted Network Rail months before the crash, warning of the deterioration in performance of track repairs.

Crisis handling analysis: Branson and Bishop

Sir Richard Branson's handling of the Virgin train crash was reminiscent of the classic 'how to' way Sir Michael Bishop responded to the BMI Boeing 737 Kegworth, UK, air disaster in 1989. The following is an analysis of the way each chairman handled his respective crisis.

Sir Richard Branson

Sir Richard Branson's response to the Virgin train crash was near textbook. At a press conference at the scene of the crash, he was visibly emotional. Every comment made was positive, complimentary and dignified, which had the effect of ensuring that Virgin maintained a good relationship with all of its stakeholders: employees, customers, train engineers, track engineers, emergency services – and, potentially, victims and the wider public.

Branson cut short a family holiday to visit the scene of the accident and visit the hospitals treating the injured. Crucially, he was swift to suggest that it was not the train's fault that it had derailed, but a fault on the track. He described the actions of the emergency services, the RAF and the police as 'wonderful'. He said: 'It is a very sad day because of the loss of one life and the injuries caused to other people.' Branson then hailed the train driver as a hero:

He's carried on sitting in his carriage for nearly half a mile, running the train on the stone – he could have tried to get back and protect himself but he didn't, and he's ended up quite badly injured. He is a definitely a hero. In the sober light of day we will have to see if he can be recognized as such.

Branson also praised the design and robustness of the train, saying that an older train would have resulted in 'horrendous' injuries and mortalities. He added that trains were 'massively safer' than cars.

Sir Richard Branson said he 'took his hat off' to Network Rail for being 'dignified' in accepting the responsibility for the accident. He said: 'It is not for us to apportion blame but rather to work closely together as train operating companies with all our partners in the industry, particularly Network Rail, to ensure that this never happens again.' And he used the opportunity to support the idea of maintenance being carried out locally rather than centrally, increasing the involvement of companies that actually use the track.

This added to the regard in which he was held by Virgin Trains' stakeholders. He was particularly careful not to criticize or alienate Network Rail, thus maintaining their working relationship and cleverly creating a situation in which the rail company was in debt to him; it is not unreasonable to suggest that, had Branson criticized Network Rail, he would have significantly perpetuated what is perceived to be a national problem – that of railway maintenance.

Sir Michael Bishop

On 8 January 1989, a British Midland Boeing 737 flying from Heathrow to Belfast crashed on the M1 motorway, killing 47 people and seriously injuring 10. The aircraft crash-landed short of East Midlands airport after engine malfunction.

Unlike the situation in previous aviation disasters when media comment had been left to lower-ranked company spokespeople, BMI (then British Midland) chairman Sir Michael Bishop offered himself openly for media enquiries. He told the media that, as the head of the company, he was responsible. On his way to the scene of the accident, Bishop gave live radio interviews from his car phone. He gave these interviews when he had no knowledge about the cause of the accident or how many had died, been injured or survived. And so he filled the information void by expressing his own feelings about the accident and outlining what he would do about it. He told of his concern and sympathy for the victims' families and kept the media constantly updated about the inquiry.

His emotional TV interviews were accepted as genuine and he received plaudits from the media and the public for his handling of the issue. He had had no formal training in talking to the media, but had years of media relations experience. British Midland suffered no subsequent loss of traffic on the Heathrow–Belfast route and maintained its level of growth prior to the accident.

Bishop said of his handling of the crash:

I suppose it was a bit of a gamble, but I had given the matter of what to do if we had a crash a lot of thought over the years and it seemed to me the best way to tackle the crisis when it actually happened. We were helped in that the crash happened just five miles away from our home base, so we could get the information quickly to pass on to the media.

He added that he had 'probably set a new style for dealing with such crises'. He had.

The *Daily Telegraph* described Bishop's handling as 'a classic lesson in how to handle a catastrophe'. It said: 'A weaker man might have hidden behind the need for an official enquiry. Instead, Bishop displayed a masterful understanding of adversity leadership: sympathetic, transparent and helpful.' *PRWeek* described his handling as 'a textbook example of how to cope with a crisis'.

Press coverage

In the *Guardian*, solicitor Louise Christian described the aftermath of the Virgin crash as 'uncomfortably similar' to that of Potters Bar. She said: 'John Armitt [the chief executive of Network Rail] appeared on television denying systemic management failure, just as happened after Potters Bar. And the claim of sabotage, unbelievably, is again surfacing through unattributable briefings of journalists and experts.' She mentioned Virgin in favourable light: 'Richard Branson spoke with dignity about his sorrow at the crash.'

A *Guardian* editorial defended rail safety over the past five years: 'In the same five years, more than 15,000 people have died on the roads and more than a million have been injured. That is the real transport-safety scandal. Most of these road accidents received no public attention at all or were only briefly noticed. But then they can only be blamed on human beings, not on wicked corporations.'

The *Independent* questioned whether the rail industry was learning from its past mistakes, and also praised Richard Branson: 'Sir Richard Branson still deserves credit for returning from his holiday early and visiting the scene of the accident, something that chief executives still too rarely do in such circumstances.'

During a PR conference, the *Independent* editor-in-chief Simon Kelner said Richard Branson's handling of the crisis was 'genius PR'. He said: 'Branson took the story away from being an institutional and public disaster and made it one about the heroism of the train driver.'

Former government communications adviser Charlie Whelan described Branson as a 'one-man PR machine' and said there was probably no public figure outside politics who is more in tune with the demands of the media. He said: 'I can't recall the owner of a train network turning up and so effectively dealing with the media.'

Conclusion

Sir Richard Branson's handling of the issue was reminiscent of Sir Michael Bishop's efforts in 1989. Branson showed the same real emotion as Bishop and communicated similar key messages. His crisis technique seemed to be as good as Bishop's, if not better – the fact that he left a family holiday to visit the crash scene and his hailing of the train driver as a hero were two human touches in a human tragedy. The now well-documented robustness of the trains used by Virgin, coupled with Branson's brilliant stakeholder relations management, has meant that Virgin customers have not been deterred. A study by academics at Harvard University concluded that Sir Michael Bishop's handling of the British Midland crash actually enhanced the reputation of the airline.

GAINING MEDIA SUPPORT

This may come as a surprise, but in our experience of dealing with the media in crisis situations their attitude will be, to begin with, at worst neutral and at best sympathetic – particularly if people have died or been injured. It is usually when the media believe the organization at the centre of the crisis is unduly slow in providing information, reticent about providing 'talking heads' for interview or thought to be withholding information, that they become hostile. The key to successful communication in crisis situations is to establish the organization at the centre of the crisis as *the single authoritative source of information about what has happened and what is being done about it.* This is precisely what Total, Virgin and British Midland achieved.

International research has shown the media to be by far the most credible sources of information throughout the Western world, well ahead of governments and, with the possible exception of Italy, the Church. By virtue of their 'believability' the media act as the most important conduit to shaping people's beliefs and behaviour.

Ultimately, newspapers, television and radio news programmes are 'products'. Those which best meet the demands of the prevailing market sell the most or are watched and listened to the most. Those that don't get it right either go out of business (the *Today* and *Sunday Correspondent* newspapers are examples) or suffer a drop in sales or audiences.

The *Sun*, for example, suffered a drop in sales when it attacked pop singer Elton John. It underestimated the singer's popularity with its readers and the libel cost it £1 million in compensation.

THE MEDIA AS AN ALLY

In most cases, the media will act responsibly if a situation is handled in an open and honest way. Public relations activity in crises must never attempt to hide the facts of what has happened; it has to act as a facilitator to explain what has happened and as a 'driver' to ensure appropriate action is seen to be taken to remedy, as far as possible, what has gone wrong. To deliberately hide the facts is complete folly. Sooner or later they will be discovered and the situation will become worse because of accusations of a 'cover-up'.

The media should be viewed as potential friends rather than potential foes. It is important to establish and track their agendas. In the Shetland Islands, during the *Braer* disaster, we regularly mixed with reporters to find out what was concerning them and what news they expected to hear next. This helped to shape what was said at press conferences and written in press releases.

On another occasion we were helping a major pet food manufacturer which had received an extortion threat. The letter said unless £50,000 was paid into an account at the Halifax Building Society by a certain date, strychnine would be injected into a leading brand of dog food. A phial containing strychnine accompanied the letter to prove the extortionist had the poison.

This was different to the Tylenol situation because the crime had not yet been committed and, dare we say it, the threat was against dogs and not human beings. If the product were recalled as a precautionary measure the extortionist could have made the same threat to another of the company's products – where would it have ended? (This kind of extortion is often known as 'sweetmail' after a blackmailer in Japan, dubbed 'the man with 21 faces', repeatedly extracted large sums of money from a Japanese confectionery company, the size of Cadbury's, until it eventually went bankrupt.)

If we told the media what was happening and the story was published, what would happen to sales of the product? Equally, if the news leaked out, the media would rip the company apart for putting profit above all else. We decided the media had to become an ally.

We agreed with officers from Scotland Yard to hold a joint press conference at which we would inform the media about the threat but ask them not to publish the story until the villain had been apprehended. Scotland Yard explained coverage of the threat would make it more difficult to apprehend the criminal, might encourage him to carry out the threat, and might encourage 'copycat' crime. In exchange, we would hold regular press briefings to keep reporters up to date with developments and they could, of course, publish the story once the extortionist had been caught.

There were no legal sanctions to prevent the media from publishing the story. There were no legal reasons to prevent them. But not one newspaper or broadcaster used the story because, we believe, the reasons given to them were entirely plausible and reasonable.

In the event, the extortionist never carried out his threat to the pet food company but switched his target to Heinz Baby Foods. Dealing with a threat to babies is entirely different from dealing with a threat to dogs. The police mounted a huge surveillance campaign at every Halifax Building Society cash dispenser and eventually the criminal was apprehended. Only then did the story become national news.

CASE STUDY: THOMAS COOK COACH CRASH

As we advocate throughout this book, a policy of open and honest communication and the preparedness to be seen to be taking the right action when a crisis hits can encourage the media to become one of your greatest allies.

The foundation then exists for an organization to emerge from the worst of all possible circumstances with its reputation intact. Evidence for this view is demonstrated by the Thomas Cook Holidays' response to the crash of a coach carrying British holidaymakers in South Africa.

On 27 September 1999 – when the public was still in shock over the Paddington rail crash, which had happened only a month previously – a coach carrying 34 elderly Thomas Cook holidaymakers, two tour guides and the driver, lost control and careered off the Long Tom Pass in the Drakensberg mountains, South Africa.

Twenty-six elderly British tourists and their South African tour guide were killed. Another tourist died two weeks later as a result of her injuries. Seven British tourists, a tour guide and the driver of the coach survived the crash, many with broken bones and head and chest injuries.

As soon as Thomas Cook Holidays received news of the accident, it initiated its crisis response plan. Simon Laxton, Thomas Cook Holidays' managing director, set up an Incident Management Team (see Chapter 11) to manage media- and relative-response teams and to deal with all other aspects of the accident.

The Incident Management Team focused first and foremost on the needs of the victims and survivors of the crash and their families. A team of trauma counsellors, mortuary technicians and legal and customer advisers was immediately sent to South Africa to counsel survivors, and to coordinate communication with the police and the media. A coach engineer accompanied the group in order to initiate an independent internal investigation into the crash. In addition, Thomas Cook Holidays consulted its insurance providers, Axa, whose employees also flew to the scene to assist with coordinating insurance and medical claims.

A relative-response hotline was quickly established to deal with the thousands of calls expected from concerned friends and relatives. The number was quickly communicated to the public via major UK television bulletins.

Despite the fact that full details of the incident weren't yet known, the Incident Management Team recognized that friends and relatives needed reassurance that Thomas Cook Holidays was doing everything possible, and that everyone involved was being treated with the utmost care.

Thomas Cook Holidays received over 2,000 calls in the first 24 hours after the crash. Simon Laxton worked with the team and answered a number of calls himself. Additional staff were drafted into the relative call centre to cope with the growing number of enquiries from concerned friends and relatives. The company made sure that *all* its staff (including those in over 700 high street branches and all bureaux de change) were contacted, briefed and updated regularly to deal with members of the public who called or visited outlets for information.

The company made immediate contact with South African Airways to make arrangements to fly relatives to Johannesburg. The terms of the insurance policies taken out by the holidaymakers varied widely. Most allowed for only one relative to fly to the scene, so Thomas Cook Holidays agreed with Axa to overwrite these, enabling distraught relatives to travel in pairs.

Contact was made with the Foreign Office, the South African government, the British High Commission in South Africa and the South African police to ensure that relatives were kept informed and that those who flew to South Africa were protected from a pack of tenacious journalists clamouring for reactions and new information.

All the necessary financial and practical arrangements were made to ensure that relatives were given all the support and information they needed while also being protected from the media glare.

Thomas Cook Holidays proactively contacted all customers booked on the same tour two weeks after the accident and offered them the opportunity to cancel their trips without charge. Only six chose to cancel, demonstrating that Thomas Cook Holidays had not lost the trust or confidence of its customers.

Media attention around the world was immediate and intense. Over 500 media inquiries were received by the media team (which was outsourced to public relations firm JGPR) in the first 24 hours after the crash. TV crews arrived at the company's headquarters in Peterborough within two hours of the crash and 'camped' for days in the car park outside the building.

The company managed an all-too-rare achievement in its response to the media. It issued its first news release via the Press Association and Reuters *before* receiving the first media call. This action ensured all the media knew which telephone number to call for information and put the company on the front foot in terms of influencing the way the story was covered.

In total, 19 statements were issued over five days. Only two of these were issued on a reactive basis, responding to specific media demands. All emphasized concern about the care and well-being of the victims' families, survivors and their relatives, as well as explaining Thomas Cook Holidays' commitment to finding out the cause of the accident as soon as possible.

Thomas Cook Holidays' lawyers, Field Fisher Waterhouse, were brought in at the outset of the incident. Their role was to ensure that all legal aspects of the coach crash were thought through, that there was immediate and professional advice available on complex issues around insurance and liability statements, and to provide immediate access to any team member with a legal query.

Simon Laxton acted as head of the Incident Management Team as well as primary spokesman for Thomas Cook Holidays. An effective spokesperson, able to convey both grave concern and decisive action, is essential in any situation involving loss of life or injury. Despite the pressure he was under, Simon Laxton made time to give all major television stations one-to-one interview slots twice a day. He showed journalists all the response teams at work and, through his honesty and transparency, won their trust.

Initial media speculation about the cause of the crash and safety record of the coach tour operator was immediately quashed by the company. Simon Laxton took care to reiterate the company's strict health and safety assessment of contracted operators and its confidence in the coach company, Springbok Atlas.

Teams flown to the scene of the accident were briefed to handle media inquiries and to protect the privacy of survivors and their relatives. A Thomas Cook representative was later based at the Millpark Hospital, Johannesburg, in order to deal with inquiries that might have been too intrusive for survivors and their relatives.

The Incident Management Team (including Simon Laxton) relocated to Johannesburg on Wednesday 29 September, three days after the crash. As the volume of calls from both relatives and the media had subsided, the team felt that it was important to address issues in South Africa directly and to be with the families who had flown out. It also wanted to give relatives direct and personal support, and to ensure victims' bodies had been correctly identified prior to their repatriation to the UK. Some members of the team remained in Peterborough to sustain the incident response in the UK.

Of critical importance was the continued day-to-day running of the business. Liz Makin, Simon Laxton's deputy, took control of the rest of the business to ensure the company's many other customers received the level of service they would normally expect – in other words, that their holidays were not disrupted in any way by the coach crash.

Even though doctors at the Millpark Hospital were confident that it was safe for survivors to return to Britain by commercial airline, Thomas Cook Holidays, in conjunction with insurers Axa, decided to use air ambulances to ensure maximum comfort for those returning home.

The company also recognized the vital role the people of Lydenburg played during the accident. Many had gone to the scene of the crash to provide assistance to emergency teams dealing with the crash. A memorial service was organized by the South African authorities and attended by Simon Laxton, who wanted to thank the townspeople 'for their overwhelming compassion and support'.

Because of Thomas Cook Holidays' open and honest communication with the media from the outset about every action it was taking, media coverage was largely neutral and quickly shifted away from the Thomas Cook Holidays brand to road safety issues in South Africa.

There was no immediate or lasting damage to the company's reputation. The company's response reinforced its reputation as a responsible company genuinely committed to its customers' safety.

There was no backlash from families and friends of the victims. From the outset, it was clear that care of the survivors and all the families involved was the absolute priority. As a consequence, there was no financial impact.

MONITORING THE MEDIA

As discussed in Chapter 5, monitoring the media on a regular basis is one important way to spot evolving issues before they become full-blown crises – sometimes we call it 'crisis creep'.

But if it *has* hit the fan, monitoring what the media is saying about the situation is a crucial part of the response. If a serious factual error is broadcast or printed then no stone should be left unturned to have it corrected. Once a serious mistake appears in print or is stated on the broadcast media it becomes set in cement and repeated everywhere. In particular, it is important to remember the print media watch the broadcast media. Anything said on television or radio is likely to surface in newspaper stories. Financial journalists talk to fund managers and investment analysts. The lay media talk to the specialist media.

Retractions are difficult to obtain. The media do not like to admit they got it wrong. A published 'letter to the editor' does not carry anything like the same weight as the original article. The first thing to decide is whether the mistake is serious enough to make a fuss. If the error is only marginal a retraction or published letter to the editor may only serve to draw people's attention to the error again.

If it is truly serious help should be sought from the Press Complaints Commission (PCC), an independent organization that regulates 97 per cent of the UK's press and magazines (but can informally respond to complaints regarding the 3 per cent that doesn't fall under its jurisdiction). The average time for a complaint to be dealt with is 35 days.

The Independent Television Commission – to which complaints about independent television companies used to be placed – has ceased to exist. Its role has been taken over by Ofcom, the Office of Communications. Ofcom is the independent regulator and competition authority for the UK communications industries, with responsibilities across television, radio, telecommunications and wireless communication services. Evidence is required before Ofcom will formally investigate a complaint. Target timings for addressing complaints are four months for disputes and six to 12 months for complaints.

The BBC also has its own internal complaints watchdog. Responses to complaints made to it are usually received within 10 days. If there is a problem with editorial standards, the Editorial Complaints Unit (ECU) should be contacted. Then, if someone disputes the ECU ruling, that person can appeal within eight weeks to the BBC Trust's Editorial Standards Committee (ESC).

People can complain about the BBC to Ofcom about all issues except impartiality, inaccuracy and some commercial issues. These remain the responsibility of the BBC Trust under the Communications Act 2003.

SUMMARY

- The media cannot ever be ignored in crisis situations.
- Begin the communications process immediately.
- Crucial to the crisis response is for the CEO to be seen to take personal charge of the aftermath and to be the principal communicator – if he or she is good at it.
- In the aftermath, focus messages on how the organization feels about what has happened and what actions it is taking to remedy the situation.
- Establish the organization as the single authoritative source of information about what has happened and what is being done about it.
- Newspapers can be boycotted in the same way as other products.
- Monitor the media constantly throughout the crisis; leave no stone unturned in obtaining retractions for seriously inaccurate reporting.

10

The legal perspective

When lawyers talk about the law normal human beings begin to think about something else.

Richard Ingrams, former *Private Eye* editor

People are often quite rude about lawyers in crisis situations and, sometimes, this includes us. When we met with the chairman of Ultramar in the Shetland Islands one of his first questions was, 'Do we need to have a lawyer with us?' Our response was, 'Only on the end of the telephone'.

The problem can sometimes be that the training lawyers receive prepares them to think about crisis situations in a completely different way. Whereas we will advocate *telling it all, telling it fast and telling it truthfully*, lawyers will often advocate *saying nothing, doing nothing and admitting nothing*. What they don't always appreciate is the long-term consequences for an organization's reputation – and the knock-on effect on its financial bottom line. These can be far more damaging than any legal consequences.

Part of the trick is to get to the CEO of the company that is in trouble before the lawyer does. If he or she has already been in the hands of lawyers for several hours it often makes it more difficult to persuade the CEO to take a more 'open' course of action. Sometimes it makes it impossible. The lawyers advising the company that owned the *Bowbelle* dredger, which tragically collided into the stern of the floating disco *Marchioness* on the Thames one summer's evening in 1989, drowning 51 young people, wouldn't even allow the *Bowbelle*'s skipper to apologize publicly. The belief was saying 'sorry' amounted to an admission of liability.

This was blatant nonsense. Admitting sorrow does not mean the company is liable. What needs to be said is: 'We deeply regret this has happened and will leave no stone unturned in establishing the cause' – as Sir Michael Bishop did after the Kegworth aeroplane crash.

The intransigence of the lawyers, and the client's 'rabbit in the head-lights' faith in all they said, caused us to walk away from the *Bowbelle–Marchioness* tragedy – one of the very few times we have done so in 20 years of advising companies in difficulty.

The other part of the trick is to marshal arguments in support of a particular course of action in the same way as lawyers do – by referring to precedents. Having a detailed knowledge of crisis case studies, of what worked well and what didn't, will provide evidence to support advice. In part, we hope this book helps in providing such evidence.

LEGAL PITFALLS WHEN COMMUNICATING IN CRISIS

From a legal standpoint there are two cardinal sins which must never be committed when communicating in a crisis. The first is *never to admit liability* for what has happened. There will always be an official investigation of some sort into what has happened and this will establish who is liable. The second is *never to speculate* about the cause of the crisis.

When something goes wrong, the first question from the media and others is: 'How on earth did this happen?' And this is the one question which will always be impossible to answer, not least because the answer will not be available. *What* has happened will be known but *how* it happened will not. As we have seen already, an essential part of the response is to describe what has happened.

Reporters will push hard for speculation about possible causes. Speculative theories make the story more interesting. They may try to flatter the spokesperson by suggesting he or she has been in the industry for a long time and, given the seniority of the position, must have some idea about the cause. The temptation is to think: 'Yes, I am a senior person with long experience and I won't look credible if I am clueless about possible causes.' This temptation must be resisted at all costs, for two reasons.

If the speculated cause proves to be incorrect it will be taken as a deliberate attempt by the organization to hide the true facts of the matter – in other words, it will be seen as a 'cover-up'. More importantly, there will be a clause somewhere in the organization's insurance policies which states the cause of any incident must be agreed with the insurers before it is made public. If it is not but is nonetheless made public, the insurance companies have the legal right not to meet subsequent claims.

In the aftermath of the *Herald of Free Enterprise* ferry tragedy, a senior spokesman for Townsend Thoresen, the ferry operator, fell famously into the speculation trap. And when we were advising the manufacturers of Cuprinol, the wood-staining and preservative product, during a crisis situation, we faced a huge dilemma with the company's insurers.

CASE STUDY: *HERALD OF FREE ENTERPRISE*

On 6 March 1987 the *Herald of Free Enterprise*, a cross-channel ferry operated by Townsend Thoresen, left Zeebrugge harbour in Belgium on a routine return voyage to Dover. Before the vessel had passed through the harbour exit it suddenly filled with water and turned over on to its side. The tragedy claimed the lives of 193 passengers and crew.

Shortly afterwards a senior executive from the company gave a television interview in which he was asked how the accident had happened. He speculated the ferry had 'hit the harbour wall' on its departure. 'Ferry hit the harbour wall' ran as the headline in newspapers for days. Thereafter the company battened down the hatches and gave few additional interviews, stating it had to deal with the operational aftermath of the tragedy.

This immediately made the media suspicious. The company's lack of communication prompted deeper investigation by reporters who soon established the ferry had not 'hit the harbour wall' but had sailed from Zeebrugge while closing its bow doors.

This caused huge quantities of water to enter the vessel and destabilize it. The media soon discovered Townsend Thoresen always operated their vessels in this way because it provided a quicker turn-round time at either end of the passage. Not only were accusations of a cover-up instantaneous but media reports claimed 193 people had died because of the company's 'corporate greed'. As with Pan Am after Lockerbie, the public lost confidence in the ferry operator and chose Sealink ferries instead.

The irony was that, just a few weeks before the tragedy, Townsend Thoresen had been acquired by the much bigger shipping line, P&O. The acquisition had been made largely because of the goodwill associated with the Townsend Thoresen name. After erosion of public confidence, however, P&O had no option but to paint out the name of Townsend Thoresen from vessel sides and replace it with its own. Townsend Thoresen, as an entity, vanished altogether.

Corporate manslaughter

The law regarding corporate manslaughter was revised in the UK in 2007. UK companies whose gross negligence leads to the death of individuals now face prosecution for manslaughter. Organizations face unlimited fines if they are found to have caused death due to gross corporate health and safety failures. Directors and other company personnel no longer face prison sentences. There is no individual liability. But the new Act (the Corporate Manslaughter and Corporate Homicide Act 2007) will make it easier to prosecute companies that fail to protect people. Companies can be held liable for manslaughter where gross failures in the management of health and safety cause death.

The Act lifts Crown immunity to prosecution – Crown bodies such as government departments and police forces will be liable for prosecution for the first time.

SO WHAT IS THE LAWYER'S ROLE IN A CRISIS?

It is about protection. Specifically, to protect:

- the company from criminal prosecution;
- the company from future liability;
- officers and employees;
- the company's position with insurers and regulators;
- documents.

In a crisis it is essential to preserve records of everything. There is a legal duty to preserve and eventually disclose in litigation relevant documents which are in the company's possession even if they are compromising or damaging. The legal process of 'discovery' demands all relevant documents to be handed over to officials investigating what has gone wrong, with the exception of 'legally privileged documents'. Legally privileged documents and communication are immune from discovery even, in some cases, from regulatory authorities.

There are two types of privilege, 'legal advice privilege' and 'litigation privilege'. Legal advice privilege is confidential communication between the client and the lawyer, whether the lawyer is from an independent firm or is the in-house counsel. Litigation privilege extends to confidential communication between the client or lawyer and third parties such as expert consultants, provided litigation has started or is in reasonable prospect.

Lawyers will advise companies to photograph or photocopy everything, particularly anything that may have to be removed by the company, the emergency services or regulators. It is also vital that any internal enquiry into an incident is led by a lawyer for it to have any legal standing. The lawyer will take detailed statements from employees, contractors and others involved in the incident as soon as possible and collect and secure any supporting documents or other form of evidence.

Counsel may want to see press releases before they are issued. This is fine if the lawyer understands the public relations requirements of a crisis. We have, however, seen clear, constructive, communicative, not legally damaging press releases turned into meaningless gobbledegook at the hands of a lawyer. The writing of press releases is the preserve of the public relations professional. Advice may be needed from the lawyer on the approach but not on the words used. One final point: press releases may be produced in court after a crisis because they provide a useful – sometimes damaging – 'snapshot' of the company's position at the time of issue – so they *do* need to be accurate.

COMPENSATION

Compensation for injured parties soon appears as an issue in newspaper stories covering a crisis. How much will be paid, by whom and how quickly?

A company that states publicly it will pay compensation to victims and their families is admitting liability for the event. So this must be avoided unless liability has been proven. On the other hand, any suggestion of callousness or complacency on the matter of compensation is out of the question. An appropriate response runs as follows:

> Right now we are doing everything we possibly can to help the families of the deceased and to ensure those injured are receiving the best possible treatment. The question of compensation will be determined by the outcome of the official investigation.

EX-GRATIA PAYMENTS

Affected families may face immediate financial hardship in the aftermath of an accident. It is wise for companies to have in place a policy – as well as a readily accessible budget – to make sums of money available to such families, for example to meet funeral expenses. These are called 'ex-gratia payments'.

Ex-gratia payments do not constitute admission of liability. They represent an act of helpfulness – and are seen as such. If, ultimately, the company that has made such payments is found not to be at fault it can reclaim its costs from the insurance companies of whoever is found to have been at fault. Never, however, reveal the amounts involved. They are a private matter between the company and families involved. This can be stated publicly in response to media questions on the subject.

SUMMARY

- The long-term consequences for an organization's reputation, and subsequent knock-on impact on its bottom line, can be more damaging than any legal consequences.
- Expressing regret for what has happened does not constitute an admission of liability.
- Refer to precedents when arguing the communications case against the legal case.
- Never, ever admit liability unless it has been proven.
- Never, ever speculate about the cause.
- If accused, use authoritative third parties to demonstrate your innocence; your own protestations will rarely be sufficient.
- Don't dodge the compensation question.
- Be prepared to make ex-gratia payments; they don't constitute liability.
- Don't have blind faith in the advice of lawyers and insurance companies; they can get it wrong too.

11

Planning for the unexpected

Today my stockbroker tried to get me to buy some 10-year bonds. I told him: 'Young man, at this point I don't even buy green bananas'.

US congressman when getting on in years

Executives, preoccupied with the market pressures of the present quarter, are not inclined to pay much attention to planning for future crises. However, it is instructive here to recall that Noah started building the ark *before* it began to rain.

Crises are often turning points in organizational life. They represent opportunities to establish a reputation for competence, to shape the organization and to tackle important issues. In most crises, because time is at a premium and resource allocation critical, company executives need strategic guidelines on what kinds of action are needed.

CALM AND POSITIVE THINKING

Taking action in a crisis can be fraught with risk. A strategy is needed for deciding when to define a situation as a crisis, when to take action and to work with others in solving the crisis. Such a strategic sense is in itself a great advantage when tension develops. The ability to keep cool when everything is collapsing is a quality valued in leaders, especially since apparent confidence by the leader is so reassuring to subordinates. Advance planning makes it more possible to concentrate on the actual problem when it peaks, and provides a framework for action.

Crisis management is about seizing the initiative – taking control of what has happened before it engulfs the organization. Planning to manage crises and issues is the key to corporate survival.

Those who are alert to the possibility that any event, even a crisis, is an opportunity to gain friends, to enlist support and, possibly, to attract new customers or shareholders, are well prepared to seize the initiative. Failure to have in place well-tried and tested contingency plans for every kind of emergency means, when the unexpected does occur, the company can only assume a combative posture; it is, of necessity, put into a defensive frame of mind.

Assuming a primarily defensive position establishes a negative attitude. It focuses thinking on reacting to conditions instead of the company acting on its own initiative. When a whole company is put into a negative frame of mind it is virtually certain to be seen as arrogant and unsympathetic to others – evidenced by Exxon Corporation's response to the *Valdez* oil spill. Instead, when positioned to deal not only with the crisis but also the inherent opportunities, a proactive posture can be established which leads to a positive attitude rather than a siege mentality.

DEEDS VERSUS DECLARATIONS

A second principle, perhaps of even greater importance, is that deeds build a reputation far more effectively than words in advertisements or glossy brochures. In today's climate of corporate accountability, promises – words alone – are greeted with cynicism or disbelief. Such an approach actually creates a target for attack should the slightest lapse in performance occur. Nothing gladdens the public heart so much as a fall from grace by the excessively righteous. Self-aggrandizement campaigns lack credibility because everyone knows the sponsor accentuates the beauty spots and hides the warts.

A record of responsible deeds is a vital ingredient for a positive image. The essence of a good reputation rests not in trying to conjure up a good story to hide substandard performance, but in sensitizing management to the need to adjust performance so the deeds speak for themselves. The guiding principles of crisis management are to:

- Develop a positive attitude towards crisis management.

- Bring performance throughout the organization into line with public expectation. Build credibility through a succession of responsible deeds.
- Seek and act on the opportunities during a crisis.

It boils down to deeds versus declarations. A record of responsible deeds is the organization's insurance policy when and if something goes wrong.

PLANNING TO MANAGE THE CRISIS

Anything which can go wrong, will go wrong.

Murphy's Law

The principles applying to crisis management planning are broadly the same for virtually all types of corporate crises. Methods for implementing the plan will not vary greatly for different types of crisis. It is usually impossible to anticipate every crisis which can arise but there are steps every company can take to prepare for one.

A coherent approach begins with the identification of potential crises. These may include:

- existing situations which have the potential to become crises;
- crises which have beset the company in the past – or other companies in the same industry – and might recur;
- planned activity which may meet with opposition from stakeholder groups.

The need is to catalogue the areas of risk: to assess the risk parameters. From this starting point it becomes easier to think through the logical series of steps which need to be taken in the crisis management planning process.

The audit process needs to be undertaken against our definition of a crisis in Chapter 6. The list then needs to be prioritized. A list which is too long will lose credibility with senior management. Since 'buy-in' from senior management is crucial to the whole process of crisis management planning, the list should be prioritized according to likely impact on the organization's financial bottom line. This will attract and sustain senior management attention.

Having identified likely areas of risk, the next questions to ask are:

1. Does the company have policies and procedures in place to prevent a risk from turning into a crisis?
2. Do plans exist for dealing with every aspect of the crisis should it occur?
3. Have the plans been tested to ensure that they work satisfactorily?

Various supplementary, but equally important, questions may be added. For example:

4. Which are the audiences most likely to be affected by the identified potential crisis?
5. Do plans include procedures for communicating effectively to these about what has happened and what is being done about it?
6. Have the communications aspects of the plan been tested, as well as the company's operational response?

In short, planning for crisis management may be summarized as:

- *cataloguing potential crisis situations;*
- *devising policies for their prevention;*
- *formulating strategies and tactics for dealing with each potential crisis;*
- *identifying who will be affected by them;*
- *devising effective communications channels to those affected so as to minimize damage to the organization's reputation;*
- *testing everything.*

How to manage the process is shown in Figure 11.1.

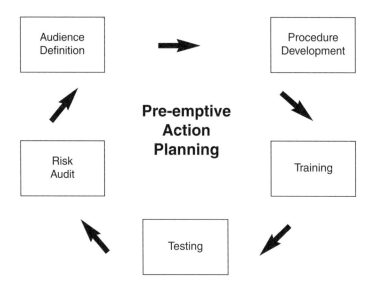

Figure 11.1 *Managing the process*

APPOINTING THE TEAMS

To manage and contain the crisis, three separate teams will be required; the Strategic Crisis Management Team, the Incident Management Team and the Communication Team (the role of the Communication Team is discussed in the next chapter).

The Strategic Crisis Management Team

This will comprise main board directors whose role is to take the 'high ground' of the crisis, considering such aspects as:

- whether the situation can worsen;
- business continuity; product sourcing and supply;
- contingency budget approvals;
- high-level communication with, for example, the overseas head office, government ministers and members of parliament;
- content of messages for institutional investors, the media, customers, employees and other affected groups;
- the insurance position; liaison with legal advisers; ex-gratia payments;
- tracking what is happening to people; preparing to make hospital/ family visits;
- *above all*, ensuring the chairman or CEO is briefed and on the way to the site, accompanied by a public relations professional, as quickly as possible, to begin the media communication process.

Members of the team need to be grouped together in a 'war room' adequately equipped with telephones, fax machines, internet access, photocopiers, a television and radio (to monitor news reports) and boards around the room on which new information and decisions are recorded. The role of the log-keeper cannot be underestimated. He or she must be a long-standing company employee, intimately familiar with the business and its technical jargon but capable of writing clearly and succinctly in lay language.

It helps to have the boards inscribed with permanent headings so information can be clearly organized, for example:

People
Incident status
Environment
Weather
Product supply

Each team member must be assigned specific, individual responsibility for these key functions. They must be aware of their responsibilities and have rehearsed them. Each member of the Strategic Team should have an 'alternative' in case someone is away. The team leader *must* chair regular information update meetings for all the team members, as often as every 15 minutes in a fast-moving situation.

The Incident Management Team

The second team to come into play is the Incident Management Team, responsible for the immediate 'hands on' operational response. The distinction between this team and the Strategic Team is crucial. Neither should interfere with the other but the Incident Management Team – which will be located at the site of the crisis – must keep the Strategic Team constantly updated with developments. *It should have a member dedicated solely to this task.* Equally, the Strategic Team – probably located at the head office – must provide the Incident Management Team with strategic advice and rapid budget approvals for urgent areas of expenditure (see Figure 11.2).

The Incident Management Team will also need a dedicated 'war room' for its members. Plans should include identification of an off-site 'war room' in case the site has had to be evacuated.

In addition to the materials and equipment already described, the 'war rooms' of each team should be equipped with plans depicting:

- locations of hazardous materials;
- sources of safety equipment;
- fire-water system and alternative source of water;
- stocks of other types of fire extinguishers;
- plant entrances and road systems, updated to include any road which is impassable;
- assembly points and casualty centres;
- location of plant in relation to the surrounding community;
- areas affected or endangered;
- deployment of emergency vehicles and personnel;
- areas where further problems may arise, eg fractured pipelines;
- area evacuated;
- other relevant information.

COMMUNICATION HARDWARE

Since the unexpected tends to happen at Sunday lunchtime or on Christmas Eve, a comprehensive, foolproof cascade call-out procedure is

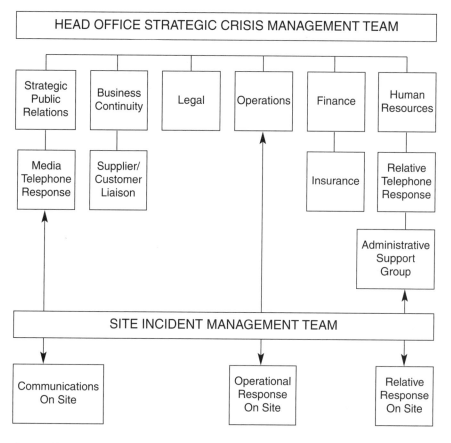

Source: Regester and Larkin training package

Figure 11.2 *Responsibilities and interactions of crisis teams*

required with back-up alternates to stand in for key individuals who are not contactable. The cascade principle involves each member of the teams having the responsibility to call out at least two other team members once he or she has been called.

Facilities and hardware for communication need to be checked. Are key individuals equipped with mobile telephones or pagers? How would the switchboard cope with floods of additional telephone calls? (Occidental Oil took 4,500 additional calls from the media and relatives in the first 24 hours after the Piper Alpha tragedy; Perrier took 3,000, over the same period, in the UK alone – see Chapter 12 for advice on handling telephone calls.)

CRISIS PREVENTION

While it will be the responsibility of the Strategic Crisis Management, Incident Management and Communication Teams to manage and contain the crisis, yet another group of people is required to ensure the crisis doesn't happen in the first place – we call this the Crisis Prevention Team. Ideally, it should be made up from members of the other three teams. It doesn't come into play when the crisis occurs but should have been instrumental in minimizing the size of the crisis if it does occur – and in preparing and rehearsing the other teams to respond effectively when it does.

Crisis Prevention Team

This team formulates and sets company-wide policies appropriate to the hazards or risks of the business. It needs to ensure managers of each part of the business have the funds and other resources required to enable them to comply with policies – *as well as responsibility for implementing them.*

Such policies need to go beyond ensuring the organization merely complies with existing regulations. They must endeavour to anticipate 'worst case' scenarios. This approach is likely to prove more costly but the cost involved of not setting such far-reaching policies can prove catastrophic in terms of human lives and the company's entire future. Developing policies against agreed company criteria will help to give them shape and depth. Such criteria can be developed by answering the following questions:

- Would this situation really affect our bottom line?
- How realistic is the identified potential crisis situation?
- Could corporate action halt or moderate the crisis?
- Does the policy stand up to public scrutiny?
- Are the resources to act available?
- Is the *will* to act present?
- What would be the effect of inaction?

A positive approach to crisis management demands the implementation of preventive policies which have been developed and checked on a regular basis. Part of the Crisis Prevention Team's remit must be to conduct audits to check policy implementation.

Take, for example, a manufacturing company being audited for implementation of policies to prevent a physical crisis. Each year the audit group might select an audit programme which examines different topics – safety and loss prevention, air and water quality, solid waste disposal, occupational health and product quality.

Sites selected for audit can be based on their risk potential, their recent performance and the length of time since last audited. To lend weight to the audit process, the Crisis Prevention Team needs to report twice yearly to the main board on the status of the risk audit programme and measures required to minimize new areas of risk.

This audit process works well because it takes an objective view of each situation and ensures appropriate standards are applied across all divisions. The continuing interest displayed by the board gives authority to the Crisis Prevention Team and ensures divisional and local management corrects deficiencies.

Auditing for potential financial crises

The same audit process can be applied to potential financial risks. For example, the Crisis Prevention Team adopts the protagonist role of an unwanted bidder and looks for tell-tale signs of weakness in the company's performance which could make it an easy prey. The danger signals are likely to include:

- static or falling earnings;
- poor return on capital;
- unhealthy dividend policy;
- bad cash management;
- too high gearing;
- poor investment policy;
- too many, difficult to justify, rights issues;
- unimaginative asset management (including well-stocked pension fund or cash mountain);
- neglected or poor communication with investors and their advisers;
- major shareholder suddenly disposing of shares;
- forthcoming tax or protectionist legislation;
- business synergy with the predator (improved earnings prospects of the combined companies);
- marketing synergy;
- knocking you out as direct competition;
- acquiring your management team;
- acquiring your production capacity.

External advisers – bankers, brokers and specialist public relations consultants – should be brought in to assist with the financial risk audit. Such advisers need to be reviewed regularly to ensure they are not also the advisers to potential predators.

The most important point to keep in mind is the worst case scenario approach. Organizations will rarely be criticized for considering every aspect of the situation and acting accordingly.

Appointment of the Crisis Prevention Team will demonstrate the organization's commitment to responsible management of its business. If it does its job effectively, the team will minimize the risk of a crisis occurring in the first place, will help to contain it if it should occur, will reduce the potential damage to the organization's reputation, and will change the organization's culture from responsive to positive. In summary, the role of the Crisis Prevention Team is to:

- anticipate, clearly and comprehensively, all forms of crisis situations;
- develop strategies and procedures for dealing with them;
- check policies and procedures are implemented;
- ensure they are rehearsed and updated on a regular basis.

SELECTING TEAM MEMBERS

Various leadership styles emerge in crisis situations. While the 'human' participative manager is generally the most effective leader, he or she can sometimes inhibit the rapid decision taking required in an emergency. On the other hand, the authoritarian leader may act decisively at the expense of demotivating the team members and inhibiting creativity. It is vital for team leaders to recognize team members' different attributes and values and integrate them to maximum advantage during the crisis.

Members of all teams involved should be chosen for their personal qualities and talents – breadth of vision, ability to stay cool, knowledge of the company and its business, and the ability to make swift, clearly expressed decisions.

Some of the styles we have seen emerge include:

- *The 'ideas' person* – a creative member who is constantly injecting new ideas and suggestions. Some of these may be far-fetched but some may have real merit. It is vital for the leader to filter out the viable ideas and discard the remainder without discouraging the flow.
- *The communicator* – the individual who helps the flow of information both within and outside the team (not necessarily the team leader, although the team leader should possess strong communication skills also).
- *The doom merchant* – the devil's advocate who brings out the negative aspects of each proposed idea or solution.
- *The book-keeper* – the neat and orderly member who wants the records and logs maintained to perfection. This individual is more comfortable in such a role than as a decision maker. Nonetheless, it is a vital role.

- *The humanist* – the people-oriented member whose solutions always focus on the human aspects of the problem – an important visionary in the heat of the moment.

PUTTING THE PLAN IN WRITING

The importance of putting the plan in writing cannot be overestimated. In our experience, too often the communication plans do not exist at all – or exist in the heads of a few individuals. Companies must overcome the 'Joe will know what to do if it happens' syndrome; Joe may be on holiday – or dead. Even if he is available, he will be too busy to explain plans which should be readily available for all concerned.

Absence of a written plan will cause hours of additional work for an already fraught management. People will fail to take basic actions; for example, failure to notify employees in an emergency will lead to a flood of unnecessary phone calls about the effect of the incident on work schedules. Valuable time will be lost and tempers grow short because names and telephone numbers are not available when needed.

Checklists of things to do and people to contact are invaluable in enabling the organization to 'hit the ground running' when the crisis occurs. In a chaotic situation it's a huge relief to be able to hand to subordinates lists of things to do, giving assurance that all the essential steps will be taken.

The plan must not be too long or rigid. It must provide the flexibility and framework which acknowledge the unpredictable aspects of any crisis situation; and give management the leeway to use common sense. It needs a structure, but a loose one.

Put the plan in writing and assign a 'champion' to ensure it is kept up to date with changes to the business and movement of personnel.

TESTING EVERYTHING

Remaining familiar with the plan's content is always a problem. The best way is through crisis exercise simulations to test effectiveness of procedures and training. But first those with key roles should receive training. There is no situation more demoralizing than running an exercise in which everyone comprehensively screws up. Worse, it puts management off doing it again. No one likes to make a fool of themselves.

A crucial ingredient to successful exercise simulations is getting the scenario right. Particularly if they have not previously participated in an exercise, management members will take part only reluctantly, believing they have 'more important things to do' and the whole business is a waste of time. If the scenario is in any way unrealistic they will refuse to continue and retire triumphant in the knowledge it *was* a waste of time.

It is also important to ensure simulations are not too complex to begin with. Testing the plan initially with a 'desktop' simulation will encourage management members to participate later in more complex, realistic simulations.

When running the simulation, a good mechanism for making the mock incident evolve over real or imagined time is to feed in printed details of each new phase of the scenario and predetermined times.

For example, the person in charge of the response will receive a message stating:

> You have just learnt from the general manager of the company's manufacturing plant in Manchester that an explosion has taken place in or near the main chemicals storage depot. Several employees are unaccounted for, feared dead or injured in the wreckage. Reporters are arriving at the factory gate and many are phoning the company. The local MP is on the phone and wishes to speak to you urgently. Take appropriate action.

He or she will receive a series of such messages, sometimes at intervals of only a few minutes, and will then activate the Strategic Crisis Management Team and Communications Team. Role-playing journalists, relatives, MPs, investors, investment analysts and environmental lobbyists start putting pressure on the company. Television camera crews arrive at the head office, as well as at the Manchester plant, demanding interviews. Every aspect of the company's response procedures is put to the test.

The simulation should last for four or five hours. It should conclude with a 'live', filmed press conference and be followed up with an immediate debrief on the response – a 'hot washup'. Later, a more considered written report should be produced clearly identifying agreed areas for improvement and whose responsibility it is for their implementation.

In our experience, those who have participated in the simulation generally rate their performance unrealistically highly. This is to be expected because of the sense of reality and unusual nature of the experience. A second evaluation needs to be provided, by qualified outside experts, which, while constructive, is more realistic. Simulations should be run once or twice a year to ensure recommendations from the previous one have been implemented and to take account of changes in the business and movement of personnel.

SUMMARY

- Develop a positive attitude towards crisis management.
- Bring the organization's performance into line with public expectation.
- Build credibility through a succession of responsible deeds.
- Be prepared to act on the opportunities during a crisis.
- Appoint appropriate teams to prevent, manage and control crisis situations.
- Catalogue potential crisis situations.
- Devise policies for their prevention.
- Put the plan in writing.
- Test, test and test again.

12

Crisis communications management

Let our advance worrying become advance thinking and planning.

Winston Churchill

The best-laid plans are worthless if they cannot be communicated.

Speed is of the essence. A crisis simply will not wait. Tell it all, tell it fast, tell it truthfully – and don't stop until the plague of locusts has had enough or found a richer source of food elsewhere. It's like wrestling a gorilla: you rest when the gorilla rests.

BACKGROUND INFORMATION TO SEIZE THE INITIATIVE

The first hour – known as the 'Golden Hour' – is critical. The 'information void' will be guaranteed to loom because of lack of hard facts about the incident. The void, however, can be bridged by offering the media background information on the company or installation which has been affected. This produces two results: the first is the creation of valuable breathing space to gather and check information about the incident before its release to the media; and it demonstrates to the media that the organization is clearly going to cooperate and communicate with them. Reporters who gather or telephone to cover the story will usually know nothing about the company, its plant and operations. Offering background information enables them to begin framing the story they will later write or broadcast.

So it is essential to keep updated background information available for the website (see page 229) about the organization and each installation or part of the operation considered potentially at risk. Information should include:

- colour and black and white photographs;
- diagrams;
- basic information about:
  - number of employees;
  - how long in business;
  - business description;
  - names of key executives;
  - safety record and practices.

Such packs located at the organization's headquarters as well as at each site at risk, where the media may descend in droves, will help the company to seize the initiative and prevent it from disappearing into the void.

SET UP A PRESS CENTRE

It may not be possible, or advisable, to hold press conferences on company premises. Reconnaissance work needs to be done near each site considered at risk and arrangements made, perhaps with a local hotel, town or village hall, which could be quickly established as a centre for the media during the emergency. The media should be informed of the times of press conferences – and these must be adhered to. They will talk to others between each conference but at least the company will have the opportunity to tell its own story once or twice a day, and to correct misinformation picked up by journalists. Around 10.30 and 15.30 are generally regarded as suitable times for holding press conferences because they meet the majority of deadlines.

MANAGING THE PRESS CONFERENCE

This can be a nightmare. Hundreds of potentially hostile journalists gathered at one location have been enough to make grown men cry. Training and preparation are the keys. The press conference site should contain:

- two entrances, one for use by management and the other by the media;
- a large diagram of the site or other visual aid material which will help to explain what has happened;
- background information press packs;
- refreshments (not alcohol);
- toilet facilities;
- adequate security measures to ensure control of persons, either on or off site, with particular regard to their safety.

Useful tips to assist with the successful management of press conferences include:

- Restrict the numbers of the management team to only those with specific knowledge of different aspects of the incident; *never* fall into the 'comfort in numbers' trap at the top table since this only provides the media with more targets to snipe at. Ensure it is chaired by a senior company executive *provided* he or she is a good communicator.
- Place a time parameter on the conference if members of management need to get back to dealing with the problem in hand; *never* less than 30 minutes. End the conference at the specified time.
- Try to issue a new press release at the *conclusion* of the conference. Have copies placed strategically at the exit door for the media so they are encouraged to use them, allowing the management to exit via their own door.

Press conferences rarely work well on television. It is best to arrange one-to-one television interviews after the conference. Never exclude television cameras from the press conference, however, as British Gas did famously when announcing the resignation of its much maligned chief executive, Cedric Brown, and the demerger of the company.

Although the company had arranged for one-to-one television interviews after the conference, broadcast journalists became infuriated when they and their cameras were excluded from the conference itself. Revenge was achieved by filming Cedric Brown leaving the conference, struggling to get through the throng of angry broadcast reporters, and being bonked on the head by a camera. A general picture of chaos – not helpful to the company's beleaguered reputation at the time – was created, which television companies delighted in showing the rest of the world on prime time news programmes.

Insist, however, that television cameras are situated at the back of the room and not allowed to gather round the table to get those nice close-up shots. This will only serve to further intimidate management and anger the print media who will not be able to see a thing.

There is another good reason for arranging television interviews after the press conference. If someone has made a mess of answering questions during the press conference the television interview provides an opportunity to rectify the error. When we were in the Shetland Islands during the *Braer* disaster, the vessel's owner was asked at one press conference: 'In the light of what has happened will you in future continue to route vessels through the narrow passage between the southern end of the islands and the north of Scotland?' He replied that thousands of vessels had plied this route for hundreds of years and he saw no reason for changing it.

This was a big mistake. The next day, the *Today* newspaper covered its front page with a huge photograph of a pathetic-looking oiled seal beneath the caption: 'I'd do it again – *Braer* vessel owner'. However, before giving a television interview for the BBC after the press conference he was suitably admonished by his public relations adviser and proceeded to provide the correct answer during the television interview: 'We will look carefully at the findings and recommendations of the official enquiry into the accident and, of course, we will adopt any recommendations which improve safety and minimize damage to the environment'. Millions more people watch television than read newspapers so, to some extent, the mistake had been rectified.

A final point to remember about giving television interviews after the press conference is that the company may be besieged with requests for such interviews and may not be able to cope because of other pressures. If this is *genuinely* the case, and can be seen as such, the 'pooling' arrangement can come into play. 'Pooling' simply means explaining to the broadcast media that there is insufficient time to meet all their demands for interviews but the company is prepared to give one interview which the broadcast media can share. The media will select from among their number who is to conduct the interview and which film crew will be used. They then share the resulting footage or radio tape.

DEALING WITH THE TELEVISION INTERVIEW

Training of television spokespeople is absolutely vital against crisis scenarios – partly to teach techniques and give confidence but also to discover who is good at it and who isn't.

Basic tips to remember are:

- Prepare three main points which, if appropriate, refer to people first, damage to the environment or property second and financial consequences third.
- If possible, rehearse the interview beforehand.
- Never speculate about the cause of the incident; instead say, 'The cause will be established once a full investigation has been completed.'
- Anticipate the worst possible questions and devise suitable answers.
- Praise the actions of third-party bodies, such as the police, fire brigade, etc.
- Never point the finger of blame at the company, employees or third parties.
- Eyeball the interviewer; never talk to the camera unless it is a down-the-line interview.
- Ensure the three main points are communicated irrespective of the questions asked.
- Jump on untruths, innuendo or misleading remarks immediately; interrupt if necessary.

COPING WITH HUNDREDS OF TELEPHONE CALLS

Few companies have more elaborate arrangements for dealing with incoming telephone calls from the media and relatives of employees than those in the oil industry. From our own experience of attempting and failing miserably to handle thousands of such telephone calls during one of the industry's worst disasters – at Bantry Bay in southwest Ireland, in January 1979, when an oil tanker, the *Betelgeuse*, blew up killing 50 people – we have helped the North Sea oil industry to pioneer a telephone response system, which is today widely used by many of the utilities, airlines, chemical, pharmaceutical, engineering and food companies. It was this system that was used so successfully during the Buncefield fire, when hundreds of media calls were received in the first 48 hours.

Since no company, whatever its industry, has a public relations or human resources department with sufficient people in it to cope with such pressure, the solution is to train employees from other disciplines within the organization in techniques for handling calls from these two vital audiences. Occidental Oil had a team of 40 trained responders in Aberdeen, and a back-up team of 20 in London, when the Piper Alpha production platform exploded late one evening in 1988. The teams helped the company to cope with some 4,500 telephone calls during the first 24 hours.

Responding to media calls

Incoming telephone calls from the media will far outweigh the numbers of reporters able to get to the site. Sometimes there is nothing to see, only people to talk to, as in the case of a company collapse or fraudulent activity. Aeroplanes, ships and oil rigs can disappear altogether. So the telephone becomes an incredibly important channel of communication.

We advise companies to designate a media telephone response room equipped with sufficient handsets and its own dedicated telephone number which can be quickly issued via the wire services in the event of an emergency. This prevents the main switchboard from becoming jammed up and allows the normal business of the day to continue. It can be a meeting room in which the handsets are stored in a cupboard ready to be plugged into jackpoints around the room at a moment's notice.

Other items to be kept in readiness for the media telephone response teams include:

- pads of numbered log sheets for each team member;
- a filing box for each individual;
- flip charts and pens;
- whiteboard and appropriate pens;
- map of the affected site;
- fax machine and photocopier;
- refreshments;
- 'fast facts' file about the company and affected installation.

'Fast facts' is a term we coined to describe the media telephone team's equivalent to the background information pack. Written in conversational language and carefully indexed, it contains the answers to every antici-pated question reporters might ask in a crisis situation. It also contains a list of questions about every conceivable kind of crisis the company may face so the answers can be filled in at the outset of the emergency. These questions act as an *aide-mémoire* to obtaining crucial information which may be forgotten in the heat of the moment.

A common mistake made by companies in crisis is to issue information to the media only via press releases. But, as we will see, press releases can take a long time to prepare and distribute in crisis situations.

There must be a constant flow of information from the Incident Management Team's 'war room' to the media responders, so it is helpful to have the two teams located close to each other. Where this is not possible there needs to be an open telephone line between the 'war room' and the media responders so new information may be constantly accessed and passed on to them. New information, which is authorized for disclo-sure, is written on the whiteboards.

Whenever new information becomes available the supervisor in charge of the media response team – ideally a public relations professional although others can be trained in the role – gives the team a signal which means 'phones off the hook'. Responders finish their telephone conversations and the new information is gone through until every team member is confident about its meaning and comfortable with words to express the information.

Such briefing periods are also used to anticipate new questions which are bound to arise from the newly issued information. For example, the new information may state the site has been evacuated, but not where it has been evacuated to. The process of obtaining answers to these questions can begin immediately and, hopefully, be received before the question is even put.

RESPONDING TO CALLS FROM RELATIVES

This is often the most ignored area of crisis communication management yet it is one of the most important, for two reasons. Any inability to respond sympathetically with information about employees to callers will only add to their anguish. And it will frustrate and anger the caller who may resort to calling a local or national newspaper thereby compounding the public relations problem.

It is also one of the most complex aspects of the crisis communications response. Few organizations have efficient systems for tracking who was on the site when it happened, although these are improving. But if the company is unable to confirm quickly whether or not an employee was present and provide the caller with information about his or her status, initial anger will turn to fury.

Many companies ask employees to fill in forms stating which family member should be notified in the event of something happening to the employee – but don't keep these records up to date. People's situations change and information may be given unwittingly to the wrong person.

When the Piper Alpha tragedy occurred Occidental Oil flew relatives of everyone who had been on board the stricken platform to Aberdeen. It took over the Skean Dhu hotel at Aberdeen airport to accommodate everyone. Generous and correct though this action was, the company failed to keep track of who it was flying to Aberdeen. Some of the men working offshore were leading complicated lives and more than one wife claiming the same husband turned up at the hotel. The rest is best left to the imagination.

When the questions come they are nearly always the same:

- Was he there when it happened?
- If he was, is he all right?

- If he is uninjured, where is he now and when can I expect to see/speak to him?
- If he has been injured, how serious are his injuries and which hospital has he been taken to?
- Will you help me to get there?

If the worst has happened and the employee has died, this information must obviously never be given down the telephone. The police will want to inform the family but, if possible, they should be accompanied by a senior company representative.

CASE STUDY: MISINFORMATION OVER MINING DEATHS IN VIRGINIA – IN A CRISIS NO INFORMATION IS MORE IMPORTANT THAN CORRECT INFORMATION TO FAMILIES

On the morning of 3 January 2006, 13 coal miners became trapped by an explosion in a mine shaft in the Sago Mine, West Virginia. The cause was suspected to have been lightning. Initial rescue efforts were called off after a build-up of dangerous gas. But this was quickly pumped out, allowing rescue efforts to resume.

Joe Manchin, governor of West Virginia, speculated that as long as the miners had survived the explosion they could survive underground for some time. This was echoed by Ben Hatfield, the head of International Coal Group (ICG), which operated the Sago Mine. The miners were equipped with basic food, water and seven hours of clean air. Hundreds of friends and relatives congregated at a nearby Baptist church to await news. A Red Cross volunteer said that several had passed out and others were crying.

On 4 January, the body of one of the 13 miners was found. Ben Hatfield admitted that hopes were 'certainly stretched thin at this point'. He added that it was a 'very good thing' that the vehicle used to transport the men in the mine was found to be empty.

Later that day, and through a process that is still not totally clear, relatives were led to believe all the men had been found alive. Joe Manchin said the news was a 'miracle'. However, about three hours later, Ben Hatfield told them that all but one had died. The news provoked an angry and emotional reaction at the church (events unfolded in the early hours of the morning, which didn't help), with one relative allegedly lunging at Hatfield. State troopers and an armed SWAT team were sent to sit near the church in case of violence. Relatives accused ICG of lying to them and were unhappy that a member of the rescue team hadn't been talking to them. They threatened legal action and vowed to shut the mine down.

Ben Hatfield blamed the reports on 'miscommunication'. He said:

ICG never made any release about all 12 miners being alive and well. We simply couldn't confirm that at that point… but that information spread like wildfire because it had come from the command centre, but it was bad information… there was desperation for good information. They wanted to share it. I don't think anyone had a clue how much damage was about to be created. And we truly regret that.

He added, 'Welcome to the worst day of my life.' Fire chief Joe Tallman of the Washington District Fire Department said that no one should shoulder the blame for the miscommunication. Governor Manchin also apologized for the mistaken information.

The ICG said that it knew within 20 minutes that reports of the survivors were inaccurate, but wanted to inform relatives and friends only when they were sure of each miner's fate. Hatfield said: 'Rightly or wrongly, we believed it was important to make factual statements to the families and we believe that word had been sent to the church to indicate that additional reports may not be correct.'

The miners had apparently survived the explosion but had been overcome by toxic fumes. The Sago Mine was listed as having 208 minor health violations in 2005.

The sole survivor of the incident wrote a letter to the relatives of the deceased that contained the allegations that at least four of the miners' air packs had failed. The ICG said the packs were checked regularly by the US mine safety authority. He also alleged that prior to the accident he noticed that a gas leak had been incorrectly plugged with glue.

Less than a month after the incident, two men died in another West Virginia mine when a fire broke out.

Media coverage

The incident was also a wrap on the knuckles for the many newspapers that carried the headlines of the initial reports of the miners surviving. The *New York Times*, *Washington Post* and *USA Today* all carried stories of survival, which were made to look woefully behind with events when read the next day. Many pundits criticized the newspapers for not waiting for more official confirmation that the miners had survived. Some newspapers later published how the story was handled, while others, notably the *Boston Globe*, said they had little other choice.

CBS News said: 'Perhaps not since "Dewey Defeats Truman" has the nation awoken to newspaper headlines so wrong.' (The *Chicago Daily Tribune* incorrectly named the winner of the 1948 presidential election.)

The *Pittsburgh Post-Gazette* said:

The sudden loss of a dozen workers is as indelible a mark on the operation as it is on the men's families. The investigations that follow this tragedy not only should seek the cause of the accident but also should explore a cruel twist that compounded the pain of the miners' loved ones: the release of erroneous information that the 12 had survived, which led to three hours of jubilation before the real and tragic news was made official.

Conclusion

The US Mine Safety and Health Administration held an investigation into the incident. It said that lightning was the likely cause and found 149 violations of mandatory mine safety and health regulations, but none of these were found to be the cause of the accident or contributed to the deaths of the 12 miners.

Republican George Miller demanded that Congress investigate 'why more wasn't done to keep these workers safe'. On 1 February, Governor Joe Manchin ordered that all coal production in West Virginia be halted until full safety checks were made. Governor Manchin also pledged to introduce legislation to ensure quicker access for rescue teams to accident sites. He wanted oxygen stations to be required by law in mines and that miners should be electronically tagged. Two of these initiatives came to pass when West Virginia legislators announced a series of measures aimed at improving mine safety, which included a rapid response system and updated tracking devices. At a Senate hearing on the incident, Senator Robert C Byrd said the deaths had been 'entirely preventable'.

The incident also affected the reputation of several US newspapers. While it is easy to criticize their lax source use and rigour, the *Boston Globe* was in its rights to point out that it and other papers had taken the news from reputable sources such as Governor Manchin and the relatives of the miners. The climactic events also came at a very awkward time for the newspapers, which had to report the latest developments before sending to print.

THE NEWS RELEASE

The news release is a key communications tool in a crisis situation. It provides the company's official explanation of what is happening and may be used for expressing quotes from senior management on how it is 'feeling' about the situation. News releases should keep coming thick and fast throughout the crisis period.

A good idea is to number, time and date them, at the top of each release. This will enable journalists to keep tabs on the chronology of events more easily. It also enables media responders to ask which was the last news release seen by the journalist – and quickly ascertain the level of knowledge currently possessed.

In some situations, it is worth thinking about who else the media will contact for information about the emergency, for example, the police, fire brigade, local hospital and other third party agencies. These can be sent copies of the company's releases in advance of sending them to the media. Such third parties are often less well geared up to respond to the media and will be grateful for copies of the company's releases to help with their own response. It helps also, of course, in attaining a consistency of message from all those involved. (In Scotland, the police have the right to vet all press releases concerning death and injury from an industrial accident.)

One final point. It is sometimes possible to prepare 'pro-forma holding statements' in anticipation of a potential crisis, for example in the case of a physical accident; here is an example.

PRESS STATEMENT

<u>Date:</u>

<u>Time:</u>

<u>No:</u>

XYZ Company confirms an incident (state what if known) has occurred (state where and when) and coordination of emergency rescue services is being controlled by the site's emergency response team.

Firm details about the incident are not yet known, but every possible action is being taken to safeguard lives and the environment.

Background information about the site is attached and more information about the incident will be released as soon as it becomes available.

The following special telephone number has been issued by XYZ Company for media enquiries relating to the incident...

-end-

Press statements should always announce news in the following order:

1. nature of the incident;
2. location of the incident;
3. details of fatalities (numbers not names);
4. details of injured (numbers not names);
5. details of areas affected;
6. details of impact on the environment;
7. details of action to be taken for customers;
8. quote from senior manager expressing regret for incident and praise for those involved in all aspects of the emergency;
9. details about follow-up investigation into the cause of the incident;
10. reminder about site's safety record (if good) prior to the incident.

KEEPING EMPLOYEES INFORMED

Following a serious incident it is vital to keep employees informed of the situation and of developments. They should not learn new information via the media, as so often happens. Employees are the company's 'ambassadors' and need to be in a position to explain to customers, family and friends what is happening.

They should have access to company press statements prior to release. Where possible, briefings should be set up to provide an opportunity to ask questions; alternatively, they can be kept informed through e-mail, letters from senior management or printed newsletters. With employees it is important to obtain a sense of common ownership of the problem. Be honest and open about decisions being taken to solve the problem and share the entire remedial plan with them. Keep them updated regularly.

There should also be a policy in place which explains it is not the role of employees to talk to the media about the problem. It is impossible and would be wrong to try to 'gag' employees, but at least they will know what is expected of them if they are aware of the company's policy. This might run as follows:

> Should you be approached by a member of the press to comment about any aspect of the company's activities, please say you are not the best person to assist with their enquiry and the journalist should contact the press office.

USING YOUR WEBSITE

In the same way that the internet has been used by activists as a highly effective global mechanism for mobilizing opinion and action against organizations, company websites can provide a fast and effective means of communicating directly to stakeholders without the risk of 'interpretation' by the media.

Increasingly used by journalists as a source of company information, websites play a crucial role in communicating to them and to other stakeholders. Use the website to post news releases and background information about a situation *in addition* to issuing news releases to papers, giving 'chat room' media interviews, responding to telephone media enquiries and holding news conferences.

Remember, though, that once information is on the website, it will be available globally. If you are dealing with a situation in which there is only local or national interest, it may be wiser to contain it to national boundaries rather than advertise it to the rest of the world.

Some companies employ the use of 'dark sites' on their website. The dark site is not normally accessible to people contacting the website; it is only activated by the company in an emergency situation. On the dark site can be 'stored' prepared news releases which anticipate the most likely events that the organization might have to face, leaving gaps for the relevant details to be added when the need arises. Additionally, 'fast facts' about the sites, products or services likely to be impacted can be kept here too. The relevant information is then released from the dark site to the main website, saving huge amounts of preparation and approval time. Once the dark site has been activated it blanks out all other information on the website.

The website can also be used by the media and other visitors to download audio comments from company spokespeople about the situation – particularly useful for radio news broadcasts.

A particular difficulty arises when the website can be updated only from company headquarters, which may be located in a different time zone. Updating websites needs to be possible in all geographical areas in which the company operates.

There are also 'smarter' ways organizations can communicate with their stakeholders using the internet during a crisis. A video file of an interview with a senior executive can be uploaded on a corporate website and viewed as a streaming video file. This won't, however, be downloadable and so cannot be reused as footage for television news programmes. If the goal is to have the footage shown on TV then it is important to ensure that the uploaded video file is downloadable. If it is necessary to keep track of who is accessing the video, then it should be stated that it is available to viewers who send in their e-mail details so the footage can be sent directly to them.

It is also worth considering staging a live webcast or 'virtual press conference' where questions are e-mailed to the conference chairperson, who will coordinate real-time responses. If a real-time press conference is held this, too, can be filmed and uploaded to the website for journalists unable to attend. Access can be controlled by issuing log-ins and passwords.

THE ROLE OF THE EMERGENCY SERVICES

The police, in particular, can be of enormous assistance in crises of a physical nature. They can absorb some of the pressure through their own press and casualty bureaux working closely with the company involved in the emergency. They will also assume responsibility for ensuring bodies are identified by next of kin and for notifying families in the event of death caused by an industrial accident. Ideally, the police officer should be accompanied by a senior company representative so immediate condolences and assistance can be offered to the bereaved family. The police will not usually inform families of the injured unless the distances involved preclude the company from visiting the family. In most cases of injury, however, it is best to break the news by telephone so relatives can get to the hospital as quickly as possible.

The police will also be in attendance when survivors arrive at the hospital, or relatives and the media arrive at the site of the accident, to ensure control. They will organize traffic flows, establish meeting points, make secure the scene of the incident and organize appropriate resources.

It is important to remember that the police and representatives of the other emergency services involved in the situation, such as the fire brigade or HM Coastguard, will wish to communicate about what has happened; about the actions, bravery and equipment of their own men and women. The key is to ensure messages are coordinated and do not conflict with those being made by the company.

Company site managers should keep in regular contact with local police and fire brigades so relationships are maintained and roles defined. Informal agreements on lines of communication, wording of press releases and the release of new information can be drawn up. Sometimes it can be useful to invite a senior representative from the emergency services to attend company press conferences in order to present a 'united front'.

WHEN IT IS ALL OVER

Experience is the name everyone gives to their mistakes.

Oscar Wilde

In the aftermath of the crisis the temptation is to forget all about it as quickly as possible; to resume normal life. But surviving a crisis provides a huge opportunity for the organization to re-examine and reorganize itself to ensure it never again finds itself in a similar position. It can represent a turning point in organizational life, present opportunities to establish a reputation for caring and competence and rise from the ashes – chastened but in better shape to tackle the challenges of the age of corporate accountability. Never forget lightning *can* strike twice in the same place.

Attention needs to be given to employees and their families in the aftermath of crisis. Some may have been traumatized by the event. Some we know have left the organization because they could not face the possibility of a similar event happening again. Families who have been bereaved will often feel colossal anger towards the organization even though it may not have been at fault. The company can help by offering professional counselling. Sometimes it is possible to redirect anger felt for the loss of a loved one into a positive energy by channelling it into finding solutions to prevent the situation from ever occurring again; to make sense of what has happened by helping others in the future.

The continued inability of organizations – whatever their sphere of operations – to regulate their activities so the chance of crisis is minimized; a failure to check constantly that their deeds match their expectations and declarations; and lassitude over plans and preparations to deal with the worst, so that crisis can be quickly contained, must inevitably lead to greater constraints being placed upon organizations of all types.

The key to crisis management is crisis prevention, whether the vigilance and preparation is self-motivated or enforced by legislation. But if a fire does break out, comprehensive contingency planning can minimize the catastrophe; and a policy of open communication can minimize damage to corporate and individual reputations.

SUMMARY

- Ensure all key players keep a copy of the crisis management plan with them at all times.
- Have background information prepared.
- Set up a press centre.
- Ensure executives are trained to manage successfully press conferences, television, radio and print media interviews – against crisis scenarios.
- Establish trained telephone response teams to cope with media and relative calls.
- Keep news releases coming thick and fast; date, time and number them.
- Company websites are a key communications tool.
- Don't forget employees – they are the company's 'ambassadors'.
- Coordinate the response of the company and third parties.
- When it's all over, review the organization from top to bottom in the light of lessons learnt – lightning *can* strike twice.

References

Anderson, S and Cavanagh, J (2000) *Top 200: The rise of corporate global power*, Institute for Policy Studies.

Association of British Insurers (ABI) (2001) *Investing in Social Responsibility: Risks and opportunities*, ABI, London.

Brown, J K (1979) *This Business of Issues: Coping with company's environments*, Conference Board Report no 758.

Buchholz, R A (1988) 'Adjusting Corporations to the Realities of Public Interests and Policy', in *Strategic Issues Management: How organizations influence and respond to public interests and policies*, Jossey-Bass, San Francisco.

Chase, W Howard (1984) *Issue Management: Origins of the future*, Issue Action Publications Inc, Leesburg, Virginia, USA.

Chippendale, P and Horrie, C (1992) *Stick It Up Your Punter – the rise and fall of the* Sun, Mandarin Paperbacks, London.

Clifton, R and Maughan, E (eds) (1999) *Future of Brands: Twenty-five visions*, Macmillan, Basingstoke.

Corporate Public Issues and their Management, **26** (1) (January 2004), Issue Action Publications, Leesburg, Virginia, USA.

Crable, R E and Vibbert, S L (1985) 'Managing Issues and Influencing Public Policy', *Public Relations Review*, **11** (2).

Department of Health (DOH) (1997) *On the State of the Public Health: The Annual Report of the Chief Medical Officer of the Department of Health for the Year 1996*, DOH, London.

Elkington, J (2001) *The Chrysalis Economy: How citizen CEOs and corporations can fuse values and value creation*, Capstone, Oxford.

Environics International, Conference Board and Prince of Wales Business Leaders' Forum (1999) *The Millennium Poll on Corporate Social Responsibility*, Environics/GlobeScan, London [online] http://www.globescan.com/news_archives/MPExecBrief.pdf.

Griffin, A (2007) *New Strategies for Reputation Management: Gaining control of issues, crises and corporate social responsibility*, Kogan Page, London.

Grunig, J E and Hunt, T (1984) *Managing Public Relations*, Holt, Rinehart & Winston, New York.

Hainsworth, Brad E (1990) 'Issues Management: An Overview', *Public Relations Review*, **16** (1).

Hainsworth, Brad E and Meng, M (1988) 'How Corporations Define Issues Management', *Public Relations Review*, winter.

Heath, R L and Cousino, K R (1990) 'Issues Management: End of First Decade Progress Report', *Public Relations Review*, **16** (1).

Heath, R L and Nelson, R A (1986) *Issues Management: Corporate public policy making in an information society*, Sage, London.

Ito, Y (1993) *Beyond Agendas: New directions in communication research from a Japanese perspective*, Greenwood Press, London.

Jones, Barrie L and Chase, W Howard (1979) 'Managing Public Policy Issues', *Public Relations Review*, **5** (2).

Kinsdorf, Marion (1990) 'Crisis Management', *Public Relations Review*, **14** (4).

Larkin, Judy (2003) *Strategic Reputation Risk Management*, Palgrave Macmillan, Basingstoke.

Management Today, July 1994.

McCue, Peter (2001) 'Preventing the Crises you Can; Managing the Ones You Can't', speech at AAMC, Georgia, March 8.

Meng, M B (1992) 'Early Identification Aids Issues Management', *Public Relations Journal*, March.

Meng, M B (1987) 'Issues Management Today', Unpublished thesis, Bingham Young University.

Midwest Academy Manual for Activists (2000) *Organizing for Social Change*, Seven Locks Press, Maryland.

Mitroff, Ian and Pauchant, Thierry (1990) *We're So Big and Powerful, Nothing Bad Can Happen to Us, an investigation of America's crisis prone corporations*, Birch Lane Press, Secaucus, New Jersey, USA.

Hanna, Nagy (1985) 'Strategic Planning and Management: A Review of Recent Experiences', World Bank staff and working papers, no 751, Washington DC.

Post, J E and Kelley, P C (1988) 'Lessons from the Learning Curve: The Past, Present and Future of Issues Management', *Strategic Issues Management: How organisations influence and respond to public interests and policies.*

Sopow, Eli (1994) *The Critical Issues Audit*, Issue Action Publications Inc, Leesburg, Virginia, USA.

SustainAbility (2001) *Buried Treasure: Uncovering the business case for corporate sustainability*, SustainAbility, London.

Taylor, Lord Justice (1990) 'The Hillsborough Stadium Disaster', Cm 962, 29 January.

Tucker, Kerry and Broom, Glen (1993) 'Managing Issues Acts as a Bridge to Strategic Planning', *Public Relations Journal*, November.

Tucker, Kerry and Trumpfheller, B (1993) 'Building an Issues Management Tracking System', *Public Relations Journal*, **49** (11), pp 36–37.

US Public Affairs Council (1978) *The Fundamentals of Issue Management.*

Wartick, S L and Rude, R E (1986) 'Issues Management: Corporate Fad or Corporate Function?', *California Management Review*, **24** (1).

Welsh Economy Research Unit, University of Wales, Cardiff Business School and Welsh Institute of Rural Studies (1996) *The Economic Consequences of the* Sea Empress *Spillage*, July.

Winter, M and Steger, U (1998) *Managing Outside Pressure: Strategies for preventing corporate disaster*, Wiley, Chichester.

Zadek, S (2001) *The Civil Corporation: The new economy of corporate citizenship*, Earthscan, London.

Index

Page references in *italics* indicate figures